praise for

LIBERTY'S BLUEPRINT

"Meyerson has written a readable book. . . . Highly recommended."
—*Choice Magazine*

"A lively account of one of the key touchstones our courts
rely upon to construe the Constitution—the Federalist Papers. . . .
Having read this engaging work, we're likely to view the debates
over the intent of the Constitution's drafters in a fresh light and
even more so to admire the product of these patriots' labors."
—*Shelf Awareness*

"Extraordinarily well written and engrossing . . . merits the
attention of all who are interested in the birth of our democracy."
—*Federal Lawyer*

"This beautifully written book vividly describes how the
Federalist Papers were written and why they are profoundly
relevant for the constitutional issues of our times. . . . Meyerson
has written a book that all students of the Constitution
and American history will enjoy and learn from."
—ERWIN CHEMERINSKY, Alston & Bird Professor of
Law and Political Science, Duke University

LIBERTY'S
BLUEPRINT

LIBERTY'S BLUEPRINT

HOW MADISON AND HAMILTON
WROTE THE FEDERALIST PAPERS,
DEFINED THE CONSTITUTION,
AND MADE DEMOCRACY SAFE
FOR THE WORLD

MICHAEL I. MEYERSON

BASIC
BOOKS

A MEMBER OF THE PERSEUS BOOKS GROUP
NEW YORK

Hardcover first published in 2008 by Basic Books,
A Member of the Perseus Books Group
Paperback first published in 2009 by Basic Books

Books published by Basic Books are available at special discounts for bulk purchases in the
United States by corporations, institutions, and other organizations. For more information,
please contact the Special Markets Department at the Perseus Books Group, 2300 Chestnut
Street, Suite 200, Philadelphia, PA 19103, or call (800) 810-4145, extension 5000, or
e-mail special.markets@perseusbooks.com.

Designed by Linda Harper

The Library of Congress has cataloged the hardcover as follows:
Meyerson, Michael.
Liberty's blueprint: how Madison and Hamilton wrote the federalist papers, defined the
constitution, and made democracy safe for the world / Michael I. Meyerson.
     p. cm.
   ISBN-13: 978-0-465-00264-1 (alk. paper)
   ISBN-10: 0-465-00264-1 (alk. paper)
     1. Constitutional history—United States.   2. Constitutional law—United States. I. Title.
KF4520.M49 2008
342.7302'9-dc22

                                                                                    2007035376

Paperback ISBN: 978-0-465-01823-9
10 9 8 7 6 5 4 3 2 1

To Lesly, William, and Andrew.
With Love.

Contents

PREFACE

One of the joys of teaching constitutional law is that every year I have the opportunity to introduce a new group of students to *The Federalist*. This collection of essays, written in 1787 and 1788 by Alexander Hamilton and James Madison (with a small assist from John Jay), was originally designed as a propaganda piece to influence the debate over ratification of the Constitution. For a modern audience, however, reading *The Federalist* is like having a private meeting with the savviest political and legal minds America has ever produced. *The Federalist* not only serves as the single most important resource for interpreting the Constitution, it provides a wise and sophisticated explanation for the uses and abuses of governmental power from Washington to Baghdad.

The Federalist was written in an extraordinary time. Just a few years after the Revolutionary War officially ended, Americans had to decide whether to accept or reject the radically new form of government devised in Philadelphia. In one sense, the battle over ratification of the Constitution can be seen as the first bare-knuckled political fight in American history. Each side suspected (with good reason) that its letters were being read, if not stolen, by postal carriers loyal to its opponents. Personal attacks and clandestine maneuvering were commonplace. Deals were struck. Promises were broken.

Yet the ratification conflict was also waged on an intellectual plane that is difficult to imagine today. Wise and educated men, many of whom were heroes of the revolution, wrote voluminously on the merits and weaknesses of this new plan of government. Both those in favor of the proposed Constitution and those opposing it believed that logic, reason, and a clear understanding of history would illuminate the discourse and lead to a proper conclusion. By far, the greatest exemplar of rational political debate was *The Federalist.*

Hamilton and Madison each expended considerable energy, physical as well as intellectual, in their struggle to secure ratification of the Constitution. In a period of seven months, from October 27, 1787, to May 28, 1788, they produced 175,000 words, explaining in detail the plan for this new form of government and expounding a sophisticated and enduring political philosophy. While it must be said that some of these papers are a bit ponderous and repetitious, and that those describing the weaknesses of the Articles of Confederation have little, if any, relevance today, the best of the Federalist papers are breathtaking in their brilliance.

When Thomas Jefferson recommended that *The Federalist* be required reading for students at the University of Virginia, he termed it "an authority to which appeal is habitually made by all . . . as evidence of the general opinion of those who framed, and of those who accepted the Constitution of the United States, on questions as to its genuine meaning." In 1821, Chief Justice John Marshall wrote that *The Federalist* was "a complete commentary on our Constitution, and is appealed to by all parties."

Both Madison and Hamilton understood that a constitution is greater than the sum of its parts. The proposed Constitution represented a radical shift in the nature of government, and they recognized the need to provide the rationale for such a markedly different governmental system. Thus *The Federalist* contains a wide array of insights on politicians, human nature, democracy, greed, and power—an array of such astuteness that Theodore Roosevelt would praise it as "on the whole the greatest book dealing with applied politics that there has ever been."

Unfortunately, much of the wisdom of *The Federalist* has been distorted by time. Many of the essays have been misread and misinterpreted. The essays are best approached with an equal appreciation of law and history. I am not a professional historian, and, as a law professor, I greatly respect the skill and discipline that historians bring to their craft. By building on their work, and conducting my own research, I have been able to arrive at a new understanding of the story and meaning of Madison's and Hamilton's astonishing creation.

But to do this requires viewing their work in its entirety, comprehending the context of each essay, and paying close attention to the arguments of the Anti-Federalists that they were trying to answer. The first goal of *Liberty's Blueprint* is to present the most important teachings of *The Federalist* to a modern audience.

It is remarkable how *The Federalist*'s analysis of the separation of powers between the president and Congress can illuminate our understanding of those same issues as they recur in the debate over Iraq or the war on terrorism. The dividing line between the federal and state governments that Madison and Hamilton labored to explicate can be seen at the heart of contemporary battles over such diverse issues as the Clean Air Act and medical marijuana. There is also much we can gain from rediscovering *The Federalist*'s observation that all power can be abused, no matter how virtuous those who are wielding it may be.

One obstacle to appreciating the wisdom of *The Federalist* is the ongoing, and increasingly heated, disagreement over whether we should rely on what is called the "original understanding" of those who drafted and ratified the Constitution in interpreting the document today. Those who call themselves originalists claim that basing our interpretation of the Constitution on such an historical understanding is the only way to stay faithful to the concept of a written constitution and the only mechanism for preventing judges from deciding cases based on their personal preferences instead of on legal principles. Opponents of the originalist approach warn that by restricting ourselves to a centuries-old interpretation of constitutional phrases such as "freedom of speech" or "equal protection of the law," we are forcing society to return to a legal system which jailed those who criticized the government, imprisoned interracial couples attempting to marry, and treated women as too weak and emotional to serve as lawyers.

A second goal of *Liberty's Blueprint* is to use *The Federalist* to bridge the gap between these seemingly irreconcilable approaches and to demonstrate how and when we should call upon the views of the framers when we interpret the Constitution. One of the extraordinary achievements of Madison and Hamilton was their ability to explain, in detail, the logic and reasoning behind the choices made by those who drafted the Constitution in Philadelphia. Equally important, they showed how these choices reflected the goals and ideals of the population of their time. From *The Federalist,* a modern reader can understand not only the workings of the Constitution but also appreciate how well the philosophy behind Madison's and Hamilton's skeptical view of power resonates with more recent lessons of history and current events.

We need to remember, though, that the Constitution analyzed by Madison and Hamilton was largely limited to issues of separation of powers and the relationship between the national government and the states. The Bill of Rights was ratified several years after *The Federalist* was written, and the Fourteenth Amendment was ratified after the Civil War. Regrettably, there was no "owner's manual" like *The Federalist* for these amendments to the Constitution. No one presented a thoughtful, comprehensive analysis of the guarantees of freedom of speech and religion contained in the First Amendment, or the Fourteenth Amendment's promise of equal protection and due process of law. We also lack any evidence that those who drafted these later amendments wrote them with the same thoughtfulness and care as the delegates to the Philadelphia convention of 1787.

Thus we are left with a surprising paradox. *The Federalist* shows that it may make sense to be a "partial originalist." We can rely, at least presumptively, on the original understanding of those who drafted and ratified the original Constitution for issues of separation of powers and federalism, yet feel freer to use our more evolved understanding for determining the contours of individual rights and equality. History, in other words, can teach when and how to use the lessons of history.

But history can never be understood as simply the development of ideas or laws. History is made by complex individuals with complicated relationships. The third aim of *Liberty's Blueprint* is to explore the lives of the authors of *The Federalist* and shed light on the unusual personal bond between Madison and Hamilton. One of the more persistent questions surrounding *The Federalist* has been how two equally brilliant men with such explosively different personalities were able to work together so successfully. Part of the difficulty of understanding their relationship is that it deteriorated so dramatically not long after the essays were completed. Moreover, the political fault lines that rose between Madison and Hamilton still divide Americans today. Contemporary fans of James Madison are drawn to his defense of individual liberty, his leading role in drafting the Bill of Rights, and his outspoken support for religious freedom. Present-day supporters of Alexander Hamilton tout his vision of economic development and fiscal responsibility. Many of the histories of Madison and Hamilton tend to be cast as either pro-Madison or pro-Hamilton, and all sides have ignored or played down the aspects of the relationship which show that, for a brief while at least, a genuine friendship existed.

Madison and Hamilton's intricate relationship is especially fascinating as it continually evolved through their joint involvement in each critical moment in the development of the American Constitution. When the two met in 1782 at the Confederation Congress, they found that they shared a common desire to strengthen the anemic powers of the national government under the Articles of Confederation. Hamilton's recklessness, however, repeatedly undermined Madison's carefully laid out attempts to forge a successful legislative compromise. At both the Annapolis convention of 1786 and the Constitutional Convention the following year, their personalities would clash, but their common goals would lead each to respect the strengths of the other. Their true friendship developed during the fight over ratification of the Constitution, when they joined forces, not only in writing the essays of *The Federalist,* but in sharing the lead in the nationwide campaign for ratification.

Madison and Hamilton were an eighteenth-century odd couple: the priggish, intellectual Madison teamed with the volatile and incautious Hamilton. At the peak of their alliance, they were able to transcend their differences, but their camaraderie was shortlived. They embraced radically different visions for the new nation and held irreconcilable political agendas. Their friendship quickly degenerated to the point that Hamilton would declare that Madison was "his personal and political enemy."

I am convinced that a study of the personal histories of Madison and Hamilton, and of the intellectual legacy of their masterwork, *The Federalist,* can teach one final, critically important lesson: it is folly to ignore the wisdom of those with whom one disagrees. My hope is that my book can contribute to an atmosphere where respectful and reasoned political discourse is considered an ideal worth pursuing.

LIBERTY'S
BLUEPRINT

INTRODUCTION

"A WELL-ESTABLISHED HISTORICAL CONTROVERSY"

SOLVING THE MYSTERY OF
WHO WROTE *THE FEDERALIST*

"Pray, if it is not a secret, who is the author or authors of Publius?" George Washington, who asked this question of Henry Knox in February 1788, was just one of many readers speculating on the identity of the writer of *The Federalist,* a series of essays dominating the debate over ratification of the Constitution. Hidden behind the pseudonym Publius, Alexander Hamilton and James Madison were turning out four essays a week, describing the nation's need for a new form of government, and explaining in detail how the new government would operate. The third coauthor, John Jay, had written only a few essays when illness forced him to leave the collaboration.

During this time, many writers weighed in on the ratification question, producing voluminous copy on both sides of the controversy. The quality of *The Federalist,* however, made it stand out. Its "greatness is acknowledged universally," wrote one enthusiastic reader. Thomas

Jefferson would declare that *The Federalist* was "the best commentary on the principles of government which ever was written."

It may seem odd that authors of such an esteemed work would mask their identity, but there were two good reasons for their use of a pen name. First, it was common for political writers in the eighteenth century to employ a pseudonym. The assumption was that this practice would highlight the importance of the ideas being conveyed rather than the reputation of the author. More important, the two main authors represented very different constituencies from different parts of the country. Hamilton often allied himself with the commercial interests of his home state of New York; Madison was a plantation owner from Virginia who habitually defended its agricultural interests. Their collaboration, if known, would represent the sort of fusion that could alienate those who were concerned only with protecting the interests of their individual states.

Hamilton and Madison worked hard to maintain their anonymity. To avoid disclosure to the prying eyes of a postal carrier, Hamilton would refer to Publius in the third person when writing to Madison. Explaining why he would be too busy for a while to write the essays, Hamilton wrote, "If our suspicions of the author be right, he must be too much engaged to make a rapid progress in what remain."

Despite the attempt at secrecy, people began guessing who Publius might be. James Kent of New York declared that "the Author must be Hamilton." Another writer suggested that "Madison has the principal hand in Publius and Hamilton assists." Henry Knox, when replying to Washington's query, correctly stated that the essays were "attributed to the joint efforts of Mr. Jay, Mr. Maddison, and Colo Hamilton."

Washington actually had more reason than most to know the identity of Publius. Both Madison and Hamilton had revealed their involvement to him. Hamilton had been subtle, simply sending the first Publius essay and remarking, "The inclosed is the first number of a series of papers to be written in [the Constitution's] defence." As Hamilton frequently sent Washington pieces of his writing, it could be expected that Washington would recognize the connection.

Madison was far more direct. Writing to Washington shortly after agreeing to join with Hamilton on the project, Madison revealed: "I will not conceal from you that I am likely to have such a degree of connection with the publication here, as to afford a restraint of delicacy from interesting myself directly in the republication elsewhere. You will recognize one of the pens concerned in the task. There are three in the whole. A fourth may possibly bear a part."

Although most of the essays were initially published in New York newspapers, they received their widest distribution when they were republished in book form. On March 22, 1788, while the essays were still being written, publishers John and Archibald McLean proudly announced their publication of "*The FEDERALIST,* VOLUME FIRST." The author was identified only as Publius. The second volume, which was released two months later, on May 28, again maintained the authors' anonymity. By the time the ratification battle was finished in mid-July, it has been estimated that "there were probably not a dozen individuals who definitely could state that Hamilton, Madison, and Jay had written [the essays]."

Once the Constitution was safely ratified, however, the identity of Publius became generally known. The three authors' names were first published in a French edition of *The Federalist.* This 1792 publication listed on its title page that *Le Fédéraliste* had been written by "MM HAMILTON, MADDISSON *et* GAY, *citoyens de* l'État *de* New York." The French thought so highly of the essays that, on August 26, 1792, they offered honorary citizenship to Hamilton and Madison, who were part of a group of men who had "brought reason to its present maturity."

The deep political and personal rift which had developed between Madison and Hamilton by this time is well illustrated by their differing reactions to this news. Madison, who was siding with France in its ongoing conflict with England, happily accepted the honor. Hamilton, who supported closer ties with Great Britain, did not even deign to respond to the French.

Even though the identity of the authors was now public, there was one further mystery to be resolved: Which of them had written which of the eighty-five essays? In 1802 an American printer, George F. Hopkins, decided to publish a new edition of *The Federalist*. When he informed Hamilton of his desire to identify the author of each individual essay, he was rebuffed. As Hopkins would later write to Hamilton's son, the proposal "met with your father's decided disapprobation." Thus the 1802 edition was released with no identification of the authorship of the individual essays.

Hamilton finally broke his vow of silence two years later. On July 9, 1804, just two days before his fatal duel with Aaron Burr, Hamilton arrived at the law office of his old friend, Judge Egbert Benson. The judge's nephew, Robert Benson, informed Hamilton that the judge was out of town, then watched as Hamilton casually walked over to a bookcase, pulled out a book, opened it, and quickly returned it to its place on the shelf. Shortly after Hamilton's death, Robert examined the same book and found the sheet of paper inserted between its pages. On this paper, Hamilton had written "Nos. 2, 3, 4, 5, 54, by J. Nos. 10, 14, 37 to 48 inclusive, M. Nos. 18, 19, 20, M. & H. jointly. All the others by H." Hamilton had ensured that he would not die without providing a way for the world to know his exact contribution to *The Federalist*. The list was placed in the New York Public Library for safekeeping but was mysteriously stolen several years later. There has been no trace of it since.

In 1810, a new edition of *The Federalist* was printed, and it specifically attributed authorship of each essay according to the list Hamilton had left behind. The result was that Hamilton was credited with writing sixty-three essays, plus an additional three jointly with Madison. Madison was allotted only fourteen solo entries and Jay, five.

Up to this point, Madison had been as scrupulous as Hamilton in keeping the specific authorship secret. In September 1788 when his ally, Tench Coxe, asked Madison which essays he had written, Madison refused to divulge the information. We do not have a copy of Madison's response, but he must have indicated in fairly strong terms that he considered himself honorbound to maintain secrecy, because Coxe immediately wrote back, apologizing for making a request that was "disagreeable and improper." Coxe begged Madison for "your pardon for the trouble I have given you on that Subject."

Years later, after completing his two terms as president, Madison was finally ready to respond to Hamilton's list. In 1818, Madison gave printer Jacob Gideon his own copy of the original edition, marked with the identity of the author of each essay. When Gideon published his edition of *The Federalist,* fifteen more essays were assigned to Madison than in the earlier edition. According to this version, a total of twenty-nine essays——numbers *10, 14, 18–20, 37–58, 62,* and *63—* were credited to Madison; numbers *2, 3, 4, 5,* and *64* (as opposed to number *54* in the Hamilton list) were allotted to Jay; and the remaining fifty-one essays to Hamilton.

Madison would later strongly reaffirm the Gideon count: "It was furnished to him by me with a perfect knowledge of its accuracy as it relates to myself, and a full confidence in its equal accuracy as it relates to the two others." Madison did not accuse Hamilton of lying to enhance his role as Publius. Hamilton's list, Madison explained, which was written "just before his death, is very erroneous, owing doubtless to the hurry in which the memorandum was made out."

Madison's account was widely accepted up until the Civil War, after which—at the urging of Hamilton's son—the question was readdressed. For the next fifty years it again became fashionable to believe Hamilton's list. Douglass Adair, an historian, tracked the changing fortunes of the lists together with the fluctuating reputations of the two authors. Through 1860, Madison was acclaimed as the father of the Constitution. He had outlived all of the other framers of the Constitution, and was revered as the last of the Fathers. The reputation of Hamilton, meanwhile, suffered the same fate as his discredited Federalist Party. He was seen as undemocratic, a particularly damning label during the rise of Andrew Jackson and a new democratic ethos. After the Civil War, however, two changes occurred. First, the reputation of Madison, a southern slaveowner, fell into disrepute, as he was seen as somehow contributing to the South's rebellion. Simultaneously, with America's increased industrialization, Hamilton's economic vision began to seem more prescient.

Now viewed as the more authentic American voice, he was seen as the more likely author of the disputed essays.

The authorship issue seemed impossible to settle. In 1904, Henry Cabot Lodge, the editor of *The Works of Alexander Hamilton*, declared that the question of who was the true author of the disputed *Federalist* essays "has fairly reached the dignity of a well-established historical controversy." In the mid-twentieth century, two historians undertook extensive studies. In 1944, Adair reviewed the content of the essays and decided that Madison's list better reflected the different policy orientations of the two. Later, Jacob Cooke reviewed the reliability of the different lists and the people who claimed to have seen them. He came to the same conclusion as Adair, namely that Madison's list was correct.

But not everyone was convinced. Robert Scigliano, who edited an edition of *The Federalist* in 2000, reviewed the scholarship of Adair and Cooke and found important gaps. Scigliano concluded that while the evidence leaned in Madison's favor, this was still "a dispute that has not yet been fully resolved."

What has finally solved the mystery of whose quill penned which essay is "stylometry," the science of using statistics to measure literary style. Stylometrics is based on the theory that writers leave "literary fingerprints" by their tendency to use simple words the same way in all of their writing. The first statistical study of *The Federalist* before the advent of computer-based stylometry was performed in 1964 and showed that, in some ways, Madison and Hamilton had strikingly similar styles. A review of the essays whose authorship was not in dispute found that the average length of a sentence was 34.59 words in Madison's essays, and an almost identical 34.55 words for Hamilton's. A review of their respective use of thirty common words showed notable differences, however, indicating that Madison, statistically, was the likely author of all the disputed essays. Since this initial study, the science of stylometry has radically advanced with the power of computers. Numerous computer-based studies have reached the same conclusion as the 1964 inquiry. In 2003, a computer scientist was able to demonstrate that by calculating the frequency with which

Madison and Hamilton used just three words—*to, upon,* and *would*—it can be established, to a mathematical certainty, that Madison was the author of the disputed *Federalist* essays.

Yet one final mystery remains. How were two people who were to become such bitter enemies able to collaborate so effectively on one of the greatest works in American political history?

PART I

WRITING *THE FEDERALIST*

1

"TESTIFYING THE ESTEEM & REGARD"

AN UNLIKELY FRIENDSHIP

*T*hey first met on November 25, 1782, when the twenty-seven-year-old Alexander Hamilton arrived on horseback in Philadelphia for his first day in Congress. James Madison, at thirty-one, was already a veteran legislator, having served in Congress since 1780. The two men presented a stark contrast from the very beginning.

Hamilton possessed a striking military demeanor. With blue eyes and gentle features, he was widely described as "handsome" and "attractive to women." While Hamilton was not particularly tall at five feet seven inches, his charisma and energetic personality led him to be known as the "little lion."

Madison, by contrast, was just "little." Variously described as between five feet four and five feet six inches, he was slight of build, never weighing more than one hundred pounds. He was often sickly and worried greatly about his health throughout his life. His private secretary, Edward Coles, noted that "his form, features, and manner were not commanding." At Madison's presidential inauguration in 1809, Washington Irving would describe him as "but a withered little apple-John." In social gatherings he was generally shy and withdrawn. One woman called him "a gloomy stiff creature"; another, who actually seemed to like him, said that he was "mute, cold, and repulsive" in public.

Madison's first serious romance did not occur until the fall of 1782, coincidentally just a few months before he made his acquaintance with Hamilton. He became smitten with Kitty Floyd, the daughter of a fellow member of Congress, William Floyd. Kitty, who had celebrated her fifteenth birthday the previous April, was less than half Madison's age. Nonetheless, by spring they were engaged to be married. Thomas Jefferson wrote a congratulatory letter to Madison on April 14, 1783, asking him to "make my compliments affectionately . . . to Miss Kitty particularly. . . . I wished [your marriage] to be so as it would give me a neighbor whose worth I rate high, and as I know it will render you happier than you can possibly be in a single state."

Madison's response to Jefferson's solicitude reveals his awkwardly formal social nature: "Your inference on that subject was not groundless. Before you left us I had sufficiently ascertained her sentiments. Since your departure the affair has been pursued. Most preliminary arrangements, although definitive, will be postponed until the end of the year in Congress."

Unlike Madison, Hamilton was passionate and exuberant. John Adams spoke disapprovingly of his "audacious and unblushing attempt upon ladies of the highest rank and purest virtue." In a particularly bitter moment, Adams attributed the source of Hamilton's political ambitions to "a superabundance of secretions which he could not find enough whores to draw off."

Hamilton married Elizabeth Schuyler, the beautiful daughter of a wealthy and politically powerful family on December 14, 1780. His letters to her were emotional and sentimental. "My heart overflows with every thing for you. . . . I would this moment give the world to be near you only to kiss your sweet hand." Hamilton's letters to her married sister, Angelica Church, interestingly enough, were no less romantic. He wrote, "I seldom write to a lady without fancying the relation of lover and mistress. . . . And in your case the dullest materials could not help feeling that propensity."

Madison's and Hamilton's widely dissimilar personalities can be traced, at least in part, to their vastly different backgrounds. Madison possessed a pedigree of impeccable southern aristocracy. When his great-great-grandfather, John Maddison, died in 1683, the family's Virginia homestead consisted of almost two thousand acres. Later generations significantly increased the size of the landholdings. The family also owned a considerable number of slaves. In fact, James Madison's father, who owned more than a hundred slaves, held the dubious distinction of being the largest slaveholder in Orange County, Virginia.

As would befit his privileged origins, Madison was classically educated. After five years at boarding school, he spent two years undergoing private tutoring on his father's plantation before attending Princeton, which was then known officially as "the College of New Jersey." He immersed himself in his studies, sleeping only four or five hours per night, and graduating in two years. Princeton's president, John Witherspoon, later said of Madison, "During the whole time he was under [my] tuition, [I] never knew him to do, or to say, an improper thing."

Hamilton's childhood was, in contrast, one of relative poverty. Born on the Caribbean island of Nevis to an unwed mother, Hamilton was, in the words of John Adams's most famous insult, "a bastard brat of a Scotch pedlar." As a child, Hamilton had no formal schooling, and was largely self-taught. After arriving in the colonies, he received his college education at King's College (later to become Columbia University). Like Madison, he was an enthusiastic student. He would later pass New York's bar examination just six months after beginning his legal studies.

The paths undertaken by Hamilton and Madison during the Revolutionary War reflected the differences in their physical and psychological natures. Madison served only briefly, as a member of the Orange County militia of which his father was the commander. He would later attribute the cause of his abbreviated service to "the unsettled state of his health and the discouraging feebleness of his constitution."

In 1776, Madison was elected a delegate to the Virginia Provincial Convention. His role as delegate was modest. His only significant achievement came during the drafting of Virginia's new constitution. The original draft had declared that "all men shou'd enjoy the fullest Toleration in the Exercise of Religion, according to the Dictates of Conscience." Madison objected on the ground that freedom of religion should be considered an inherent right possessed by each individual in society, not merely an activity permitted due to the "tolerance" of the government. Madison convinced the convention to amend the provision's language to declare that "all men are equally entitled to the free exercise of religion."

The provincial convention was later restyled as the House of Delegates, and in 1777 Madison ran for reelection. His campaign was severely hampered by his refusal to participate in the local custom in which, he said, candidates "recommend themselves to the voters . . . by the corrupting influence of spirituous liquors, and other treats." Unwilling to trade alcohol for votes, Madison lost the election to a tavern-owning opponent, Charles Porter, who had no such scruples.

Madison's political career was, of course, far from over. In November 1777, he was elected to the governor's primary advisory board, the Council of State. Two years later, the Virginia State Assembly elected him to serve in Congress.

Hamilton's wartime course to Philadelphia was far more glamorous. In March 1776, he became the captain of an artillery company; within a year, he was promoted to lieutenant colonel and became George Washington's aide-de-camp. Hamilton quickly developed into an indispensable and trusted assistant and adviser; Washington referred to him as his "principal and most confidential aide."

Nonetheless, Hamilton was desperate to leave the command post and see real combat. He repeatedly requested permission to lead troops in battle. Washington refused, saying he needed Hamilton's services, which frustrated and angered the young officer. Tensions between the two intensified, culminating in a final bizarre confrontation on February 16, 1781. Washington informed Hamilton that he wanted to speak with him, and Hamilton, by his own admission, did not hurry to the appointment. Washington was left waiting impatiently in the farmhouse which they were using as headquarters. According to Hamilton, the altercation was brief:

> I met him at the head of the stairs, where, accosting me in an angry tone, "Col. Hamilton (said he) you have kept me waiting at the head of the stairs these ten minutes. I must tell you, Sir, you treat me with disrespect." I replied, without petulancy, but with decision "I am not conscious of it, sir; but since you have thought it necessary to tell me so, we part." "Very well, Sir (said he) if it be your choice" or something to this effect, and we separated.

Despite attempts by Washington to reestablish a warm working relationship, Hamilton remained aloof and distant. He wrote to his father-in-law that he "always disliked the office of an aide-de-camp as having in it a kind of personal dependence." Thus, Hamilton continued, he would not accept Washington's entreaties as "I was always determined, if there should ever happen a breach between us, never to consent to an accommodation."

After stepping down as aide-de-camp, Hamilton continued to badger the commander-in-chief for a combat position. He was finally given command of a light-infantry unit that would play a major role in the Battle of Yorktown. When Hamilton learned of his assignment, he raced to his quarters yelling "We have it! We have it!" During this decisive battle, Hamilton led a battalion in a dangerous but successful assault on key British fortifications.

Shortly after his military triumph, Hamilton was appointed receiver of continental taxes for New York State by Superintendent of Finance Robert Morris. He had served for barely one month when he was elected by the New York State legislature to serve as a delegate to Congress.

In Congress, Madison's and Hamilton's tumultuous collaboration centered on the mission of financing and empowering the impoverished "continental" government. Congress's political weakness stemmed from its governing document, the Articles of Confederation. This charter, which was designed to tie the thirteen former colonies together as loosely as possible, was approved by the Continental Congress on November 15, 1777. The Articles of Confederation were sent to the states for ratification with little fanfare or debate. As indicative of the states' dismissive attitude toward centralizing authority, the articles remained unratified for almost four years until March 1, 1781, when Maryland finally agreed to sign the document after receiving land concessions from Virginia.

The articles were crafted so as to preserve the maximum amount of individual state autonomy. Immediately after proclaiming that this new nation would be called "The United States of America," the articles made clear that the emphasis should be on the word "States" rather than "United": "Each state retains its sovereignty, freedom, and independence, and every power, jurisdiction, and right, which is not by this Confederation expressly delegated to the United States." In actuality, very little was expressly delegated to the federal government. Congress was given the power to wage the war against Great Britain, but it fell to each individual state to "raise the men and cloath, arm and equip them in a solid-like manner." More important, although all the costs of war, as well as other common expenditures, were to be charged to the national treasury, Congress could not act on its own to raise the money to pay these costs. Instead, it was required to request funds from the states, and wait impotently for each to pay its allotted share.

Although the Articles of Confederation were not ratified officially for most of the Revolutionary War, Congress, as well as the individual states, largely carried out the task of governing as if they were already in place. Thus, Congress was able to incur enormous wartime expenses without the means to pay them. When loans from European countries proved insufficient, it tried to pay its debts by printing more money. The inevitable economic effect of flooding the market with new currency was rampant inflation. By 1779, the currency was trading for only one-thirtieth its stated value. General George Washington pleaded with the president of the Continental Congress, John Jay, to "restore the credit of our currency." Washington warned that the situation had reached the point where "a wagon-load of money will scarcely purchase a wagon-load of provisions."

Unable to borrow sufficiently and unwilling to print more devalued currency, Congress turned to the states. Under a system known as "requisition," Congress asked each state to collect its share of the national budget from the citizens living within that state's borders. Because state compliance was strictly voluntary, it was unreliable at best. State tax collection officers would sometimes collect the requested money and turn it over to the state treasury instead of Congress. Robert Morris, the superintendent of finance, grumbled that while this system "confers on Congress the privilege of asking everything, it has secured to each State the prerogative of granting nothing."

James Madison, who had taken his seat in Congress for the first time on March 20, 1780, was appalled to find "the public treasury empty, public credit exhausted." A week after his arrival, he wrote to Virginia Governor Thomas Jefferson, expressing his fears that if the states were unwilling to provide the needed funding, "we are undone." As for the prospects of the states voluntarily paying their fair share, Madison could only say, "I look forward with the most pungent apprehensions."

Within a year, Madison was arguing that Congress should use military might to blockade recalcitrant states and force them to pay the requisitioned amount. In an ironic foreshadowing of some of his most contentious battles over the interpretation of the Constitution, Madison argued that Congress, under the Articles of Confederation, had "implied powers," specifically the "implied right of coercion" against "any of the States which shall refuse or neglect to abide by such their determinations." Doubting that he would be able to convince others to agree that Congress could be empowered by implication, Madison proposed amending the articles to empower Congress explicitly "to employ the force of the United States, as well by sea as by land, to compel [states] to fulfill their federal engagements." The plan was considered so extreme, it was never even debated in Congress. Instead, Congress decided that the best way to resolve its financial difficulties was to obtain for itself the power to raise money through a 5 percent tax on imports. On February 2, 1781, it approved a measure requesting the states "to vest a power in Congress" to levy what became known as an "impost." Supporters of the impost faced one particularly serious obstacle: The Articles of Confederation required the unanimous approval of all thirteen states before the impost could go into effect. If even one state objected, the proposal would die.

By the end of 1781, ten states had approved the impost, but three, Georgia, Massachusetts, and Rhode Island, had not. Superintendent of Finance Morris wrote an urgent letter to the governors of these states, stressing that the War of Independence was not yet won and that continued military success required secure funding. In a particularly graphic indictment, Morris declared, "He who opposes the grant of such revenue not only opposes himself to the dictates of justice, but he labors to continue the war, and, of consequence, to shed more blood, to produce more devastation, and to extend and prolong the miseries of mankind."

By the end of the summer of 1782, only tiny Rhode Island still refused to approve the impost. On November 1, the Rhode Island legislature voted officially to reject the proposal, declaring that the impost was "repugnant to the liberty of the United States" because an independent power to raise money would render Congress "independent" of the states. On November 26, Madison wrote a letter to his ally, Edmund Randolph, bemoaning Rhode Island's action, stating that "the most enlightened patrons of the foederal interests . . . pronounce it a blow to our credit abroad as well as our future credit at home." His letter concluded by matter-of-factly informing Randolph: "Col. Hamilton took his seat in Congress yesterday as a Delegate for the State of N. Y."

Hamilton's arrival in Congress brought an energetic and passionate ally to the fight to strengthen the powers of Congress. Unlike Madison, whose shyness and diffidence had kept him from uttering a word of debate in his first six months in Congress, Hamilton entered

Congress ready to make himself heard. He gave his first speech in Congress the day after presenting his credentials, and quickly joined with Madison in the fight to save the impost. On December 6, Congress accepted Hamilton's proposal to send a three-man delegation to Rhode Island to try to persuade its legislature to reverse its decision. Next, Hamilton and Madison were named to a committee, along with Thomas FitzSimons of Pennsylvania, to prepare an answer to Rhode Island's stated objections.

Hamilton, though the junior member of the committee, took the lead, and within a few days had written his first major report for Congress. In this report, he laid out a principle which he would repeat a few years later in *The Federalist*: If a government is given a particular task, it must, by necessity, have been given the powers necessary to accomplish that task. In a long and forceful statement, he declared that it is "pernicious to leave any government in a situation of responsibility disproportioned to its power." Without the ability to raise adequate funds, Congress would be "rendered incapable of providing for the interior harmony or the exterior defence of the State."

Armed with Hamilton's analysis, the congressional delegation left Philadelphia for Rhode Island on December 22. After riding less than ten miles, they learned that Madison's home state of Virginia had rescinded its previous approval of the impost. It quickly became obvious that their trip was useless. Even in the unlikely event that Rhode Island approved the impost, Virginia's action meant that the impost would still fail for lack of unanimity. The delegation turned around and returned to Congress in Philadelphia. Supporters of the impost were distraught. According to Madison, "The most intelligent members were deeply affected & prognosticated a failure of the Impost scheme, & the most pernicious effects to the character, the duration, & the interests of the confederacy."

Within a few days, however, their prospects began to improve. On December 29, a delegation of three army officers rode into Philadelphia to plead the case for the back pay the soldiers were owed and the pensions they were promised. The very different reactions Madison and Hamilton had to the news of the officers' arrival reveal their contrasting personalities and political instincts. For Madison, the army's plight was further proof of the need for Congress to have its own source of funding, so that it could pay its debts. It became the centerpiece of his defense of the impost. To Hamilton, however, the army presented an opportunity to radically alter the terms of the debate in order to frighten and intimidate opponents of the impost and, finally, to force the approval of the long-sought economic measures.

The officers' complaints were well founded. Many had not been paid for a very long time, some for as long as six years. Moreover, even though in 1780 Congress had pledged that soldiers would be granted a retirement pension at half pay, retired soldiers were not receiving any payments, and some state officials were now suggesting that the pension should not be paid at all.

The delegation of officers came armed with a petition drafted by Major General Henry Knox, which they presented to Congress on January 6, 1783. The petition warned that "we have borne all that men can bear." With so little pay for so long, "our property is expended, our private resources are at an end, and our friends are wearied out and disgusted with our incessant applications." Further delay in payments, they declared, could be dangerous for the nation: "The uneasiness of the soldiers, for want of pay, is great and dangerous; any further experiments on their patience may have fatal effects."

Superintendent of Finance Morris could envision the potential political utility of a band of soldiers who were armed, angry, and out of patience. He realized that a powerful political force could be created if the army would join with the public creditors—those wealthy citizens who had either loaned money to the Treasury or provided goods on credit to the army. Morris met with the delegation to convince them that their only hope of redress was to work with the other creditors to gain approval of Morris's economic plan; relief for the army could come only from the central government. In order to increase pressure on the officers, Morris warned them that if they tried to have their debts paid by the individual states instead of by Congress, they would be opposed until "all prospect of obtaining continental funds" had been exhausted.

Robert Morris had two important allies in his attempt to use the officers for political advantage. He was joined both by Hamilton and by the assistant superintendent of finance, Gouverneur Morris (who, despite the shared last name, was not related to his boss). Gouverneur Morris had been a friend of Hamilton's since the beginning of the Revolutionary War. Both men were strong supporters of Robert Morris's plan to combine the interests of the army with those of the other public creditors. Each was determined to make more immediate the implicit threat in the army's discontent.

On January 1, 1783, just days after the officers' delegation had arrived in Philadelphia, Gouverneur Morris wrote an almost gleeful letter to John Jay. "The army," he wrote, "have swords in their hands. You know enough of the history of mankind to know much more than I have said, and possibly much more than they themselves think of." He hinted that he was actively manipulating the situation: "Depend on it, good will arise from the situation to which we are hastening. And this you may rely on, that my efforts will not be wanting." Morris ended this note by acknowledging the risks in his plan and explaining that "although I think it probable, that much of convulsions will ensue, yet it must terminate in giving to government that power, without which government is but a name."

Hamilton's initial involvement with the delegation does not seem to have involved the encouragement of "convulsions." Nevertheless, he utilized his influence from the outset to further the superintendent of finance's plan. At the time of their arrival in Philadelphia, each member of the officers' delegation could claim a warm personal relationship with Hamilton. The leader of the group, General Alexander McDougall, had been Hamilton's sponsor, helping him get his start in the military during the Revolutionary War by recommending to the New York Provincial Congress that Hamilton be named captain of an artillery company. The second, Colonel Mathias Ogden, was the brother-in-law of Francis Barber, who had run a New Jersey college preparatory program which Hamilton attended from 1772 to 1773. The third member was Colonel John Brooks, an "intimate friend" of Hamilton's.

Hamilton met with his three friends prior to their formal meeting with Congress. Shortly thereafter, General McDougall announced his full support for the plan "to unite the influence of Congress with that of the Army and the public Creditors, to obtain permanent funds for the United [S]tates, which will promise ultimate security to the Army."

On the evening of January 13, 1783, the army delegation met with a Grand Committee of Congress, which included one delegate from each state. Both Madison and Hamilton were among those who attended this meeting. The officers, using the advice they had received, made clear the threat of military unrest if the financial issues were not resolved. They warned that if the army was not paid, "the most serious consequences were to be apprehended." General Mc-Dougall reported that the army was "verging to that state which we are told will make a wise man mad." One member of Congress asked what would happen if no payments were immediately advanced. The officers responded menacingly that "at least a mutiny would ensue." Immediately after the officers left the meeting, the unsettled Grand Committee voted to create a subcommittee made up of Hamilton, Madison, and John Rutledge of South Carolina to work with the superintendent of finance to respond to the officers' demands.

On January 24, the subcommittee reported back to Congress. But before their report was presented, the superintendent of finance increased the pressure on Congress by giving it an ultimatum in which he demanded that it either make "permanent provision for the public debts of every kind" or else he would resign. He closed his plea with this stark declaration: "I will never be the minister of injustice."

According to Madison, "This letter made a deep & solemn impression on Congress." It quickly and unanimously approved Hamilton's report, which proposed that Congress should be responsible for the claims of the troops and should obtain from the states "funds adequate to the object of funding the whole debt of the U.S." As an astounded Madison wrote in an aside, "even Rhode Island concurring in it."

Turning this principle into a plan of action, however, presented a far more divisive question. Many in Congress were strongly opposed to any funding scheme which would alter the existing balance of power between Congress and the states. Their goal in the ensuing debate was to preserve state autonomy and to ensure that Congress would not be empowered to invade state sovereignty. It would fall to Madison to try to mollify their fears while reining in Hamilton, his overly enthusiastic ally.

On January 27, 1783, Congress began its funding debate. James Wilson of Pennsylvania, who would later attend the Constitutional Convention and serve on the Supreme Court, proposed "the establishment of general funds to be collected by Congress." This proposal embodied two significant and controversial changes: Congress would be able to raise funds directly as well as control the actual collection of taxes.

Hamilton eagerly supported this proposal. In the first of several long speeches, he defended both the concepts of creating a permanent source of revenue and of having that revenue collected by agents appointed by Congress. Congress, not the states, should collect the monies, he said, because that method would be simpler, more economical, and less subject to state manipulation. After he spoke, several delegates took the floor, each voicing a "strong dislike" for the concept of officers appointed by Congress collecting taxes.

The debate continued into the following day. Finally, Madison, fearful that the very concept of establishing a source of funding for Congress was in jeopardy, rose to offer a compromise, which would split Wilson's original motion in two. In the first part, Congress would vote on the proposition that "the establishment of permanent and adequate funds, to operate generally throughout the United States, is indispensably necessary." The even more contentious issue of whether such funds were "to be collected under the authority of Congress" was left to be debated afterward. Madison's strategy was to try to reassure the opponents of granting taxing power to Congress that the plan need not intrude on the autonomy of the individual states.

Even Madison's compromise ran into opposition. Many delegates continued to argue that the taxing power should stay with the states. Hamilton delivered another lengthy speech, again emphasizing the necessity of a permanent source of general funds. He ended his remarks by bringing up the issue of having Congress appoint the tax collection officers. Hamilton said that the federal government lacked "the energy . . . necessary for pervading and uniting the states." This problem could be ameliorated, Hamilton concluded, by introducing into the states "the influence of officers" whose jobs depended on the goodwill of Congress, and hence would be "interested in supporting the power of Congress."

Caught in the passion of his argument, Hamilton unwittingly had just handed his adversaries the weapon they needed. He had made Madison's compromise proposal appear to be merely the first step of a nationalist plot to "pervade," "unite," and ultimately subsume the states. Madison, when describing the congressional debate, said, "This remark was imprudent, and injurious to the cause which it was meant to serve." Madison added that two strong opponents of the plan, Theodorick Bland and Arthur Lee, came to him in private and gloatingly told him that "Mr. Hamilton had let out the secret." Madison's modified funding proposal was defeated, and the congressional debate over funding continued for several more months.

Hamilton appears to have been unaware that Madison blamed him for "injuring" the cause. Madison never confronted him with his concerns. Hamilton, in a pattern that would be repeated in 1788, seemed oblivious to Madison's anger and continued to view him as an ally. In fact, the next day, Hamilton singled him out to share some sensitive news he had obtained. Madison wrote in his notes that, during a congressional discussion about a treaty with Holland, Hamilton "told him privately" of the potentially serious objections that the secretary of the French legation had raised to Hamilton about the treaty.

Congressional debate over funding grew more and more frustrating for Madison. On February 4, he complained that, while most delegates supported a system of federal revenue, such plans were thwarted by their "despondence & timidity." A week later, Madison wrote that "we seem only to have gone round in a circle."

Hamilton was not content to wait for Congress to reach a consensus. Instead, he, along with Gouverneur Morris, decided to use the army's discontent to increase the pressure on Congress. In early February, Colonel Brooks was given two letters to deliver, one from Hamilton and one from Morris. Morris wrote to Major General Henry Knox, telling him that once peace came and the army was no longer considered useful by the states, "they will see you starve rather than pay a six Penny tax." Thus, Morris continued, "the only wise mode is for the army to connect themselves with the public creditors of every kind both foreign and domestic and unremittingly to urge the grant of general permanent funds." He offered a military allusion to describe his scheme: "The army may now influence the legislatures and if you will permit me a metaphor from your own profession after you have carried the post the public creditors will garrison it for you."

Hamilton had a far more delicate assignment. His task was to write George Washington and convince him to manipulate the increasingly impatient troops and direct their anger into more productive channels. This was to be Hamilton's first direct communication with his former supervisor in over a year. Hamilton laid out the ambitious financial plan to Washington: "The great desideratum at present is the establishment of general funds, which alone can do justice to the Creditors of the United States (of whom the army forms the most meritorious class), restore public credit and supply the future wants of government. . . . In this the influence of the army, properly directed, may cooperate."

Hamilton explained how the army's anger might be beneficial, as it could frighten those opposed to the federal funding plan: "The claims of the army, urged with moderation, but with firmness, may operate on those weak minds which are influenced by their apprehensions more than by their judgments." The army, said Hamilton, "may add weight to the applications of Congress to the several states." The plan did not require a mutiny or armed insurrection. Hamilton's goal was to use the mere threat of such activity to play on the "apprehensions" of the opposing legislators.

But an angry collection of armed soldiers presented an obvious danger as well. Hamilton knew they must keep a "complaining and suffering army within the bounds of moderation." And Hamilton saw how the task of inciting yet controlling the army could be done: "This," he told Washington, "your Excellency's influence must effect." He urged Washington not to suppress the army's activities, "but rather by the intervention of confidential and prudent persons, to take the direction of them." Hamilton knew that Washington's position as commander-in-chief would make a public leadership role politically unfeasible. So he reminded Washington that the general's involvement "must not appear." Instead, he suggested that Washington should attempt surreptitiously to control the army's threatening behavior. Hamilton added a postscript to his letter concerning Henry Knox, whom Gouverneur Morris simultaneously was trying to recruit into the plan. Hamilton wrote to Washington that Knox was trusted by the army and that "he may be safely made use of."

When Hamilton had not received a reply within a few weeks, he became increasingly anxious. Finally, on March 5, he wrote another note to Washington, stating that he had written "on a very confidential subject and shall be anxious to know as soon as convenient whether the letter got safe to hand."

Washington had, in fact, already sent a response declining Hamilton's invitation. Washington decried the idea that a collection of soldiers would act in concert to influence the government: "It would at this day be productive of Civil commotions & end in blood. Unhappy situation this! God forbid we should be involved in it." Washington then declared that he would not participate in any such plan: "I shall pursue the same steady line of conduct which has governed me hitherto."

Gouverneur Morris was similarly unable to convince either General Knox or another Revolutionary War hero, General Nathaniel Greene, to join the plan. While each agreed with the principle that the army shared a common interest with the other public creditors, they strongly disapproved of any plan to use the threat of armed insurrection as a lobbying tool. As Greene warned Morris, "When Soldiers advance without authority, who can halt them?"

The hope that politics would lead to a solution dimmed when Congress learned on February 13 that King George had given a speech stating that preliminary agreement had been reached on a peace treaty with the United States. The end of the war seemed to embolden those who wanted to maintain the power of the states in financial matters. In response, several of the delegates who were most in favor of increasing the power of Congress held an emergency strategy meeting on the evening of February 20. The meeting was held in the home of Thomas FitzSimons and was attended by Madison and Hamilton, as well as Daniel Carroll, Richard Peters, and Nathaniel Gorham.

Hamilton warned the group that the army was secretly plotting to refuse to lay down their arms unless provision was made to ensure that they would be paid. Moreover, Hamilton stated, Washington was becoming increasingly unpopular among the troops, and plans were being made to replace him with someone who was not as disinclined to "unlawful proceedings." Hamilton also disclosed, in the most general terms, that he had written to Washington, urging "him to be the conductor of the army in their plans for redress, in order that they might be moderated & directed to proper objects."

After much discussion, all in the group but one reached the disappointing conclusion that it had become impossible to convince Congress to impose any tax beyond the impost and that it was now necessary to compromise with the legislative opponents. Only Hamilton continued to believe that their original broader vision was still obtainable.

This evening meeting marked a turning point in the roles of Madison and Hamilton in the impost debate. Madison would from then on take the lead in forging a legislative compromise, one which Hamilton was determined to oppose.

Fresh from the evening meeting, on February 21, Madison announced that he was ready to acquiesce in many of the demands of his former adversaries. While saying he had wished for an arrangement in which the federal government was able to obtain all of the funding it needed through its own taxing power, Madison now conceded that

Congress was not ready to accept such a plan. He stated that he would limit the proposal so that Congress would be empowered only to raise revenue from the impost, and that the rest of the money needed to pay back the creditors would be derived from "a revenue established within each State separately & appropriated to the Common Treasury." As part of this new spirit of compromise, Madison pledged to support "no measure tending to augment the power of Congress which should appear unnecessary."

After much discussion, Congress finally voted to create a committee, which included Madison and Hamilton, to propose a funding plan. In his final attempt at compromise, Madison wrote the committee's report, proposing that Congress be given the ability to impose a 5 percent import tax, but instead of a permanent grant of power, this authority would expire within twenty-five years. The import tax was to be collected not by federal officials but by collectors "appointed by the states." Finally, this proposal would not take effect until approved by every one of the thirteen states.

Hamilton never would accept this compromise. He later attempted, unsuccessfully, to postpone the vote on the proposal and replace it with his own plan for more extensive federal taxing powers.

Meanwhile, the situation with the army took an extreme and sinister turn. On March 10, an anonymous document began circulating among the troops stationed in Newburgh, New York. Later determined to have been written by John Armstrong, a disaffected twenty-six-year-old army major, the address called for a meeting of officers to discuss what measures the troops should take to obtain the money which they were owed. The simple act of calling such a meeting was disturbing because—as it was not sanctioned by the commanding officer, George Washington—the meeting was illegal. The tone of Armstrong's address was simultaneously angry and threatening. The officers were told to confront "a country that tramples upon your rights, disdains your cries and insults your distresses." Now was the time to change their tone, to alter their "appeal from the justice to the fears of government." The troops were called on to declare that they would refuse to lay down their arms if peace came, but if the war were to resume, they were to refuse to fight, and "retire to some unsettled country, smile in your turn, and 'mock when their fear cometh on.'" The address included a veiled threat to General George Washington himself: "Suspect the man who would advise to more moderation and longer forbearance."

Superintendent of Finance Robert Morris knew of the blossoming conspiracy. Officers at Newburgh were said to have sounded him out and reported that he was not hostile to their aims. An army supplier in Newburgh later reported that Morris, when asked how an army which was opposed by the country could be fed, replied, "I will feed them."

When Washington learned of the March 10 address, he acted quickly to regain control of the situation. He issued his own order the next day, condemning the "irregular invitation" to "such disorderly proceedings," and called instead for a meeting on March 15. He indicated that he would not attend this meeting but that the presiding officer would "report the result of the deliberations to the Commander in Chief."

On the morning of Saturday, March 15, a tense and angry group of officers from every unit crowded into a newly constructed building. The seventy-by-forty-foot wood structure had been designed to serve as both a social meeting place and a place of worship for the soldiers and was commonly called the Temple of Virtue. The meeting was called to order by Major General Gates, who was probably one of the ringleaders of the anti-Washington forces. Suddenly, without advance notice, Washington entered the building, and requested the opportunity to address the surprised troops. He began by attacking the anonymous document for proposing that the army should ever consider threatening "the dreadful alternative, of deserting our country in the extremest hour of her distress or turning our arms against it," a proposal he called "so shocking . . . that humanity revolts at the idea."

When he finished his prepared remarks, Washington orchestrated one of the great melodramatic moments in American history. To demonstrate the commitment that many in Congress felt to the officers' cause, he began to read a letter from delegate Joseph Jones. Washington then paused, and the crowd grew restive as they watched him reach into his vest pocket. For the first time in public, he put on his new reading glasses (which had been sent to him by the astronomer David Rittenhouse). Turning to the assembled soldiers, Washington apologized and said softly, "Gentlemen, you will permit me to put on my spectacles, for I have not only grown gray but almost blind in the service of my country." The effect was immediate and overwhelming. As one officer, Major Samuel Shaw, would later write, "There was something so natural, so unaffected in this appeal as rendered it superior to the most studied oratory. It forced its way to the heart, and you might see sensibility moisten every eye."

The uprising was over. Washington left the room and the officers soon approved a resolution not only supporting him but declaring their "unshaken confidence in the justice of Congress and their country." They further pledged that "no circumstances of distress or danger shall induce a conduct that may tend to sully the reputation and glory which [the officers] have acquired."

Washington would turn to Hamilton with his suspicion that the aborted mutiny had been instigated by those outside the military, and that politicians had manipulated the plight of the officers to achieve their own political aims. On March 12, the day after the "irregular" call for the officers' meeting, Washington wrote, "There is something very mysterious in this business. It appears reports have been propagated in Philadelphia, that dangerous combinations were forming in the Army. . . . That some member of Congress wished the measure might take effect, in order to compel the public, particularly the delinquent states, to do justice." Washington concluded that "it is firmly believed by some, the scheme was not only planned, but also digested and matured in Philadelphia."

On March 17, Hamilton responded with a partial confession. He wrote that he, along with others, had urged "the propriety of uniting the influence of the public creditors, & the army as a part of them, to prevail upon the States to enter into their views." He tried to explain that this had all been just a harmless attempt to combine "the personal influence of some, the connections of others, and a sense of justice to the army, as well as the apprehension of ill consequences, [which] might form a mass of influence in each state." Hamilton added that, of course, he would never be in favor of the use of force which "would only be productive of the horrors of a civil war, might end in the ruin of the Country & would certainly end in the ruin of the army."

Washington replied that even if the civilians did not plan to use force, dire consequences could flow from the misuse of the army. The army, he warned, "is a dangerous instrument to play with." Washington added that "some men (& leading ones too) in the Army" believed that Congress intended that the army was "to be made use of as mere Pupp[e]ts to establish Continental funds; & that rather than not succeed in this measure . . . they would make a sacrifice of the Army and all its interests." Without indicating whether he shared this view, Washington concluded by singling out Robert Morris, asserting that "the Financier is suspected to be at the bottom of this scheme."

Hamilton's defense is an interesting one. Rather than directly state that there had been no attempt to manipulate the officers, he simply declared that the allegation could not be proven: "The necessity and discontents of the army presented themselves as a powerful engine. But Sir these Gentlemen would be puzzled to support their insinuations by a single fact." He similarly did not assert the innocence of either Robert Morris, or his assistant, Gouverneur Morris. Instead, Hamilton told Washington that these men should be viewed as allies: "The men against whom the suspicions you mention must be directed are in general the most sensible[,] the most liberal, the most independent and the most respectable characters in our body as well as the most unequivocal friends to the army. In a word they are the men who think continentally."

Whether as a result of Madison's legislative actions or Hamilton's extracurricular activity, Congress at last began to make progress on reaching an agreement on funding. First, on March 22, exactly one week after Washington's address to the troops at Newburgh, Congress resolved one major sticking point by agreeing to what was called "commutation," or liquidating the former promise to soldiers of half pay for life to a guarantee of five year's pay. Then, on April 18, Congress finally approved an impost program. Based largely on Madison's proposal from February, the final plan gave Congress the authority to impose a 5 percent import tax for the limited time of twenty-five years, with the tax to be collected by state officials. The rest of the money to pay off the federal debt was to be the responsibility of the individual states. The proposal would not go into effect until it received the approval of every state.

The congressional vote in favor of the proposal was overwhelming. The only negative votes were cast by the two delegates from Rhode Island, Stephen Higginson of Massachusetts, and, stubborn to the end, Alexander Hamilton. A frustrated and bitter Madison wrote to Thomas Jefferson that this defection was due to "the rigid adherence of Mr. Hamilton to a plan which he supposed more perfect."

While Madison did not hide his disappointment in Hamilton, neither did he mask his own misgivings about the final compromise. Congress authorized Madison to prepare an "Address to the States" urging them to approve the impost. His letter revealed his own ambivalence about the fact that the impost was limited to twenty-five years and would not be collected by federal officials. "If the strict maxims of national credit alone were to be consulted," he wrote, "the revenue ought manifestly to be co-existent with the object of it, and the collection placed in every respect under that authority which is to dispense the former, and is responsible for the latter." Madison urged the states to view the compromise as proof that the delegates in Congress recognized that they were subservient to the wishes of the states and thus were willing "to attend at all times to the sentiments of those whom they serve."

As the states began considering the proposal, peace finally was officially declared. With the war over, however, the troops were faced with an order to disband before what Washington called the "debt of honour" was repaid. On May 26, Congress approved a compromise proposal by Hamilton that the troops be "furloughed," that is, sent home but not formally discharged. No provision was made for the immediate payment of the soldiers.

While most of the army begrudgingly accepted the situation, a small contingent from Pennsylvania was so fearful that they would never be paid that they decided to take aggressive action. Disobeying orders from their commanding officers, about eighty soldiers left Lancaster, Pennsylvania, early on the morning of June 17 to march to Philadelphia and, as they described it, "to obtain Justice." It has never been entirely clear who their target was, since Congress was not the only governmental body in Philadelphia; Pennsylvania's governing body, the Supreme Executive Council, was also based in Philadelphia, and both bodies met in the Pennsylvania State House.

As the Lancaster troops neared Philadelphia, the president of Congress, Elias Boudinot, appointed a three-member committee for the purpose of meeting with the president of Pennsylvania's Executive Council, John Dickinson, to take "such measures as they should find necessary" to deal with the threat posed by the mutinous troops. Boudinot named Hamilton to chair the committee, and Hamilton quickly assumed responsibility for handling the impending crisis. Hamilton's audacious maneuverings during the next few days would lead many to question his character and judgment.

On Thursday, June 19, Hamilton met with Dickinson and the state's Executive Council and strongly urged that the Pennsylvania state militia be called out to stop the Lancaster soldiers. The Pennsylvanian authorities obstinately refused to call out the militia until "some outrage should have been committed by the troops." Hamilton responded by ordering, in the name of his committee, Assistant Secretary of War William Jackson to meet the troops outside the city limits and order them to return to Lancaster. Hamilton was now in control of managing the crisis; he did not even deign to seek Congress's approval before issuing the order to Jackson. The troops ignored Jackson's plea, and on the morning of Friday, June 20, marched into Philadelphia and joined other troops who were housed in the Philadelphia barracks.

The next day was Saturday, and Congress, which had adjourned on Friday, was not scheduled to meet again until Monday. The Pennsylvania Executive Council, however, had scheduled a Saturday session, and at midday their meeting was interrupted by the ominous sounds of drumbeats and fifes. A group of thirty soldiers approached the State

House. Speaking for the soldiers, Sergeant Ebenezer Robinson presented a demand to President Dickinson and the Executive Council: either permit them to appoint their own officers to lead their battle for the money they were owed, or "we shall instantly let in those injured soldiers upon you, and abide by the consequences." Shortly thereafter, 250 more soldiers arrived and surrounded the building.

Meanwhile, Hamilton had learned of the problems with the troops. It is unclear whether he had simply heard rumors in the morning of trouble brewing or if he knew that the soldiers had in fact arrived at the state capitol. In any event, he spoke with the president of Congress, Elias Boudinot, who shortly thereafter called for an emergency meeting of Congress. Congress again asked for Dickinson to call out the militia. He again refused, saying that "without some outrages on persons or property the temper of the militia could not be relied on."

The soldiers, meanwhile, were raucous but generally well behaved, despite the fact that, in the words of Madison, "spirituous drink from the tipling houses adjoining began to be liberally served out to the Soldiers." Apart from occasionally shouting offensive words and waving their bayonets in the air, there was no serious misbehavior by the soldiers. At three o'clock, Congress adjourned and left the building. A few soldiers harassed Elias Boudinot as he left, but they were quickly admonished by a superior officer. Other than that, the soldiers presented no greater threat than "offering a mock obstruction" and they permitted the members of Congress to leave the State House without further incident.

Congress reconvened at six in the evening to discuss how to deal with this situation. The delegates voted to urge, once more, President Dickinson to call out the state militia. Hamilton's committee was authorized to meet again with Pennsylvania officials and, if the committee concluded that there was inadequate state action for "supporting the dignity of the federal government," they were to advise Congress to leave Philadelphia and meet in either Trenton or Princeton, New Jersey.

The next day, Sunday, Hamilton met with the state Executive Council at Dickinson's house. Hamilton demanded that the state militia be called and declared that "vigorous measures should be taken to put a stop to the further progress of the evil." He also reported that Congress was "unwilling to expose the United States to a repetition of the insult" and would not meet again in Philadelphia until the crisis had ended. The Executive Council requested a day to ascertain the "disposition" of the state militia. On Monday, they informed Hamilton that, in their opinion, the militia was "disinclined" to enter the fray.

Hamilton received more bad news the following day. The officers whom the soldiers had selected to represent them had apparently drawn up a new list of demands and seemed disinclined to end the standoff quickly. Reports emerged that the soldiers "were getting Drunk very fast." At two o'clock in the afternoon, Hamilton wrote his formal statement to Boudinot recommending that Congress leave Philadelphia. Following Hamilton's advice, Boudinot quickly issued an order for Congress to reconvene in two days in Princeton.

With Congress truly gone from the city, Pennsylvania finally called out its militia. Immediately, the uprising ended. The two main leaders, Captain Henry Carbery and Lieutenant John Sullivan, fled, and the rest of the soldiers quickly submitted to the orders to return to their base.

As for Congress, its relocation to Princeton was not a pleasant one. As delegate Eleazer McComb of Delaware complained, "This Town is too small for our Accommodation." Princeton, at the time, was a "small scattered village, consisting of about 50 houses." Most of these were in disrepair, and many of the new ones were not yet finished. The delegates were scattered throughout the town and its surroundings, many living in farmhouses, miles apart from one another.

James Madison appears to have had a particularly bad time of it. After much searching, he and fellow Virginian delegate Joseph Jones were able to find only a single room to share, one that was "scarcely ten feet square." To Jefferson, Madison complained that the room was so small that it lacked a desk or "a single accommodation for writing." To his father he added that "we are exceedingly crowded in this place; too much so . . . for our own comfort," especially since Madison and Jones, who was six feet tall, were forced to spend the nights together, "in one bed."

The citizens of Philadelphia also did not take well to the new arrangement. While some blamed President Dickinson and the Executive Council, many accused Congress of overreacting. In the sneering words of Pennsylvania's secretary of state, John Armstrong, "The grand Sanhedrin of the Nation, with all their solemnity & emptiness . . . have removed to Princeton, & left a State, where their wisdom has been long questioned, their virtue suspected, & their dignity a jest."

The anger soon focused on Hamilton, who was accused of acting precipitously. He was suspected of plotting to move the capital permanently out of Philadelphia and into his home state of New York. The French foreign minister wrote that he believed that Hamilton had deliberately "soured the climate by spreading rumors" so that Congress eventually "would reside in his State." The same accusation, though more colorfully stated, came from an anonymous newspaper writer who described the "ship Congress" as being sunk, with some of its members "privy to the sinking" in the hope that the ship would be "moored hereafter, at a new wharf lately built on the North [Hudson] River."

The irony here is that it was not Hamilton, but congressional President Elias Boudinot who most appears to have been motivated by the desire to move Congress to his native state. Boudinot, who was from New Jersey, had written to his brother even before the final decision to leave Philadelphia had been made and told him, "I wish Jersey to shew her readiness on this occasion, as it may fix Congress as to their permanent residence." Hamilton, in contrast, expressed his willingness to move Congress back to Philadelphia as soon as the crisis with the soldiers had passed.

The more serious charge against Hamilton was that, in advising Boudinot to call Congress into a special session on Saturday, June 21, Hamilton had precipitated the crisis by putting Congress in the path of the mutinous soldiers. One historian, Kenneth Bowling, concluded that Hamilton deliberately inserted Congress into the middle of the troops because he "hoped perhaps that a military demonstration against Congress would be the source of badly needed public support for the federal government." If so, it should be pointed out, the plan failed; no great outpouring of support for Congress materialized.

Hamilton was desperate to clear his name. He needed a witness to verify that he had not been in an unseemly rush to leave Philadelphia, but had delayed as long as possible. He turned to James Madison and, in a letter dated July 6, pleaded with him to "vindicate myself from the insinuation" that he had been "influenced by the desire of getting Congress out of the city." Be specific, asked Hamilton: "What appeared to be my ideas and disposition respecting the removal of Congress? Did I appear to wish to hasten it, or did I not rather show a strong disposition to procrastinate it?"

Hamilton's letter was lost in the mail for several months. It finally reached Madison in October, and Madison wrote back immediately. He provided a complete defense, stating that Hamilton was "opposed to the removal of Congress, except in the last necessity; that when you finally yielded the measure it appeared to be more in compliance with the peremptory expostulations of oth[ers] than with any disposition of your own mind; and that after the arrival of Congress at Princeton your conversation shewed that you received the removal with regret than with pleasure." Madison ended by noting that, though his letter might no longer be necessary after the extensive delay, he did not want to miss the "opportunity of testifying the esteem & regard" in which he held Hamilton.

By the end of October, both Madison and Hamilton had left Congress to return to their home states. Despite their efforts, the Congress they left behind was homeless, penniless, and powerless to solve any of the serious problems facing the nation. The impost for which they had fought so passionately was destined never to be approved by the states. Congress itself became a restless vagabond, embarking on an odyssey that took it over the next several years to Annapolis, Trenton, and New York.

A complex personal and political relationship, however, had begun. As historian Jack Rakove has noted, Madison and Hamilton were not joint partners in a "nationalist party" in Congress, planning and plotting the centralization of power. Neither were they close, intimate friends. Nonetheless, the early indications of a powerful collaboration are apparent.

Many of their contemporaries did not hesitate to assume that Madison and Hamilton were working together as effective and companionable partners. For example, on July 15, 1783, Robert Livingston, the secretary for foreign affairs, wrote to Madison in Princeton asking for help in convincing Congress to permit Livingston to sign the formal peace treaty with England before leaving office. In his attempt to lobby Congress, Livingston mentioned to Madison only one other member of Congress. Livingston wrote, "I should write Coll Hamilton also on this subject . . . if however he should still be with you . . . . I pray you to show him this." A few days later, it was Hamilton who responded to Livingston. He wrote that Madison had indeed shown him the letter and that "we have talked over the subject of your letter to him, and need not assure you how happy we should be to promote your wish." Hamilton concluded, "You shall hear me further on the subject. Mr. Maddison does not write himself as the letter contains both our ideas."

On a more personal level, Hamilton's turning to Madison for support and validation after the Philadelphia mutiny demonstrates the respect and trust in which he held Madison. Madison's response, in return, reveals that, despite his misgivings over Hamilton's impetuousness and occasional inflexibility, he, too, had begun to see in Hamilton a colleague and potential ally.

2

"To Cement the Union"

SOUNDING THE CALL FOR A CONVENTION

Upon leaving Princeton, Madison returned to Virginia. He originally had hoped to travel to New York to be reunited with his young fiancée, Kitty Floyd. During the summer of 1783, however, she sent Madison a letter (sealed, according to Floyd family legend, with a lump of rye dough), informing him that she was breaking off their engagement. A dejected Madison wrote to his friend Thomas Jefferson informing him that his relationship had ended. Madison, in his characteristically awkward manner, told Jefferson of "the uncertain state into which the object I was then pursuing has been brought by one of those incidents to which such affairs are liable." Madison was hardly devoid of feeling. He would, late in life, scratch out most of his letter to Jefferson rendering it unreadable, until biographer Irving Brandt, in 1948, was able to decipher some of the concealed writing. Among the phrases that emerged was Madison's rueful description of "a profession of indifference at what has happened."

Hamilton, meanwhile, traveled north to New York, where he was reunited with his wife, Elizabeth, and their first child, Philip. Before joining Congress, Hamilton had written to the Marquis de

Lafayette describing his life as "rocking the cradle and studying the art of fleecing my neighbors." When Hamilton left Congress, his plan was to resume that existence. He declined requests to run for the New York State Assembly, choosing instead to focus his attention on his legal career.

From his New York City office, Hamilton became known as one of the premier lawyers of his day. His specialty was one that would raise questions about his commitment to the American democracy: defending British loyalists against claims from both the patriotic citizens of the city of New York and the state itself. New York had enacted several laws which singled out loyalists for particularly harsh treatment. New York's Confiscation Act, which had been passed in 1779, permitted the state to seize the property of anyone found to have "adhered to the Enemy." The Trespass Act, passed in 1783, permitted "patriots" to sue "loyalists" for any damage allegedly done to their property.

While defending loyalists, particularly wealthy ones, was a lucrative enterprise, Hamilton justified his role as a matter of principle. To Hamilton, New York's laws raised both practical and policy concerns. He argued that excessively punitive measures would drive a "great number of useful citizens" out of the state and into Canada, where they would provide unnecessary competition for New York businesses. Hamilton also believed that generous treatment of those who had been defeated would improve the standing of the United States in the world: "Those who consult only their passions might choose to construe what I say as too favourable to a set of men who have been the enemies of the public liberty; but those for whose esteem I am most concerned will acquit me of any personal considerations and will perceive that I only urge the cause of national honor, safety and advantage. We have assumed an independent station; we ought to feel and to act in a manner consistent with the dignity of that station." Hamilton also contended that both of New York's laws violated the Treaty of Paris, which ended the Revolutionary War. Article 6 of the treaty specifically stated that "there shall be no future confiscations made, nor any prosecutions commenced" against those who opposed the revolution. Hamilton wrote that pursuant to this language, "the disaffected were secured from every future deprivation and injury whatever."

The most important case Hamilton argued challenging these laws was *Rutgers v. Waddington* in 1784. This lawsuit was brought by Elizabeth Rutgers, who had left New York City, abandoning her brewery and malt house, when British troops took over the city. Her properties were subsequently commandeered by the British commissary general, and handed over to a British merchant, Joshua Waddington, who took possession on August 13, 1778. In 1780, the British commander-in-chief assumed control of commandeered property and charged Waddington rent through March 1783. The British then left the city, and Waddington eventually returned the property to Rutgers. She sued under the Trespass Act to recover damages for the taking of her property.

Rutgers v. Waddington was widely seen as a test case, one which might determine the relative power of the state and national governments, and determine whether the Trespass Act, enacted by the State of New York, could withstand a challenge that it conflicted with the Treaty of Paris, which had been ratified by Congress. In his arguments before what was then known as the New York Mayor's Court, Hamilton presented a comprehensive analysis of two issues that would become essential components of his later writings in *The Federalist:* the supremacy of national laws over contradictory state laws, and the authority of courts, using the power of judicial review, to strike down acts of a legislature. Hamilton argued that unless Congress had the right to bind a state in its "internal police," the confederation was nothing more than "the shadow of a shade!" The treaty ratified by Congress was "a law Paramount to that of any particular state," and "the Legislature of one state cannot repeal a law of the United States." When faced with a direct conflict between the nation's treaty and a state's law, courts were duty bound to disregard the law and follow the treaty, for "that which relates to the most important concerns ought to prevail." In such a case, "a law from a particular state derogating from its constitutional authority *is no law.*"

Although Mayor James Duane, who also served as chief judge of the Mayor's Court, agreed with much of what Hamilton said, he was unwilling to embrace the full scope of the argument. Duane authored a long, convoluted opinion in which Hamilton's client won a partial victory. Waddington was relieved of all liability for his use of the Rutgers property for the period of 1780–1783, since under the "law of nations" the British commander-in-chief had the authority to control the property occupied by his troops. Waddington, however, was ordered to pay for his pre-1780 occupancy, since the commissary's actions were not pursuant to a similar military authority and thus were not similarly covered by the "law of nations."

Duane appears to have accepted Hamilton's argument on the supremacy of Congress's treaty power: "The foederal compact hath vested Congress with full and exclusive power to make peace and war. . . . And we are clearly of the opinion, that no state in this union can alter or abridge, in a single point, the foederal articles [of Confederation] or the treaty."

Duane tried to sidestep the more volatile question of judicial review and whether a judge could declare a state law which attempted to alter a treaty void. In fact, Duane at one point seemed to say the opposite, declaring that "the supremacy of the Legislature need not be called into question; if they think fit *positively* to enact a law, there is no power which can controul them." That may have been mere window dressing because, as many New York politicians noted, Duane's decision had the indisputable result of depriving New York's law of its full intended effect. Melancton Smith, who would later become a leading Anti-Federalist opponent of the Constitution, criticized the ruling on the ground that "the Mayor's court have assumed and exercised a power to set aside an act of the state." The New York State Assembly agreed, and passed an angry resolution, condemning the decision as "subversive of all law and good order." The resolution warned that if courts "may take upon them to dispense with, an act in direct violation of a plain and known law of the state, all other Courts either superior or inferior may do the like . . . and Legislatures become useless."

Despite Duane's attempt to finesse the issue, in practical terms, Hamilton's theory of judicial review had been vindicated.

Madison, as well, was immersed in several disputes that would leave a lasting imprint on American constitutional law. In April 1784, Madison had been elected a delegate to the Virginia State Assembly, where he would serve for the next three years. During that time, Madison would take the lead in historic controversies involving freedom of religion and the call for the Constitutional Convention in Philadelphia.

The battle over religion pitted Madison against the politically powerful orator Patrick Henry. Henry was a strong supporter of a tax that would fund "teachers of the Christian religion." This bill would have imposed a tax on all Virginians, who were permitted to designate which denomination or "society of Christians" was to receive the tax revenue. Madison argued that this bill would violate Section 16 of the Virginia Declaration of Rights, which he had helped draft. The Declaration of Rights provided that "religion, or the duty which we owe to our Creator and the manner of discharging it, can be directed by reason and conviction, not by force or violence; and therefore, all men are equally entitled to the free exercise of religion, according to the dictates of conscience."

Madison was unable to find enough supporters to defeat the tax bill. It appeared headed for passage until he used a parliamentary procedure to have the final vote on the bill delayed for eleven months, until November 1785. During that time, Madison helped rally opposition to the bill, and on June 20, 1785, he presented his "Memorial and Remonstrance against Religious Assessments." This petition has become one of the fundamental documents explaining, if not actually creating, the American concept of separation of church and state.

Madison declared that the government should not be involved in promoting religion, stating that "in matters of Religion, no man's right is abridged by the institution of Civil Society and that Religion is wholly exempt from its cognizance." He cautioned that they were on a slippery slope. If government could favor one religion, it could also favor one denomination or even one chosen sect: "Who does not see that the same authority which can establish Christianity, in exclusion of all other Religions, may establish with the same ease any particular sect of Christians, in exclusion of all other Sects?" He also argued that nonbelievers have the same right to their beliefs as those who belong to the majority religion: "Whilst we assert for ourselves a freedom to embrace, to profess and to observe the Religion which we believe to be of divine origin, we cannot deny an equal freedom to those whose minds have not yet yielded to the evidence which has convinced us."

Finally, Madison made an observation that he would build upon in his famous *Federalist* essay, *Federalist 10*. Peace could not be obtained from a majority, religious or otherwise, mandating uniformity of belief. Only a system which provided for a freedom that permitted multiple religions to coexist could prevent religious warfare: "Torrents of blood have been spilt in the old world, by vain attempts of the secular arm, to extinguish Religious discord, by proscribing all difference in Religious opinion. Time has at length revealed the true remedy. . . . The American Theatre has exhibited proofs that equal and compleat liberty, if it does not wholly eradicate it, sufficiently destroys its malignant influence on the health and prosperity of the State."

Madison's effort at coalition building led to the withdrawal of the bill to fund Christian teachers. Late in life, he would recall how his "Memorial and Remonstrance" had "met with the approbation of the Baptists, the Presbyterians, the Quakers, and the few Roman Catholics, universally; of the Methodists in part; and even of not a few of the Sect [Episcopal Church] formerly established by law." He proudly recalled that "When the Legislature assembled, the number of Copies & signatures prescribed displayed such an overwhelming opposition of the people, that the proposed plan of a genl assessmt was crushed under it."

Madison's other great battle in the legislature did not begin as auspiciously. He was unable to convince his fellow delegates to approve any increase in Congress's power. He was, however, instrumental in creating a series of meetings that led to the Constitutional Convention.

The first meeting grew out of George Washington's desire, first articulated in 1770, to make the Potomac River "the Channel of conveyance of the extensive and valuable Trade of a rising Empire." The Potomac River served as the boundary between Maryland and Virginia and, according to the Charter of 1632 to Lord Baltimore, the entire river belonged to Maryland. In order for Washington's plan to transform the Potomac into the major trade route for the interior of the country to become a reality, Maryland and Virginia would have to work together. In 1784, both states agreed to charter the Potomac Company, with Washington as its president, for "opening and extending the navigation of the Potomac River."

Madison was then chairman of the Virginia Assembly Committee on Commerce. He drafted a resolution, approved on December 28, 1784, which called for four commissioners from Virginia—Madison, Edmund Randolph, George Mason, and Alexander Henderson—to meet with commissioners from Maryland to discuss the proper regulation of the Potomac. The Maryland delegation wrote to Virginia's governor, Patrick Henry, proposing that the meeting be held in Alexandria, Virginia, on March 21, 1785. Governor Henry, no supporter of either Madison or interstate compacts in general, neglected to inform the Virginia commissioners of this letter. Thus, the Maryland delegation arrived in Virginia for the meeting without the knowledge of any of the Virginia delegation. As they rode to Alexandria, the Marylanders happened to pass by George Mason's home at Gunston Hall. Once he realized what was happening, Mason was able to contact a fellow commissioner, Alexander Henderson, who lived nearby. After waiting several days in Alexandria, the two Virginians concluded that Madison and Randolph, who were still in Richmond, must have been, like them, unaware of the scheduled meeting. They decided to proceed with the meeting rather than send the Maryland delegation back empty-handed. George Washington, eager to ensure the meeting's success, had his carriage bring both delegations back to his home in Mount Vernon for a more comfortable negotiation site. The new venue must have been effective, since "the most amicable spirit is said to have governed the negociation."

On March 28, 1785, at what has become known as the Mount Vernon conference, the commissioners signed a compact. Among the major provisions agreed upon was that each state would refrain from imposing tolls on vessels sailing from the other state, and that both states would share the costs for building and maintaining lighthouses on the Chesapeake Bay. Even though he did not attend the conference, Madison enthusiastically supported the "Mount Vernon Compact" and spearheaded the effort which obtained legislative approval for the agreement by the end of 1785. Madison believed that this cooperative spirit could be built on to develop closer bonds between states. He suggested to Washington that "advantage should be taken of the occasion . . . to urge on the Legislatures the adoption of measures of relief to a greater extent than was generally contemplated."

The Virginia legislature was not interested in adopting such measures and blocked Madison's proposed bill to expand Congress's taxing power. Madison again tried to gain Virginia's approval of a change in the Articles of Confederation to authorize Congress to levy the impost directly. Madison's proposal also would have authorized Congress to prohibit foreign vessels from countries, such as Great Britain, which did not have a commercial treaty with the United States. In an attempt to assuage the fears of opponents in the assembly, Madison added a provision stating that no congressional action under this new authorization could last longer than twenty-five years unless renewed by a vote of two-thirds of the states. When opponents in the assembly amended his bill to remove the renewal clause and limit any congressional action to thirteen years, Madison voted, along with a majority of the assembly, to table the bill. As Madison wrote to Washington on December 9, explaining his vote to kill his own legislation, "I think it better to trust to further experience and even distress, for an adequate remedy, than to try a temporary measure which may stand in the way of a permanent one."

At the time he wrote this letter to Washington, Madison was already considering alternative approaches for increasing Congress's powers. John Tyler had proposed that Virginia issue a call for commissioners from every state to meet to discuss proposals for "the requisite augmentation of the power of Congress over trade." As Madison explained to Washington, this plan to discuss commercial issues "will have fewer enemies" than the impost proposal because "it seems naturally to grow out of the proposed appointment of Commssrs from Virga. & Maryd, concerted at Mt. Vernon for keeping up harmony in the commercial regulations of the two States."

For the next month, Madison was involved in constant battles in the legislature and saw the defeat of many of his proposals, most notably a total revision of the state's legal code. Nonetheless, when he wrote his summary of the legislative session to Thomas Jefferson on January 22, 1786, he was able to inform him of two significant successes. First, Madison had been able to build on the momentum from the defeat of the bill to fund Christian teachers to push through a law, originally proposed by Jefferson seven years earlier in 1779, called the Bill for Establishing Religious Freedom. This law declared that freedom of religion was among "the natural rights of mankind," and that for any government "to compel a man to furnish contributions of money for the propagation of opinions which he disbelieves, is sinful and tyrannical." Accordingly, the law provided that "no man shall be compelled to frequent or support any religious worship" nor "suffer on account of his religious opinions or belief." In his letter to Jefferson, a jubilant Madison wrote, "I flatter myself [that this act has] in this country extinguished forever the ambitious hope of making laws for the human mind."

Madison was somewhat less enthusiastic about the second positive outcome of the legislative session. After recounting his inability to persuade the legislature to approve any increase in Congress's taxing power, Madison wrote that the proposal for a "general meeting of Commssrs from the States to consider and recommend a foederal plan for regulating Commerce" had been presented in December but was "left on the table" until the last day of the session. Finally, "it was found that Several propositions for regulating our trade without regard to the other states produced nothing. In this extremity [the] resolution was generally acceded to."

The plan was exceedingly mild in scope. The commissioners from the different states were to assemble, at a place and time not yet specified, with the limited mandate to discuss only commercial issues. They were to "examine the relative situations and trade of the said

States [and] to consider how far a uniform system in their commercial regulations may be necessary to their common Interest and their permanent Harmony." The end product was to be a proposal, directed to the states, for increasing the power of Congress to regulate trade.

Late in life, Madison would say that the call for this meeting had been "kept in reserve" in case, as it turned out, the legislature rejected his proposal to directly expand the powers of Congress. Part of the reason for the assembly's acceptance was that it was proposed by John Tyler who, unlike Madison, had never served in Congress. Because Tyler was "a highly respected member who, having long served in the State councils without participating in the Federal," his proposal would not "subject him to the suspicion of a bias in favor of that body."

Madison was decidedly ambivalent about the fallback position he had supported. On the same day that he wrote to Jefferson, he also wrote to James Monroe, expressing his concerns. Madison stated that "the expedient [of such a meeting] is no doubt liable to objections and will probably miscarry." He further worried that the Virginia legislature had named too many commissioners, eight in all, including himself: "It is not unlikely that this multitude of associates will stifle the thing in its birth." Nonetheless, he permitted himself some hope that this meeting, even with an agenda limited to trade, could lead to further, more expansive changes in the future: "It is better than nothing, and as a recommendation of additional powers to Congress is within the purview of the Commission it may possibly lead to better consequences than at first occur."

On March 1, 1786, Edmund Randolph informed Madison that several of the commissioners had met and decided that the meeting should be held in Annapolis, Maryland, on the first Monday in September. As Madison would later explain to Jefferson, Annapolis had been chosen over Philadelphia and New York because it was "thought prudent to avoid the neighbourhood of Congress, and the large Commercial towns, in order to disarm the adversaries to the object, of insinuation of influence from either of these quarters."

Madison continually expressed his doubts about whether any good would come out of the Annapolis convention. In March 1786, he wrote to Jefferson and expressed his growing fears: "I almost despair of success. It is necessary however that something should be tried & it is the best that could possibly be carried thro' the Legislature here." Similarly, he told James Monroe that he was "far from entertaining sanguine expectations" about Annapolis. With obvious ambivalence he stated that he "cannot disapprove of the experiment." Perhaps, he said, something will be done concerning commerce, but if not, "If nothing can be done we may at least expect a full discovery as to that matter from the experiment, and such a piece of knowledge will be worth the trouble and expense of obtaining it."

By contrast, Alexander Hamilton approached the Annapolis convention with enthusiasm. While he had been pursuing his legal career, Hamilton had continued to maintain a close watch over the political scene. He had convinced three of his friends, Robert Troup, William Duer, and William Malcolm, to run for the New York State Assembly, in May 1785. As Troup would later recall, the three had been "sent to the state legislature as part of the city delegation, and we were to make every possible effort to accomplish Hamilton's objects." They failed in their first attempt, as they were unable to convince the New York legislature to support the federal impost. They next turned their attention to Virginia's call for states to join the Annapolis convention. According to Troup, "We went all our strength in the appointment of commissioners to attend the commercial convention, in which we were successful." Most significantly, Hamilton's friends were able to have him included among the list of New York commissioners.

From the outset, Hamilton had far more ambitious plans for the meeting than did Madison. At this point, at least, Madison was content to limit the Annapolis convention to commercial matters. Madison told Monroe that the Virginia legislature never would have approved a broader mission: "They would have revolted equally against a plenipotentiary commission to their deputies for the Convention." Madison explained his rationale for caution: "I am not in general an advocate of temporizing or partial remedies. But a rigor in this respect, if pushed too far may hazard every thing."

Madison reaffirmed his view in August, one month before the convention, that the Annapolis convention should be limited to commercial matters. He wrote to Jefferson that he had visited New York and that "Many Gentlemen both within and without Congs. wish to make this Meeting subservient to a Plenipotentiary Convention for amending the Confederation. Tho' my wishes are in favor of such an event, yet I despair so much of its accomplishment at the present crisis that I do not extend my views beyond a Commercial Reform. To speak the truth, I almost despair even of this."

It is likely that George Washington was thinking of Madison when he wrote of those who were in favor of limiting the scope of the Annapolis convention: "It is regretted by many, that more objects were not embraced by the meeting. A General Convention is talked of by many for the purpose of revising and correcting the defects of the foederal government; but whilst this is the wish of some, it is the dread of others from an opinion that matters are not yet sufficiently ripe for such an event."

Hamilton, however, was intent on using the Annapolis convention to achieve his long-standing goal of calling a convention of the states to revise the entire Articles of Confederation. As early as 1780, Hamilton had suggested "calling immediately a Convention of all the States, with full authority to conclude finally upon a General Confederation." Two years later, in July 1782, Hamilton and his father-in-law, Philip Schuyler, prepared a resolution which was passed by the New York legislature, calling for a "general Convention of the States, specifically authorised to revise and amend the Confederation."

The next year, while serving in Congress, Hamilton again proposed a "General Convention" to revise and amend the Articles of Confederation. Madison's notes on the congressional debates reveal an intriguing split between himself and Hamilton. The debate, which took place on April 1, 1783, involved a proposal for Massachusetts and New York to meet, with other states present, to discuss "regulating matters of common concern." According to the minutes, "Mr. Madison & Mr. Hamilton disapproved of these partial conventions . . . [as]exciting pernicious jealousies; the latter observing that he

wished instead of them to see a General Convention take place."
Note that it is only Hamilton who is calling for the broader convention; Madison was not yet prepared to join him in this call.

After the Philadelphia mutiny, Hamilton grew even more frustrated
with what he termed the nation's "constitutional imbecility." He
drafted a new proposal for a convention to propose "such alterations"
to the Articles of Confederation as they thought necessary. He detailed
the numerous weaknesses of the current system: "confining the power
of the foederal government within too narrow limits"; "confounding
legislative and executive powers in a single body"; "withholding from
them all controul over either the imposition or the collection of the
taxes"; and "not vesting in the United States a general superintendence
of trade." At the top of the page, Hamilton wrote his own disheartened epitaph for his plan: "Resolution intended to be submitted to
Congress at Princeton in 1783; but abandoned for want of support."

When the Annapolis convention was called, Hamilton saw it as the
springboard for his broader vision. According to Egbert Benson, the
New York attorney general who attended the convention and rode with
Hamilton from New York City, Hamilton arrived at Annapolis determined to take full advantage of "the present opportunity for obtaining a
Convention to revise the whole of our mode or system of General Government." His friend Robert Troup agreed, stating that Hamilton had
no "partiality in a commercial convention otherwise than as a stepping
stone to a general convention to form a general constitution."

Many of the commissioners prepared for the convention on the
assumption that it would be limited to commercial concerns. Hugh
Williamson, who had been appointed a commissioner from North
Carolina, told the governor of his state how he had needed to go to
"some trouble" to collect "a full account of our exports by which the
relative Importance of our Commerce might in some measure be
ascertained." Similarly Edmund Randolph reported that he was going
to Annapolis "with as accurate a state of the exports, and imports, as
can be collected."

Interestingly, while Madison was expecting, and advocating for, a
convention limited to commercial matters, his preparation was of a

far different nature. Rather than examine the details of trade and commercial data, he embarked on an extraordinary study of the history of confederated governments.

Madison had been planning this project for several years. In 1784, when Thomas Jefferson left for France to serve as minister, he and Madison had made a deal: Madison would oversee the education of Jefferson's nephew, Peter Carr, and Jefferson would procure for Madison the "occasional purchase of rare and valuable books." Madison told Jefferson that he was most interested in books that explored the various historical instances when other nations tried to create loose confederacies, so that he could compare their experiences with those of the United States under the Articles of Confederation. Madison expressed his desire for "whatever may throw light on the general Constitution & *droit public* [public law] of the several confederacies which had existed. . . . The operations of our own must render all such lights of consequence." In April 1785, Madison repeated his request that Jefferson get him "such books as may be 'either old & curious or new & useful,'" especially, he added, "treatises on the antient or modern foederal republics—on the law of Nations—and the history natural and political of the New World; to which I will add such Greek and Roman authors where they can be got very cheap." Toward the end of the Virginia legislative session in January 1786, Madison received the news that a ship had come ashore carrying two trunks of books from France. Madison wrote Jefferson that he was having the trunks forwarded to his house, so that he would not "be deprived of the amusement they promise me for the residue of the winter."

Once home, Madison took advantage of his free time to engage in his studies in earnest. By the middle of March, he was able to report to Jefferson that he had finally "had the leisure to review the literary cargo." By the time of the Annapolis convention, Madison had written a forty-three-page exposition which he titled "Ancient & Modern Confederacies." In this document, Madison methodically reviewed the history of confederated governments, from the amphictyonic confederacies, which had been formed around 300 BCE, to the German empire, which was then still in existence. In careful detail, Madison described the legal organization of each confederacy, ending with a section entitled "vices." Each of the confederacies he reviewed seemed, in one way or another, to share a common vice with the United States under the Articles of Confederation. All of them exhibited a deliberate weakness of the central authority which led to "jealousies" among the constituent parts, inefficiency, corruption, and conflict. Madison would later use this study in both the debates at the Constitutional Convention and as the basis for three of his essays in *The Federalist.* For the moment, it permitted Madison to attend the "commercial convention" with a deeper understanding of the underlying flaws of the Articles of Confederation.

Around the nation there was much suspicion as to the real motivation behind the proposed Annapolis convention. Some, such as Stephen Higginson, who had been appointed a Massachusetts delegate to the convention, assumed that there was a secret agenda to overhaul the entire political system: "When I consider the men who are deputed from New-York, Pennsylvania and Virginia, and the source of whence the proposition was made, I am strongly inclined to think political Objects are intended to be combined with commercial, if they do not principally engross their Attention. . . . Few of them have been in the commercial line, nor is it probable they know or care much about commercial Objects."

Others thought the opposite, that the convention was just a meaningless ploy to defeat any serious attempt to increase congressional power. Theodore Sedgwick, a Massachusetts member of Congress, warned that "no reasonable expectations of advantage can be formed from the commercial convention. The first proposers designed none. The measure was originally brought forward with an intention of defeating the enlargement of powers of Congress. Of this I have the most decisive evidence."

This same suspicion—that the convention would result in a lessening of congressional power—led to the first major setback for Madison and the others involved in building support for it. On March 11, 1786, Maryland voted to reject Virginia's invitation to attend the convention despite the fact that it was the host state, with its capital city being the host city. The Maryland Senate explained its decision as due to concern that the gathering of commissioners to consider commercial regulation might "give umbrage to Congress, and disquiet the citizens of the United States, who may be therefore led erroneously to suspect that the great council of this country wants either the will or wisdom to digest a proper uniform plan for the regulation of their commerce." In a surprisingly prescient coda, the Maryland Senate voiced concern that, should this convention take place, it "may produce other meetings, which may have consequences which cannot be foreseen." Maryland's decision not to attend raised deep fears over whether the convention would turn into a catastrophe. Edmund Randolph expressed his concerns to Madison: "But what a dreadful chasm will the refusal of Maryland create? A chasm more injurious to us, than any other of the delegates."

Several other states also chose to decline the invitation to attend the Annapolis convention. Connecticut, South Carolina, and Georgia, either by direct action or deliberate inaction, indicated that they would not be sending commissioners to Annapolis.

On the plus side, as September approached, the other nine states had indicated their willingness to participate. Although it was not to be a full representation, these nine represented more than two-thirds of the nation. Moreover, nine was a politically significant number; it was enshrined in the Articles of Confederation as the minimum number of state congressional delegations required for approving the spending and borrowing of money.

On September 4, 1786, Madison rode into Annapolis and took up residence at Mann's Tavern, also known as the City Hotel. Mann's Tavern, which had been the site of George Washington's farewell dinner in 1783, when he resigned his commission as commander-in-chief of the Continental Army, was an elegant establishment, with "one hundred beds and stabling for fifty horses." An English traveler described it as "an excellent publick house" whose "Lodging Rooms, all wainscoted to the ceiling, might vie with any tavern in England."

Madison did not have much company when he arrived at the tavern. Only two other commissioners, both from New Jersey, were there. A few days later, Hamilton arrived with Egbert Benson.

Although there had been some limited correspondence between Madison and Hamilton since leaving Princeton in 1783, this was probably the first time they had met since then. While some later commentators accused Hamilton and Madison of plotting together from the initial call for the Annapolis convention in January as part of a plan to obtain a general revision of the Constitution, there is absolutely no evidence that they had been in communication during that time, let alone conspired between themselves.

There is also no evidence that Madison initially viewed the low turnout in Annapolis as the opportunity it became. On Friday, September 8, Madison wrote a worried letter to his brother that "the prospect of a sufficient no. to make the Meeting respectable is not flattering."

By the end of the weekend, only twelve commissioners were in Annapolis. Just three states, Virginia, New Jersey, and Delaware, were even represented by a quorum, the number necessary to be able to vote officially on behalf of a state. New York was one vote shy, while Pennsylvania was represented by only a single commissioner. Nonetheless, on Monday, September 11, the commissioners began their formal meeting. They gathered in the Old Senate Chamber of the Maryland State House, where the Continental Congress had met from November 26, 1783, to August 13, 1784, after departing from Princeton, and before heading for Trenton and New York. The first act of business for the commissioners was to elect as chairman of the convention John Dickinson of Delaware, who had been the primary author of the Articles of Confederation.

There are no official records of the debates at the Annapolis convention, and none of the participants left detailed notes on what transpired. It is clear, however, that early in the proceedings Hamilton took charge and was able, with a final assist from Madison, to achieve his ultimate goal: a call for another convention authorized to revise the entire frame of government.

At the beginning of the debates, Tench Coxe of Pennsylvania attempted to raise the "commercial" issue of discriminatory duties. Several states, he said, placed unequal taxes on goods and ships, benefiting merchants from the home state while penalizing those from other states. He was surprised to be informed that the convention would not be dealing with commercial topics after all. Declaring that it would be "inexpedient for this Convention in which so few States are represented to proceed in the Business committed to them," the commissioners voted instead to create a committee to prepare a report for dissemination to the states which appointed them. Edmund Randolph was named the chair of this committee and began drafting the report. Almost immediately, Hamilton managed, at least figuratively, to take the pen out of Randolph's hand and write his own draft report. It is unknown precisely how Hamilton succeeded in wresting the task from Randolph, but the feat is all the more remarkable considering that Hamilton was not even on the committee charged with drafting the report.

Equally impressive was how quickly Hamilton was able to have the convention complete its work. In the 1780s, meetings that required members to travel across the entire nation rarely began on time. For example, at the Constitutional Convention, which was held the next year, only a few delegates were in place on its scheduled starting date, May 14, and it was not until almost two weeks later, May 25, that a quorum finally appeared. It was common custom that meetings as important and diverse as the Annapolis convention would wait a reasonable time to allow all who were interested in attending to arrive.

Just to be sure, the Massachusetts delegation, who had begun their long journey from Boston on September 2, wrote to Hamilton as they were about to leave New York City on September 10. They asked him "to communicate to the Convention if it should open before we arrive there, that we shall set off from this Place to morrow to join them" and that they expected to arrive by the end of the week. They also mentioned that the Rhode Island delegation was on its way.

Meanwhile, another commissioner, Hugh Williamson, was traveling from North Carolina carrying the results of his arduous research, all of the "papers and other information respecting the State of our Commerce as I had been able to Collect." He arrived in Norfolk,

Virginia, on September 7, where he was forced to wait a week through stormy weather for a boat to take him to Annapolis.

The late-arriving commissioners fully expected that their fellow commissioners would wait for them. Thus, on Friday, September 15, the Massachusetts delegation was "exceedingly surprised" when, barely thirty miles from the town of Rock Hall, Maryland, where they were to take a boat to Annapolis, they came face to face with the New York and New Jersey delegates heading home. Williamson was similarly amazed to find upon reaching Annapolis the same day that Mann's Inn was deserted.

It seems strange, if not downright rude, for those attending the Annapolis convention to have ended it so abruptly, with full knowledge that other commissioners were on the way. The haste seems even more peculiar considering that a third New York delegate, Robert C. Livingston, had virtually completed his journey and was getting ready to board the boat to Annapolis at Rock Hall, when he encountered fellow New Yorkers Hamilton and Benson getting off the boat. Suspicions were raised about the motivation for the convention's precipitous behavior. During the debates over ratification of the Constitution the following year, a leading Anti-Federalist writer, who signed his name "Federal Farmer," would criticize the manner in which the Annapolis convention had "hastily" acted, especially because "this was done before the delegates of Massachusetts, and of the other states arrived."

The most likely reason for the unseemly haste appears to be that the Hamilton-led commissioners wanted to complete their call for a second, broader convention without the need to worry about possible objections that the latecomers—especially those from Massachusetts—might raise. This does not mean that they had all arrived in Annapolis with this plan in mind. Rather, through discussion and persuasion, a consensus quickly formed within the walls of the Old Senate Chamber. According to Madison, momentum developed among the commissioners for a "more radical reform," with "each being fortified in his sentiments and expectations by those of others." Tench Coxe would later describe to Madison how his mind had been changed by the discussions in Annapolis: "Since my Journey to Annapolis . . . I have deemed capital Alterations in our general government indispensably necessary."

On Wednesday, September 13, Hamilton produced his draft report, and its inflammatory language nearly destroyed this newly created consensus. While a complete copy of this draft has been lost to history, it was apparently a remarkably strong statement on the weaknesses of the current system and the need for a substantially stronger central government. In describing the proposed scope of responsibility for the next convention, Hamilton even repeated a provocative phrase from his congressional debates over the impost, concerning the need for "all such Measures as may appear . . . necessary to cement the Union of the States."

It appears that many of the Commissioners had expected the convention to produce much more understated language. The recent converts to the idea of a significantly broader reform of the national government did not yet share Hamilton's disdain for the Articles of Confederation. Edmund Randolph, perhaps still smarting over losing the opportunity to write the report, was especially hostile to Hamilton's draft. Hamilton continued to insist on retaining his original language. Finally, Madison pulled Hamilton aside and, pointing to Randolph, said, "You had better yield to this man, for otherwise all Virginia will be against you."

This time, Hamilton followed Madison's advice. He permitted his draft to be altered, and the amended report was approved unanimously the next day, September 14. This final version carefully avoided any detailing of the numerous controversies over the defects in the Articles of Confederation, stating instead, "Your Commissioners decline an enumeration of those national circumstances on which their opinion respecting the propriety of a future Convention, with more enlarged powers, is founded; as it would be an useless intrusion of facts and observations."

The report also had to confront the legalistic question of how a commercial convention would be justified in calling for a wider revision of the Articles of Confederation. That problem was neatly surmounted when it was realized that New Jersey, unlike the other states which authorized delegations for Annapolis, had empowered its commissioners, "to consider how far an uniform system in their commercial regulations and other important matters, might be necessary to the common interest and permanent harmony of the several States." Emphasizing the phrase "and other important matters," the report stated that the New Jersey description, "was an improvement on the original plan," and should be incorporated into instructions for the next convention.

What followed has been called "an infinity of circumlocutions and ambiguous phrases" masking the real reason for the call for a new convention. Avoiding any mention of "cementing the union" or "amending the Articles," the report's recommendation was far more subtle, stating simply that the next convention should "devise such further provisions as shall appear to them necessary to render the constitution of the Federal Government adequate to the exigencies of the Union." Also, to avoid the risk of confusion and delay, the report specified a time and place for the next meeting, "at Philadelphia on the second Monday in May next."

The report was sent not only to the governors of the five states represented at the Annapolis convention but to all thirteen governors plus Congress. At the top of the report were the names, by state, of all those in attendance. The list was not in alphabetical order; the first state listed was New York. The names were not listed in alphabetical order either; the first name listed, implicitly proclaiming his primary role, was that of Alexander Hamilton.

3

"BETTER THAN NOTHING"

THE DRAFTING OF THE CONSTITUTION

The call for a new convention with broader powers has been accurately termed "a gamble." There was no guarantee that the commissioners would be able to convince their home states, the other states, and Congress to accept the plan.

Yet Madison was able to secure Virginia's approval quickly. As he wrote Jefferson, "The recommendation from the Meeting at Annapolis of a plenipotentiary Convention in Philada. in May next has been well recd. by the Assembly here." On November 6, 1786, Madison presented a bill to the Virginia House of Delegates to implement the Annapolis convention report, which was signed into law a few weeks later. The bill called for the appointment of seven delegates. The list was headed by George Washington and included George Mason; Edmund Randolph, who was then governor; George Wythe, who is considered the first law professor in the United States; John Blair, a state judge; and James Madison. Patrick Henry was chosen but refused to attend, saying later that he suspected that the convention planned to radically increase the power of the federal government. Or, as he put it more succinctly, "I smelt a rat."

Five other states—New Jersey, Pennsylvania, North Carolina, Delaware, and Georgia—also appointed delegates for the upcoming convention. The remaining states, including New York, were waiting to see how Congress responded to the call from Annapolis.

The early congressional reaction had been quite hostile. Congress received the report on September 20, 1786, less than a week after the Annapolis convention had ended. On October 11, 1786, it appointed a committee to consider the report, but the committee did not meet for four months.

Fortunately for those hoping to overcome the inertia, on February 12, 1787, James Madison arrived in New York to resume his service as a member of Congress. By the end of the month, Congress had approved a call, albeit halfheartedly, for the new convention. The resolution did not even mention the Annapolis convention or its report but simply declared that "in the opinion of Congress it is expedient that on the second Monday in May next a Convention of delegates who shall have been appointed by the several States be held at Philadelphia for the sole and express purpose of revising the Articles of Confederation."

In New York State, Governor George Clinton was still reluctant to move forward. When Clinton received the report of the Annapolis convention, Hamilton would later write, the governor "expressed a strong dislike of its object, declaring that, in his opinion the confederation as it stood was equal to the purposes of the Union." Hamilton was prepared to battle Clinton directly. In April 1786, as the New York Assembly was debating whom to send to Annapolis, Hamilton decided that he needed to be more involved in the state's day-to-day political infighting. He confided to Robert Troup that he intended to run for the legislature in order to "render the next session subservient to the change he meditated," specifically, "a radical change in the frame of our general government."

Hamilton won his election and attended his first legislative session on January 12, 1787. Within a week he had his first confrontation with Clinton, over the long-standing proposal to give Congress the power to impose the import tax. Virtually every other state had approved the impost. New York had nominally given its approval but had placed so many conditions on its approval that Congress considered its actions invalid. Congress requested that Clinton call a special session of the legislature to reconsider New York's position. When Clinton refused, Hamilton responded on January 19 with the first of two lengthy speeches castigating the governor for his "singularly forced" reasoning and "most unreasonable extreme" interpretation of the New York State Constitution. On February 15, Hamilton tried again to garner support for the impost. In an impassioned oration that lasted a full hour and twenty minutes, Hamilton warned that rejection of the impost would lead to the loss of our national character, the dissolution of the Union, war among the states, and war with all the great powers in Europe. His speech was met with "contemptuous silence" by his fellow assemblymen. Without an opponent even deigning to respond, the impost was defeated and laid to rest for all time, by a vote of 38 to 19.

Hamilton then turned his attention to other means for increasing national power. Eleven days after the vote to kill the impost and five days after Congress's resolution authorizing the new convention, Hamilton introduced a resolution calling for New York to send five delegates to Philadelphia. Lacking the votes to defeat the measure, Governor Clinton managed to reduce the number of New York delegates to three. After vigorous politicking, the legislature voted to send Hamilton and two close allies of Governor Clinton, Robert Yates and John Lansing. Hamilton attempted to convince the legislature to send two more delegates, particularly citing the "tried integrity and abundant experience" of John Jay. The Clintonians refused to expand the delegation, guaranteeing that Hamilton would be a lonely minority voice at the convention. In a letter to Washington, Madison expressed his concern that their ally Hamilton would be hamstrung by the hostile Yates and Lansing who were "likely to be a clog on their Colleague."

At the same time, Madison was preparing for the convention. According to historian Jack Rakove, Madison understood that the "prevailing mood of uncertainty" would give a significant advantage to "anyone who seized the initiative in defining the issues confronting the Convention." Madison believed that "a man who did his homework and thought through issues and alternatives before debate began could often lead his lazier colleagues—of whom there would always be many—along the avenues he had selected." Thus, Madison resumed the intensive reading and analysis which he had begun the year before and which had already resulted in his study, "Ancient & Modern Confederacies."

In a one-month period, from March 19 to April 16, 1787, Madison wrote three letters that described his growing understanding of the changes that would need to be made in the structure of the American government. The letters serve as a window into Madison's mind, revealing how his thinking continued to evolve. With each one he grew more confident in his understanding and more detailed in his approach.

The first of these letters was to Thomas Jefferson. Madison told his friend that any new system would need to be ratified "by the people themselves" to make the new document "clearly paramount to their Legislative authorities." Next, he wanted to institute a division of the national powers into "separate departments," and change the voting in Congress from one vote per state to a system of proportional representation. Additionally, he hoped to increase the national powers in two key ways. First, he wanted Congress to possess the power to regulate trade and other matters "in which uniformity is proper." Even more important, said Madison, he wanted to grant Congress the power to veto any bill passed by a state legislature. He told Jefferson that such a veto was necessary in order for the national government to be able to defend itself against state encroachment and, as an added advantage, prevent states from harming other states and even local political minorities.

About three weeks later, on April 8, Madison wrote to Edmund Randolph, explaining that delegates to the convention would expect "leading propositions" to come from Virginia, the first state which had voted to attend the convention. Madison said that he would "just hint the ideas" he had developed. In addition to reiterating his desire for proportional representation and a national veto on state law, Madison, for the first time, predicted that the Articles of Confederation might be replaced rather than merely amended. Saying that major changes were inevitable, Madison concluded that it might be "best to work the valuable articles into the new System, instead of engrafting the latter on the former." He envisioned a new relationship between the national and state government, with a strong central government and the states in a decidedly secondary role. He called for a system which would provide "a due supremacy of the national authority, and leave in force the local authorities so far as they can be subordinately useful."

He then described what he believed should be the three branches of the new national government. Congress would be divided into two houses. A national judiciary would be created, especially for disputes involving "foreigners, or inhabitants of other States." Finally, there would have to be a "National Executive." Despite his extensive study, Madison had not begun to focus on the role of a chief executive in a national government: "I have scarcly venturd to form my own opinion yet either of the manner in which it ought to be constituted or of the authorities with which it ought [to be] cloathed." One year later, when he and Hamilton would share the writing of *The Federalist,* Madison would leave the analysis of the constitutional role of the president to his coauthor.

Madison's last letter in this series was to George Washington on April 16. He repeated his call for proportional representation, calling it the "ground-work" for all of the other changes he was proposing. He offered his proposal for a national veto of state legislation, saying that "without this defensive power, every positive power that can be given on paper [to the national government] will be evaded & defeated."

The most important new idea expressed in this letter was Madison's first tentative discussion of his theory of how to prevent "the aggressions of interested majorities on the rights of minorities and of individuals." This theory would eventually blossom into his brilliant analysis in *Federalist 10* on the virtues of the "extended republic." For the moment, though, Madison simply stated that a veto over state laws would permit the national government to serve as a "disinterested & dispassionate umpire in disputes between different passions & interests in the State."

While Madison was writing these three letters, he was also completing his own personal study of what he termed the "Vices of the Political System of the United States." By now his reading had expanded far beyond history to include the philosophers of the Enlightenment, with a particular focus on the writings of David Hume. Madison's extraordinary accomplishment in this memorandum was that he was able to transcend mere theory and combine the philosophy he was reading with the real-world politics he had experienced, both in Congress and in the Virginia Assembly. The result was essentially a sequel to "Ancient & Modern Confederacies." Just as each section of that work had ended with the specific "vices" of a particular confederacy, this study listed the numerous vices inherent in the Articles of Confederation, such as "Encroachments by the States on the federal authority" or the "Multiplicity" and "Mutability" of state laws. After describing each vice, Madison gave specific illustrations from recent American experience and, most important, explained why such vices were inevitable unless a radically new form of government was implemented.

For example, one of the "vices" Madison listed was the inability of the national government to force states to follow national law. State disobedience to such laws was inevitable, Madison maintained. The economies of the individual states were dependent on different sources of income, he argued, so that states would always be impacted to differing degrees by each piece of national legislation. The states most adversely affected by any particular measure would be more likely to refuse to comply with it. Additionally, he said, there would always be some local political leaders who would try to gain popularity by "exaggerating the inequality," and to lead their states in opposition to the contrived national unfairness. Finally, Madison asserted, due to what we now call the "free rider" problem, even states which supported a measure might be reluctant to comply voluntarily, suspicious that other states might choose to take the benefit, without the burden, of such compliance. Thus, said Madison, "Here are causes & pretexts which will never fail to render federal measures abortive."

Similarly, Madison explored another "vice," the "Injustice of the laws of States." Here he expanded on the discussion in his letter to

Washington on the problem of the abuse of political power by majority interests. He described some of the different "factions" into which society is divided, such as creditors versus debtors and merchants versus manufacturers, as well as those distinctions based on religion or geography. Noting that, in a republic, laws are written by the largest faction, Madison declared, "Whenever therefore an apparent interest or common passion unites a majority what is to restrain them from unjust violations of the rights and interests of the minority, or of individuals?" His proposed solution, which became the heart of *Federalist 10,* was that an "enlargement of the sphere," an increase in the size of the political entity, would impede the ability of different factions to combine into a governing majority.

"Vices of the Political System of the United States" was not compiled for public consumption. Rather, Madison was putting together a comprehensive analysis, for his eyes only, so that he could both appreciate the full rationale for creating a radically new political system and understand what changes were needed to ensure that the vices did not recur.

Those necessary changes were the major subject of discussion when the Virginia delegation arrived in Philadelphia, well in advance of most of the other delegates, in early May. Madison arrived first, on May 5. For the next two weeks the rest of the Virginia delegates— George Washington, George Mason, Edmund Randolph, George Wythe, and John Blair—trickled into town. They would meet every day for two or three hours, and ultimately produced the proposal which was to form the basis of discussion at the convention, the "Virginia Plan." Madison was not the sole author of the Virginia plan, but it was his preparatory work that served as the starting point for the group's deliberations. More important, his major proposals, including broad legislative power for a two-house Congress, a separate executive branch and an independent judiciary, proportional representation in Congress and a national veto of state law, were all incorporated into the plan.

Hamilton arrived in Philadelphia on May 18. Unlike Madison, he faced total opposition to his goals from his companions. The New

York delegation, with two members opposed to any significant change in the Articles of Confederation, would be largely irrelevant in Philadelphia, and Hamilton was generally marginalized for most of the convention.

The convention formally began on May 25, with George Washington unanimously elected its president. Madison obtained for himself a front row seat, "in front of the presiding member," so that he would be in a "favorable position for hearing all that passed." From this favored perch, Madison kept the most complete notes of what was said during the next four months of debate. Madison was determined that future students of history would have the kind of record of the creation of the American republic that he had wished for in his studies of earlier governments. These notes were especially important, since the convention was closed to the public, and the delegates were sworn to secrecy. In fidelity to his project, he later wrote that he "was not absent a single day, nor more than a casual fraction of an hour in any day, so that I could not have lost a single speech." Madison would also say that he rewrote his notes each night to ensure accuracy; this labor "almost killed him . . . but that having undertaken the task, he was determined to accomplish it."

Throughout the early stages of the convention, Hamilton and Madison would meet and discuss the ongoing struggle to create the new governmental structure. They held long conversations during afternoon breaks in the proceedings. A particularly intriguing indication of their relationship can be seen in the notes Hamilton took during the convention. Compared with Madison's notes of the convention, Hamilton's were shorter, less complete, and more impressionistic. They were written for his use, not for posterity, and Hamilton would often place his own opinion of a speaker's ideas next to his summary of the speech itself.

In his notes of June 1, Hamilton summarized Madison's views, beginning with his description of Madison's newly minted theory of factions: "The way to prevent a majority from having an interest to oppress the minority is to enlarge the sphere." What is revealing about this note is that Madison did not present this theory to the convention, including the phrase "enlarge the sphere," until June 6. It is therefore apparent that Madison had discussed his novel theory with Hamilton privately, earlier in the convention, and Hamilton's notes had anticipated by five days Madison's actual convention speech.

Conversations Hamilton was having with his two New York colleagues did not go as well. As predicted, he was repeatedly outvoted by Lansing and Yates. As those two would later write to Governor Clinton, they fervently opposed any attempt to strengthen the national government and were "of the opinion that the leading feature of every amendment ought to be the preservation of the individual states in their uncontrolled constitutional rights."

Delegates with similar views saw their prospects brighten on June 15, when William Paterson of New Jersey proposed an alternative to the Virginia plan. The so-called New Jersey plan sought to preserve much of the Articles of Confederation. Most significantly, it would have maintained the one-state, one-vote regimen of the Articles of Confederation. The small-state delegates, in particular, were determined not to create a system in which the larger states would have the ability to overwhelm the smaller states and ignore their needs. As John Dickenson of Delaware remarked to Madison, "We would sooner submit to a foreign power than submit to be deprived of an equality of suffrage."

Over the next several days, the convention was effectively paralyzed, as neither the proponents of the New Jersey plan nor those of the Virginia plan retreated from their positions. Suddenly, on June 18, Alexander Hamilton rose to deliver what was probably the strangest speech of the convention. For most of the preceding three weeks he had been largely and uncharacteristically silent, in part because of his expectation that he would be opposed by his two fellow New York delegates. Unable to contain himself any longer, Hamilton apparently decided it no longer made sense to edit himself. He proceeded to unleash a Herculean five-hour oration, the substance of which would haunt him for the rest of his career.

He began by declaring his opposition to both the New Jersey and the Virginia plans, and then detailed the sort of system he would prefer. In a statement that forever led his political opponents to call him a "monarchist," Hamilton declared that "the British Govt. was the best in the world" and said that he "doubted much whether any thing short of it would do in America." He extolled the virtues of the hereditary monarchy, claiming that the "interest of the King was so interwoven with that of the Nation, and his personal emoluments so great, that he was placed above the danger of being corrupted from abroad." Hamilton also praised the House of Lords as a "most noble institution" which prevented the poor from oppressing the aristocracy. Acknowledging that America would never accept a hereditary form of government, Hamilton proposed what he described as a system as close to it "as republican principles will admit." His plan was for one house of the legislature to be elected for three-year terms, with the second house and chief executive to be elected for life.

According to Robert Yates, Hamilton concluded his remarks by condemning both of the plans before the convention for ceding too much power to the populace without the sorts of protections found in England. The New Jersey plan, Hamilton warned, would not eliminate the dangers caused by "an excess of democracy." Hamilton added that the Virginia plan also was inadequate to prevent such excess: "And what even is the Virginia plan, but pork still, with a little change of the sauce?"

Hamilton's speech was met with stunned silence. The delegates immediately voted to adjourn for the day, and the debate resumed the following day as if Hamilton had never spoken. A perhaps too generous delegate from Connecticut, William Samuel Johnson, would remark a few days later that Hamilton's speech "has been praised by everybody," but somehow "he has been supported by none."

It fell to Madison to lead the fight against the New Jersey plan. On June 19, Madison delivered his longest speech of the convention, methodically drawing from the analysis he had crafted in his spring research, the "Vices of the Political System of the United States," to expose the flaws in the New Jersey plan. As in his prior study, he denounced the "multiplicity" and "mutability" and "injustice" of state laws. To illustrate how states would "trespass" on the rights of other states, Madison even attacked the Mount Vernon Compact, whose approval in the Virginia legislature he had engineered. In Philadelphia, Madison criticized the compact for authorizing Virginia and Maryland to give "a preference to their own Citizens in cases where the Citizens of other States are entitled to equality of privileges by the Articles of Confederation."

Madison was successful in one aspect; the convention voted to reject the New Jersey plan. He was unable, however, to gain approval for the Virginia plan. The stalemate over representation persisted into July. For almost seven weeks, Madison led an attempt to use "persuasion, rational argument, and appeals to principle," to win support for proportional representation.

Hamilton grew impatient with the prolonged debate and frustrated with what he saw as the direction in which the convention appeared to be turning. On June 29 he left Philadelphia and returned to New York and his legal practice. On July 3 he wrote to Washington, describing his mood: "I am seriously and deeply distressed at the aspects of the Councils which prevailed when I left Philadelphia." Hamilton complained that the convention was in danger of letting "slip the golden opportunity of rescuing the American empire from disunion, anarchy and misery."

A week later, Washington wrote back. While sharing Hamilton's concerns, Washington admonished him that "no opposition . . . should discourage exertions til the signature is fixed." In simple terms, Washington urged Hamilton to return: "I am sorry you went away. I wish you were back." Despite these entreaties, Hamilton did not return to Philadelphia until the beginning of August; after one more week at the convention he would leave for New York again.

During Hamilton's first absence, on July 16, the convention reached "the Great Compromise," voting to approve the so-called Connecticut plan, in which there would be proportional representation in one house, while in the second, each state would have an equal vote. Madison remained adamant in his opposition to giving states equal representation in either house of the legislature, denying to the end that there was any "ground of compromise."

Even more disheartening for Madison was the fate of his proposal for a national veto of state laws. Madison argued in vain that "the negative on the laws of the States [was] essential to the efficacy & security of the Genl. Govt." Nonetheless, on July 17, the day after the vote to approve the Connecticut plan, the convention voted, seven states to three, to reject Madison's plan.

While Madison is often referred to as the father of the Constitution, he actually disagreed with many of the decisions made in the convention. One historian, Forrest McDonald, has calculated that Madison was unsuccessful far more often than not in Philadelphia: "Overall, of seventy-one specific proposals that Madison moved, seconded, or spoke unequivocally in regard to, he was on the losing side forty times." It would be a mistake to make too great a use of these numbers, however. Despite his setbacks, Madison had a significant impact on the convention and played a fundamental role in persuading it to agree to replace, rather than merely amend, the Articles of Confederation.

Nonetheless, Madison's disappointment in the overall work of the convention was revealed in a letter to Thomas Jefferson. Writing on September 6, while the convention was nearing completion, Madison described his pessimistic view of the proposed Constitution: "I hazard an opinion . . . that the plan, should it be adopted, will neither effectually answer its national object nor prevent the local mischiefs which every where excite disgusts agst the state governments."

September 6 also marked Hamilton's return to Philadelphia. Despite his opposition to much of what had transpired, Hamilton realized that the convention's handiwork was to be of historic importance, and he was determined to be a part of it. While in New York on August 20, he had written to Rufus King, who was representing Massachusetts at the convention, and pleaded with him "to let me know when your *conclusion* is at hand; for I would choose to be present at that time." Once he returned, Hamilton continued to express "his dislike of the Scheme of Govt. in General" while declaring that he intended "to support the plan to be recommended, as better than nothing."

On the last day of the convention, September 17, the delegates debated the form in which the Constitution should be presented to the public. There were several difficulties. First, because Yates and Lansing had left the convention in July, never to return, New York State did not have the minimum two delegates present to constitute a quorum. Hamilton, by himself, was unable to vote on New York's behalf and New York could not be counted as voting for the Constitution.

A second problem arose from the fact that not all of the delegates still in Philadelphia supported the Constitution. Two Virginia delegates, George Mason and Edmund Randolph, along with Elbridge Gerry of Massachusetts, announced their opposition. Mason's opposition came primarily from the convention's rejection of his last-minute proposal that a bill of rights be added to the Constitution.

Several delegates, led by Benjamin Franklin, tried to persuade them to sign. Franklin stated that "I confess that there are several parts of this constitution which I do not at present approve, but I am not sure I shall never approve them." He concluded by urging that "every member of the Convention who may still have objections to it, would with me, on this occasion doubt a little of his own infallibility—and to make manifest our unanimity, put his name to this instrument."

Hamilton followed by warning that a lack of unanimity "might do infinite mischief by kindling the latent sparks which lurk under an enthusiasm in favor of the Convention which may soon subside." He reiterated his strong ambivalence toward the Constitution: "No man's ideas were more remote from the plan than [my] own were known to be." Still, he explained, he supported the final product as better than the alternative, describing the delegates' option as deciding "between anarchy and Convulsion on one side, and the chance of good to be expected from the plan on the other."

Gerry, Mason, and Randolph refused to reconsider, but the convention created an ingenious way to present a unanimous face to the world. To avoid drawing attention to the fact that the New York delegation had not officially approved the Constitution, the signature page was introduced by the phrase "Done in Convention by the Unanimous Consent of the States present the Seventeenth Day of

September." Since New York, with only one delegate in attendance, was not present in the legal sense of the word, the declaration of unanimity among the states present was technically correct.

Next, it was decided that delegates would not be listed as approving or disapproving the proposal. Gerry, Mason, and Randolph would not be given the opportunity to attest to their opposition. Rather, in another creative piece of ambiguous language, those signing were merely attesting to the fact that all of the states present had approved the Constitution: "In Witness whereof We have hereunto subscribed our Names."

When the time came for the formal signing ceremony, Hamilton made sure that he would be forever associated with the drafting of the Constitution. He obviously could not be the first person to sign; that honor would have to go to the president of the convention, George Washington. Hamilton did the next best thing. He managed to seize the quill and performed the task of scribe, carefully writing the names of each state, listed before the signatures of the individual delegates. Hamilton's handwriting on America's founding document can still be seen at the National Archives.

4

"ESTABLISHING GOOD GOVERNMENT FROM REFLECTION AND CHOICE"

PRODUCING *THE FEDERALIST*

The battle over ratification of the Constitution began inauspiciously during the summer of 1787, while the delegates to the Constitutional Convention were still debating in secret. Alexander Hamilton, in New York during his extended absence from Philadelphia, launched an emotional, ill-advised attack on his leading political adversary, Governor George Clinton. In a letter published on July 21, 1787, in New York's *Daily Advertiser,* Hamilton accused Clinton of pledging to fight any plan the convention might produce. Such opposition from a leading political figure, especially since no proposal had even been issued, was, according to Hamilton, "unwarrantable and culpable in any man." Clinton's "dangerous predetermination" to oppose any change in the Articles of Confederation, Hamilton concluded, "argues greater attachment to his own power than to the public good."

The governor's allies quickly retaliated. They accused Hamilton of being part of a "certain Aristocratic junto, who appear determined, by their writings, to silence, and traduce every person who will not subscribe to every part of their political creed." The attacks on Hamilton were often quite personal. One of Clinton's defenders wrote a poem that contained the couplet "To Hamilton's the ready lies repair; Ne'er was lie made that was not welcome there."

The most vituperative of these attacks came in a series of anonymous articles published under the name Inspector. These particularly scatological pieces referred to Hamilton as "Tom Shit" (which appeared in the *New-York Journal* as "Tom S**t"). According to Inspector, Tom Shit was a "superficial, self-conceited coxcomb," born out of wedlock, with George Washington as his "immaculate daddy." Hamilton was also described as a "mustee," that is, a white person with at least one black great-grandparent. Of all the charges leveled against him by Inspector, Hamilton was most unsettled by accusations that he had been rejected as unworthy by Washington during the Revolutionary War.

Hamilton wrote to inform Washington of the charge that Washington had "dismissed" him: "This I confess hurt my feelings," Hamilton said. He pleaded with Washington for a letter of support, to affirm that Hamilton had never "palmed" himself off on the general and had left the position of aide-de-camp on his own accord.

Washington wrote back with a chastening response. While acknowledging that all the charges against Hamilton were "unfounded," he criticized Hamilton for his role in instigating the dispute with Governor Clinton. Washington wrote that "when the situation of this country calls loudly for unanimity & vigor, it is to be lamented that Gentlemen of talents and character should disagree in their sentiments for promoting the public weal."

Washington's concern was well founded. The fight for ratification would prove to be difficult enough without needlessly inflaming the opposition.

Less than a week after the conclusion of the convention in Philadelphia, Madison received a panicked letter from New York. Edward Carrington urged him to race back to New York to save the Constitution from being buried in Congress by fellow Virginian Richard Henry Lee: "Least, however, you may, under a supposition that the State of the delegation is such as to admit of your absence, indulge yourself in leisurely movements, after the fatiguing time you have had, I take this precaution to apprise you that . . . Mr. R. H. Lee is forming propositions for essential alterations in the Constitution, which will, in effect, be to oppose it."

After attacking the convention for exceeding its mandate by replacing, rather than merely altering, the Articles of Confederation, Lee raised the issue that would haunt the Federalists for the duration of the ratification battle. He proposed that Congress add a bill of rights to the Constitution prior to approving the document. Madison saw this proposal as a subtle strategy for derailing the ratification process, since any alteration by Congress would transform the Constitution into a "mere act of Congress," requiring the assent of all thirteen states.

To maintain the appearance of congressional unanimity in the face of serious opposition, Madison and his allies devised a means to mask the disagreement. As drafted, the Constitution did not require congressional approval at all; Article VII of the Constitution specified that it would become effective upon ratification by specially elected conventions in nine states. Thus, supporters of the Constitution decided that Congress could simply forward the document to the states without any recommendation. On September 28, 1787, Congress passed a resolution transmitting the proposed Constitution "to the several legislatures in Order to be submitted to a convention of Delegates chosen in each state by the people thereof." The fight for ratification would now be waged state by state.

One of the more remarkable features of the ratification battles was that, in addition to the normal political tools of lobbying, threats, and compromise, the conflict was also one of ideas. Those who opposed the Constitution began to fill newspapers with arguments explaining why it should not be ratified. Some of these pieces tended toward the caustic. "Centinel," of Pennsylvania, on October 5, 1787, attacked one of the leading strengths of those in favor of the Constitution: the support of two American icons, George Washington and Ben Franklin. Centinel's approach was direct. He dismissed Washington as naïve; readers were told that his "unsuspecting goodness and zeal . . . has been imposed on." Franklin, meanwhile, was just a doddering fool, suffering "the weakness and indecision attendant on old age."

Other writers provided far more substantial reasons for opposing the Constitution. Two who appeared in the New York newspapers under the names Federal Farmer and Brutus were particularly effective. In three articles that ran from October 8 through October 10, Federal Farmer argued that the new Constitution violated fundamental principles of separation of powers because the Senate's power of impeachment, combined with its ability to reject both treaties and presidential appointments, would give it virtual control over the new chief executive: "The president is connected with, or tied to the senate; he may always act with the senate, but never can effectually counteract its views." Brutus, who began to publish his articles the next week, contended that the population and size of the United States were too large for any form of government but a tyranny: "A free republic cannot long subsist over a country of the great extent of these states."

Hamilton and Madison watched the development of opposition articles with increasing anxiety. In early October they were still optimistic, as Hamilton wrote to Washington that "the new Constitution is as popular in this city as it is possible for anything to be, and the prospect thus far is favorable to it throughout the state." On October 14, Madison reported that while the Constitution had "in general been pretty well recd. . . . Opposition however begins to shew itself." A few days later, Madison expressed more concern to George Washington when he stated that "the Newspapers here begin to teem with vehement & virulent calumniations of the proposed Govt." Nonetheless, Madison was pleased to say that "the reports however from different quarters continue to be rather flattering." By October 21, Madison recognized that the supporters of the Constitution faced a serious threat. He was especially concerned about Brutus, whom he described as "a new Combatant . . . with considerable address & plausibility, [who] strikes at the foundation." Finally, on October 30, Hamilton wrote to Washington to tell him that while there had been strong initial support for ratification, "the artillery of its opponents makes some impression." These attacks on the Constitution would not go unanswered. Hamilton placed with his letter a copy of a newspaper column and noted, "The inclosed is the first number of a series of papers to be written in its defence." With that, George Washington received the first essay of *The Federalist.*

Because of the secrecy with which *The Federalist* was written, much of its initial planning must be divined from snippets of contemporary evidence and from documents written long after the memory of the collaboration of Hamilton and Madison had been colored by partisan bickering. Nonetheless, a reasonably clear picture can be created.

Hamilton spent the first part of October 1787 in Albany, New York. After the convention, he had resumed his law practice, and needed to be in Albany to attend the October session of the New York Supreme Court. He returned to New York City shortly after the session ended on October 16.

When Hamilton journeyed between New York City and Albany, he usually traveled by sloop. In those days, the trip on the Hudson River, then called the North River, was a leisurely affair. For up to a week, the seventy-foot vessel with its large mainsail would meander past farmland, towns, and verdant hillsides, and the wealthier passengers, such as Hamilton, could repair to their cabins. It was there that Hamilton prepared the outline for a series of essays that would not only demonstrate the need for a stronger federal government but carefully explain how the individual sections of the new Constitution would work to create a national government that was strong enough to protect the nation's interests yet able to avoid the pitfalls of despotism and aristocracy.

As his pseudonym, Hamilton selected Publius, also known as Publius Valerius, a Roman ruler from approximately 500 BCE. This choice was especially apt. Upon assuming power, Publius had been forced to confront the suspicions of the people, many of whom feared he would end their republic. According to the classic telling of the story by the Roman historian Livy, "It was rumoured that he was aiming at monarchy." To dispel the rumors, Publius ordered that his house, an "impregnable fortress" located on top of a high hill, be torn down and a new structure built at the bottom of the hill. As Publius told the onlookers, "you may dwell above the citizen whom you suspect." Publius proved to be so just a ruler that he was given the name Publicola, or lover of people. The appeal for Hamilton of such a story is not difficult to understand.

Hamilton also needed a title for his series of articles. He selected the designation which had been adopted generally by those who supported ratification: *The Federalist.* The terms "Federalist" and "Anti-Federalist" had been in use since at least 1786, with the former used to describe those in favor of increased power for the federal government. Nonetheless, the labels greatly distressed those who were opposed to ratification. First, they claimed, with some validity, that those who supported the loose confederation of states under the Articles of Confederation should be considered the true federalists and that those who wanted a strong national government should be viewed as nationalists. Even more frustrating to those who were trying to prevent ratification was that they were saddled with "the odious term anti-Federalists." It was a textbook example of what today would be termed political branding.

Federal Farmer unsuccessfully lobbied for different terminology, writing that "if any names are applicable to the parties, on account of their general politics, they are those of republicans and anti-republicans," with, of course, the Anti-Federalists being the Republicans. Elbridge Gerry, one of the three delegates who had refused to sign the final document at the convention, was still complaining a year after the Constitution had been ratified. Arguing that the true division was between supporters and opponents of ratification, he bemoaned, "Their names then ought not to have been distinguished by federalists and anti-federalists, but rats and anti-rats."

In such a heated environment, Hamilton decided to implement an approach very different from his ill-fated attack on Governor Clinton a few months earlier. In his very first essay as Publius, published in New York's *Independent Journal* on October 27, 1787, and addressed "To the People of the State of New York," Hamilton described how *The Federalist* would be different from other entries in the debate. His approach, he told his readers, would be one of "candor." He would strive to convince his audience with honest, dispassionate reasoning.

Hamilton attempted to establish his credibility from the start by explicitly rejecting a tactic used by several Anti-Federalists. Many opponents of ratification began their essays by proclaiming that they were undecided on the issue and were merely offering their disinterested musings. Thus, Federal Farmer began his attacks by writing, "I do not mean, hastily and positively to decide on the merits of the constitution proposed." In contrast, Hamilton forthrightly declared his support for ratification. He wrote, "I will not amuse you with an appearance of deliberation, when I have decided." Hamilton said that he would "frankly acknowledge to you my convictions," and explain "the reasons on which they are founded."

In another, perhaps unexpected, burst of candor, Hamilton conceded that the battle could not be characterized as one between virtuous Federalists and their evil opponents. Rather than demonize the Anti-Federalists, Hamilton stated that there are "wise and good men on the wrong as well as on the right side of questions, of the first magnitude to society." Moreover, he warned, even those who supported him might have been doing so for improper reasons: "Ambition, avarice, personal animosity, party opposition, and many other motives, not more laudable than these, are apt to operate as well upon those who support as upon those who oppose the right side of a question." Pledging to avoid an "intolerant spirit," Hamilton modestly promised that his arguments would "at least be offered in a spirit, which will not disgrace the cause of truth."

His plan was ambitious. He stated that the series of essays would cover the entire range of issues involved in the ratification debate. He listed six broad topics:

The utility of the Union to your political prosperity—
The insufficiency of the present Confederation to preserve that Union—
The necessity of a government at least equally energetic with the one proposed to the attainment of this object
The conformity of the proposed constitution to the true principles of republican government—
Its analogy to your own state constitution—
The additional security, which its adoption will afford to the

preservation of that species of government, to liberty, and to property—

He further pledged to respond to the charges leveled by the Anti-Federalists: "In the progress of this discussion I shall endeavor to give a satisfactory answer to all the objections which shall have made their appearance."

Hamilton initially underestimated the size of this undertaking. Rather than the eighty-five essays that ultimately made up *The Federalist,* he told printer Archibald McLean that he expected the work to "consist of twenty Numbers, or at the utmost twenty-five." Nonetheless, Hamilton knew that to complete even this quantity rapidly enough to affect the ratification debates would require coauthors. He first sought out fellow New Yorkers with whom he had worked before. Hamilton recruited his old ally, Gouverneur Morris. After Morris declined, he was "warmly pressed" by Hamilton to reconsider, but the lure of a lucrative business deal with Robert Morris outweighed any desire he might have had to help obtain ratification for the document he had helped draft. Hamilton was more successful in his other two initial choices for collaborators, William Duer and John Jay. Their subsequent experiences, however, did not bode well for the project's completion.

William Duer, an old friend of Hamilton, had served in the Continental Congress and was one of the signatories of the Articles of Confederation. His marriage to Catherine Alexander Sterling, known as Lady Kitty, was particularly fortuitous. Not only was she wealthy and well connected—at her wedding she was given away by George Washington—she was also a cousin of Hamilton's wife.

Duer was a Hamilton loyalist. In 1785, as a member of the New York legislature, Duer had been instrumental in securing Hamilton's appointment to attend the Annapolis convention. Duer did not attend the Philadelphia convention, and by all accounts showed very little interest in its goings on, but Hamilton asked him to participate in the writing of *The Federalist* anyway.

Many years after the fact, Madison would describe Duer's involvement in the project, saying that his pieces, "tho' intelligent &

sprightly, were not continued; nor did they make a part of the printed Collection." A review of Duer's essays reveals that Madison was being exceedingly charitable and that Hamilton was quite wise in rejecting them.

Duer's first attempt was an awkward essay which contradicted both itself and the thoughtful tone that Hamilton was trying to present. Duer's main point was that state officials opposed the Constitution for selfish reasons. The Constitution, Duer wrote, would result in a "diminution of State authority" which would then lead to a "diminution of the POWER of those who are invested with the administration of that authority" and might actually "annihilate the offices themselves." Apparently realizing that the "annihilation" of state offices played into the fears of the Anti-Federalists, Duer appended a final not very reassuring paragraph, asserting that the state offices that would be affected by the Constitution "though of considerable importance are not numerous" and that "most of the departments of the State Governments will remain, untouched."

Even though it would never become enshrined as part of *The Federalist,* Duer's essay did reach print. It was published on October 30, 1787, under the name Philo-Publius, appearing the day before the second *Federalist* essay appeared. Philo-Publius wrote three other very short and forgettable pieces which appeared in New York papers through December 1, and was otherwise silent during the ratification debate.

This was not the last time that Duer would disappoint Hamilton. When Hamilton became secretary of the treasury in 1789, one of his first decisions was to appoint Duer as assistant secretary. Duer served for only seven months, but in that short time he managed to become America's "first inside trader." At the same time that he was working closely with Hamilton, Duer became one of the most aggressive speculators in government securities. Utilizing his knowledge of Hamilton's plans, and ignoring the fact that it was illegal to traffic in government securities while on the federal payroll, Duer led a syndicate which roamed throughout the country purchasing government paper. He also shared privileged governmental information with his friends.

Noah Webster was able to write to his future brother-in-law of the still-secret interest rate the government was going to pay on its debts, and attributed his information to "the outdoor talk of Col. Duer, the Vice-Secretary."

Not surprisingly, Duer amassed an enormous fortune. He lived, as one contemporary described it, "in the style of a nobleman." Duer employed fifteen liveried servants in his mansion overlooking the Hudson River and traveled with "a coat of arms emblazoned upon his carriage." The opulence of Duer's lifestyle was described by a guest at one of his famous gatherings, who remembered a meal with "not less than fifteen different sorts of wine at dinner and after the cloth was removed, besides most excellent bottled cider, porter, and several other kinds of strong beer."

After leaving government service, Duer continued his speculation, including a plan to buy up shares of the Bank of New York and sell them at inflated prices. Thomas Jefferson, who despised such "gambling scoundrels," dubbed Duer, "the king of the alley." Hamilton recognized that Duer was engaging in a dangerous scheme and wrote to his friend that he "had serious fears for you—for your purse and for your reputation." But Hamilton's warning was not heeded. In 1792, Duer, who was heavily in debt, became caught in a credit squeeze. He not only owed large sums to other speculators but also to "shopkeepers, Widows, orphans—Butchers, Carmen, Gard[e]ners, market women, & even the noted Bawd Mrs. Macarty."

Unable to pay his creditors, Duer was sentenced to debtors' prison. From his cell he could hear an angry mob throw stones at the jail and yell for vengeance: "We will have Mr. Duer, he has gotten our money." Duer remained in prison for seven years, and was released in February 1799, only after becoming seriously ill. He died destitute three months later.

John Jay should have been a much better choice than Duer as coauthor. At forty-two, he was older and, at the time, better known and better respected than either Hamilton or Madison. He had helped draft the New York State Constitution and served as both president of the Continental Congress and chief justice of New York.

Experienced in foreign affairs, he had been minister to Spain and, with Benjamin Franklin and John Adams, had negotiated the Treaty of Paris, which formally ended the Revolutionary War. Beginning in 1784, he served as secretary of foreign affairs and later as secretary of state, until Thomas Jefferson succeeded him in 1790. The only reason that Jay did not attend the Constitutional Convention was that his nomination had been blocked by New York's Governor Clinton.

Jay, nonetheless, had an excellent understanding of the issues facing the delegates in Philadelphia. His negotiations with foreign governments had been continually sabotaged by the unwillingness of the states to work together under the Articles of Confederation. He also appreciated the necessity for a separation of powers rather than their conglomeration in the Continental Congress. As he wrote to George Washington prior to the convention, "Let Congress legislate. Let others execute. Let others judge."

Jay wrote his essays for *The Federalist* quickly, completing his first four in just ten days. These pieces were concerned with the need for unity, and more importantly, set a strongly positive tone for the rest of the essays. In *Federalist 2*, he extolled the virtues of nationhood and described what he saw as America's divine nature:

> This country and this people seem to have been made for each other, and it appears as if it was the design of Providence, that an inheritance so proper and convenient for a band of brethren, united to each other by the strongest ties, should never be split into a number of unsocial, jealous and alien sovereignties.

Jay's next three essays discussed the dangers that a divided United States would face from foreign nations. Not only would the individual states be more vulnerable to foreign attack, they would likely be drawn into opposing alliances: "Different commercial concerns must create different interests, and of course different degrees of political attachment to and connection with different foreign nations." According to Jay, the inevitable result would be that states would have even more to fear from one another than from the outside world.

After these first few essays, Jay's contribution to *The Federalist* came to an abrupt halt. A short time after his *Federalist 5* appeared on November 10, Jay was incapacitated by a bout of rheumatoid arthritis. He was unable to resume writing for several months.

Coincidentally, the Anti-Federalists began a campaign of disinformation about Jay. At the end of November, a Baltimore newspaper announced that Jay was opposing the Constitution because it was "as deep and wicked a conspiracy as has been ever invented in the darkest ages against the liberties of a free people." Washington was unsettled by this story. He wrote to Madison for reassurance: "I am anxious . . . to know, on what ground this report originates." Madison wrote back, telling Washington that the story was an "arrant forgery" and complaining that "tricks of this sort are not uncommon with the Enemies of the new Constitution."

By midwinter, Jay had recovered sufficiently to write one more *Federalist* essay. On March 5, 1788, in *Federalist 64*, Jay relied on his personal experience to defend the treaty provision of the Constitution. Noting that "we heretofore suffered from the want of secrecy and dispatch" in negotiations, he praised the Constitution for providing that the president would be responsible for future negotiations. He added that the convention had wisely placed a check on the president's power by requiring the consent of two-thirds of the Senate before any treaty would be effective.

Any possibility that Jay would write additional *Federalist* essays was ended by one of the first riots in American history, the so-called Doctors' Riot of 1788. The name is actually misleading, since it was the doctors who were the target of the rioters. On Sunday, April 13, a group of young boys climbed a ladder in order to peer through a window of New York Hospital, located on the corner of Broadway and Pearl Street. From their vantage point, they were able to observe medical students dissecting a cadaver. Noticing the boys spying on them, one young doctor-in-training with a peculiar sense of humor picked up an amputated arm, waved it at the children, and said, "This is your mother's hand." Unbeknownst to the medical student, the mother of one of the boys had recently died. Distraught and in tears, the child ran to tell his father what he had just seen. His father proceeded to his wife's grave, which had, coincidentally, recently been emptied by robbers.

The man then gathered his friends, and very quickly a large crowd ransacked the hospital, hoping to take vengeance on both the medical students and any doctors they could find. The students and most of the doctors escaped, though "sundry doctors and others were considerably mauled." Four other physicians were rescued and, for their protection, locked inside the city jail on lower Broadway.

The next day, a large crowd gathered outside the jail, shouting, "Bring out your doctors! Bring out your doctors!" Local political leaders, including Governor Clinton and Alexander Hamilton, accompanied the local militia to protect the jail. General Matthew Clarkson, racing to the scene, saw John Jay leaving his house and said, "My God, Jay, the mob is surrounding the jail! They're going to break in and rip up the doctors. If they succeed we'll have murder and universal confusion. There's not a minute to lose. Can you let me have a sword?" Jay went back to his house, returned with two swords, and the two men hurried off to join the others defending the jail.

The mob quickly turned violent. Men began throwing bricks and stones. Jay was hit in the head and knocked unconscious. As he was rushed away for emergency medical attention, the militia began firing on the crowd, killing three and dispersing the rest. Jay was carried home with "two large holes in his forehead." For several days, doctors feared he had suffered serious brain injury. Though Jay recovered fully in time to attend the New York ratifying convention, *The Federalist* would be completed without any more of his assistance.

Thus it was James Madison who would serve as the primary coauthor of *The Federalist*. Late in life, when discussing how he came to participate, Madison wrote that "the undertaking was proposed by A. Hamilton to J. M. with a request to join him & Mr. Jay in carrying it into effect." The exact timing and nature of the request is unclear, but Madison's letters written in September and October of 1787 permit a general understanding of the chronology.

By the time Congress had completed its vote to send the Constitution on to the states, Madison and Hamilton had not only grown closer personally, they were seen as joint leaders of the national ratification campaign. At the end of September, Tench Coxe of Pennsylvania sent some essays favoring ratification to Madison, and asked him to discuss with Hamilton the best strategy for disseminating them in New York and Virginia: "I beg the favor of your perusing them with Col. Hamilton . . . and if you and he think they will be of any Service be pleased to have them reprinted in the papers of those States." On October 1, Madison wrote back to inform Coxe that Hamilton was out of town but that "as soon as he returns your commands with respect to him shall be executed."

A few weeks later, on October 21, Coxe sent some additional articles supporting ratification to Madison, again stating his "wish that you and Col. H. may make any use of them, which you think will serve the cause." On October 26, Madison wrote back to tell Coxe that "Col. Hamilton had returned to the City which gave me the opportunity of immediately putting into his hands such of them as were destined for him. I have no doubt he will make the best use of them." What is most interesting about these letters is not merely that they demonstrate that people understood that Madison and Hamilton were working together in the struggle for ratification. The timing of the letters also reveals that the two men met right before the publication of Hamilton's first *Federalist* essay on October 27.

At this time, Madison had not yet agreed to participate in the writing of *The Federalist*. Sometime after November 8, he left New York to go to Philadelphia and was uncertain whether he would return to New York. As he wrote to Edmund Randolph on November 18, "I returned hither [New York City] yesterday from Phila. to which place I had proceeded under arrangements for either going on to Virginia, or coming back as I might there decide." There is no question that by the date of his return to New York, Madison had decided to join with Hamilton. The same day he wrote to Randolph, Madison also wrote to Washington and sent him the first seven *Federalist* essays. In asking Washington to place the essays in Virginia newspapers, Madison revealed that he was joining Publius: "I will not conceal from you that

I am likely to have such a degree of connection with the publication here, as to afford a restraint of delicacy from interesting myself directly in the republication elsewhere."

While we do not know precisely when Hamilton first approached Madison, it is clear that Hamilton was delighted with Madison's decision to join the project. The same day that Madison returned to New York City, November 17, Hamilton announced a change in the writing schedule that Publius would follow. The essays would now appear twice as frequently. Instead of two essays a week, Hamilton wrote at the end of *Federalist 7*, "it is proposed to publish them four times a week." As historian Douglass Adair has noted, it could only have been "Madison's definite promise of aid" that would have permitted Hamilton to make such a bold promise.

Even with two capable and determined authors, the writing was hectic. In the six months from October 1787 through March 1788, Madison and Hamilton wrote almost one thousand words a day. Publication deadlines would often arrive before the day's essay was complete. According to Madison, "It frequently happened that whilst the printer was putting into type the parts of a number, the following parts were under the pen, & to be furnished in time for the press." The printer would sometimes be standing anxiously by Hamilton's desk as he completed an essay. One friend saw the printer, Samuel Loudon, "in the General's study, waiting to take numbers of the Federalist as they came fresh from the General's pen, in order to publish them in the next paper."

Hamilton intended that *The Federalist* would dominate New York's discussion of the Constitution. He arranged to have the same essays appear in four of the five city newspapers. The constant republication of the essays led a group of readers who identified themselves as "Twenty-seven Subscribers" to write to one newspaper, pleading with the publisher to stop "cramming us with the voluminous PUBLIUS."

Madison and Hamilton were able to produce their papers so quickly because of the research and planning each had done to prepare for the Constitutional Convention. As Madison later remarked, "the performance must have borne a very different aspect without the aid of historical and other notes which had been used in the Convention and without the familiarity with the whole subject produced by the discussions there." Hamilton's essays that followed Jay's, for example, were based almost entirely on the notes he had put together for his notorious June 18 speech in the convention, although this time he omitted his praise of the monarchy. The arguments and historical examples in *Federalist 6–9*, used to describe the "dangers from dissensions between the States" and "the consequences of hostilities between the States," were taken almost verbatim from Hamilton's convention notes. Madison's first essay, the famous *Federalist 10*, similarly drew on the speech he had given on June 6 in the convention concerning the dangers of factions. In fact, virtually all of the opening essays, at least through *Federalist 22*, the end of the section dealing with the "insufficiency" of the Articles of Confederation to preserve the union, were based on Hamilton's and Madison's prior research.

The other noteworthy aspect of these opening essays was that Hamilton and Madison worked together so closely in their preparation. Madison would leave his lodgings at 19 Maiden Lane and walk to Hamilton's house, which was located at the corner of Wall Street and Broadway, to discuss the day's piece before publication. As Madison later described their routine, "In the beginning it was the practice of the writers . . . to communicate each to the other, their respective papers before they were sent to the press." Later, the crush of their schedules made such close work impossible. The discussion of their work prior to publication was ultimately "rendered so inconvenient, by the shortness of the time allowed, that it was dispensed with."

The results of their initial collaborative effort can be seen in several of their early essays. Hamilton's *Federalist 9*, which discusses the dangers of factions, is largely an introduction for the much more detailed analysis of factions Madison provides in *Federalist 10*. *Federalist 18–20*, dealing with the lessons to be learned from the history of the world's earlier confederacies, was the subject of negotiation between the two coauthors. By the beginning of December, both men had started working on the topic. It was decided that Madison, who had done far more extensive research when preparing his forty-three-page study, "Ancient & Modern Confederacies," prior to attending the Annapolis convention, should write on the topic. According to Madison, "What had been prepared by Mr. Hamilton, who had entered more briefly into the subject, was left to Mr. Madison, on its appearing that the latter was engaged upon it, with larger materials, and with a view to a more precise delineation, and from the pen of the latter the several papers went to press."

At about this time, Hamilton and Madison made an important decision about *The Federalist* that would fundamentally alter the impact of the project. The essays had begun to receive significant positive feedback, and the coauthors decided that they could have even more impact if they bound their work in book form. Thus, on December 2, Madison promised Virginia Governor Edmund Randolph that "the Printer means to make a pamphlet of them, when I can give them to you in a more convenient form." Although they knew copies of the book would be sent to Virginia, Hamilton and Madison initially saw the work's primary audience as the voters of New York. An early advertisement for the book identified the essays as written "By a Citizen of New-York." Madison and Hamilton soon realized, however, that *The Federalist* was having an effect on the ratification process throughout the country, and as Madison later noted, since the essays were already being "republished in other States and were making a diffusive impression in favor of the Constitution, that limited character was laid aside." By the time the book appeared in March 1788, the author was again identified as Publius.

As plans for the book progressed, Hamilton and Madison embarked upon a more formal division of their labor. By December 18, 1787, they had reached the third item on Hamilton's original agenda, the need for a strong national government or, as the topic was described in *Federalist 23*: "THE necessity of a Constitution, at least equally energetic with the one proposed, to the preservation of the Union." Hamilton was chosen to write the essays on the topics with which he was most concerned, the power of the sword and of the purse. In the next several essays, Hamilton explained why it was essential for the federal government both "to be clothed with all the powers requisite to" the care of the common defense, and to possess "a general power of taxation."

On January 11, 1788, with *Federalist 37*, Madison took over the writing. Through February 20, while Hamilton attended to his legal practice, Madison would write the next twenty-two essays. He began by discussing the nature of the Constitutional Convention. Without acknowledging that he himself had been a member of the convention, Madison described the hard work, integrity, and spirit of compromise that characterized the delegates. Citing the extraordinary difficulty of reconciling so many competing interests in producing the final document, Madison declared, "It is impossible for the man of pious reflection not to perceive in it, a finger of that Almighty hand."

In his next essay, Madison addressed the greatest fear of those supporting the Constitution: that their opponents would succeed in calling for amendments prior to ratification. By mid-January, five states (Delaware, Pennsylvania, New Jersey, Georgia, and Connecticut) had ratified the Constitution. In each of these states' ratifying conventions, the vote in favor was more than twice that opposed. Massachusetts, the next state to decide, provided a more challenging battleground. Anti-Federalists in Massachusetts stalled the ratification process by arguing that problems such as the lack of a bill of rights, in addition to concerns over the specific powers being given to the federal government, should be addressed before the state would grant its approval. On January 20, Madison wrote to George Washington, expressing concern that prospects in Massachusetts had become "very ominous."

In *Federalist 38*, Madison answered those calling for prior amendments. He derisively catalogued sixteen different and contradictory objections which had been expressed by various Anti-Federalists and concluded that there was no semblance of agreement by the opponents of the Constitution as to how it should be amended. Were the nation to grant the Anti-Federalists the opportunity to devise amendments prior to ratification, Madison warned, "the discord and ferment that would mark their own deliberations" would kill all hope of creating an alternative to the Articles of Confederation.

The Federalists in Massachusetts were able to negotiate a compromise which avoided that scenario. They convinced Governor John Hancock to present a proposal for nine "subsequent amendments" and promised that they would see that these were adopted as soon as the Constitution went into effect. Even with this maneuver, the vote in the Massachusetts ratifying convention was the closest to date. On February 6, 1788, Massachusetts, by a vote of 187–168, became the sixth state to ratify the Constitution.

Madison, meanwhile, returned in his essays to describing how the Constitution would function. He devoted several essays to the relationship between the state and national government. He explained that the Constitution created a complex structure, one in which the federal government would have significant power and the states would be preserved as sovereign entities with their own separate sphere of power. Moreover, in many areas, federal and state powers would be intermingled. The Constitution, Madison concluded, is "neither a national nor a federal constitution; but a composition of both."

With *Federalist 47*, Madison introduced his analysis of the distribution of power at the national level with a discussion of his theory of separation of powers. For five essays, he explained that a constitution which did nothing beyond declaring that governmental power should be separated would create a mere "parchment barrier" to those who wanted to usurp the power of other branches. The only way to prevent the ultimate and total consolidation of governmental power was through the Constitution's system of checks and balances.

Madison then turned to a discussion of the legislative branch, the segment of government which he had studied most closely and with which he was most concerned. *Federalist 52* marked the beginning of the final major phase of work done by Publius, the minute dissection of the organization, power, and limitation of each part of the federal government. For the next seven essays, Madison focused on the House of Representatives. After discussing both how representatives would be elected and the rationale for biennial elections, Madison addressed the topic which may have caused him the most discomfort: slavery.

The Constitution provided that the number of representatives allotted to each state would be calculated "according to their respective Numbers." Each state's number was to be calculated "by adding to the whole Number of free Persons . . . three fifths of all other persons." In other words, for purposes of representation, slaves counted as only three-fifths of a free person.

It was perhaps inevitable that Madison would be the one to defend the three-fifths compromise. Hamilton was strongly opposed to slavery. Both he and Jay were leading members of a group organized to end slavery in New York, the "New York Society for the Manumission of Slaves and the Protection of such of them as had been or wanted to be Liberated"—more generally known as the New York Manumission Society. Shortly after the group had formed, Hamilton exposed the hypocrisy of some members by proposing that anyone who wanted to participate in the society be required to free their own slaves. The proposal failed.

During the convention, however, Hamilton was not as forthright. Unlike several other antislavery delegates, Hamilton was unwilling to jeopardize the chance for a new governmental structure by challenging the institution of slavery. His friend, Gouverneur Morris, had announced to the convention that "he never would concur in upholding domestic slavery. It was a nefarious institution. It was the curse of heaven on the States where it prevailed." Hamilton, in contrast, never made such a statement in Philadelphia. In fact, when the Manumission Society drafted an antislavery petition to be delivered to the convention, Hamilton convinced them to withhold it. The minutes for August 17, 1787, of the Manumission Society reported that a committee had completed drafting the petition but had decided not to send it after being "informed that it was probable the Convention would not take up the Business."

Madison's view of slavery was even more convoluted. Like his friend Thomas Jefferson, he recognized that slavery was "the great evil under which the nation labors"; yet, unlike George Washington, he never freed his slaves, even in death. Late in life, when he contemplated the eventual end of slavery, he could not envision an integrated society. Madison saw free Blacks as "idle and depraved" and eventually joined the colonization movement to send freed slaves to Liberia.

Nonetheless, Madison won a victory in Philadelphia that would become a significant part of the abolitionist movement's linguistic arsenal. He successfully fought to prevent the word "slavery" from appearing in the final document. Madison told the convention that it would be "wrong to admit in the Constitution the idea that there could be property in men." Thus, the Constitution did not say that "the slave trade" could not be prohibited before 1808; instead, the limitation on Congress's power was placed on the awkwardly phrased "importation of such Persons as any of the States now existing shall think proper to admit."

This was not a hollow victory for Madison. Because of Madison's "scruples against admitting the term 'Slaves' into the Instrument," Frederick Douglass, the former slave who became a leader in the abolitionist movement, was given an important rhetorical tool. He could declare in 1863 that "the Federal Government was never, in its essence, anything but an anti-slavery government." Noting the absence of the word "slavery," Douglass argued, "Abolish slavery tomorrow, and not a sentence or syllable of the Constitution need be altered. It was purposely so framed as to give no claim, no sanction to the claim, of property in man."

Madison's ambivalent feelings toward slavery are nowhere more evident than in his tortured *Federalist* essay discussing the three-fifths compromise. Madison could not bring himself to defend the provision directly, so he invented a fictitious advocate, whom he described as "one of our Southern brethren," to attempt the job for him. According to this hypothetical speaker, the three-fifths ratio reflected the legal reality that slaves had a "mixt character of persons and of property." They could be sold and forced to labor, but they also were protected in some ways against being attacked personally. Moreover, those states which held a slave legally accountable for wrongdoing were treating that slave "as a moral person, not as a mere article of property." Perhaps sensing that this argument was not particularly convincing, Madison had his "Southern brethren" plead with his reader: "Let the case of the slaves be considered as it is in truth a peculiar one. Let the compromising expedient of the Constitution be mutually adopted, which regards them as inhabitants, but as debased by servitude below the equal level of free inhabitants, which regards the *slave* as divested of two fifth of the *man*."

The voice of Madison or, more precisely, Publius, then returned to conclude the essay. Commenting on the twisted logic of the "Southern brethren," Madison lent his clearly unenthusiastic support: "Such is the reasoning which an advocate for the southern interests might employ on this subject. And although it may appear to be a little strained in some points, yet on the whole, I must confess that it fully reconciles me to the scale of representation, which the convention have established."

On February 22, 1788, after an absence of almost two months, Hamilton returned, providing Madison a brief respite. In Hamilton's next three essays, *Federalist 59–61*, he discussed the ability of Congress to regulate the "time, places and manner" for the election of representatives and senators.

Madison, who had been averaging more than three essays a week, finally had a week off to recover. His next two essays, *Federalist 62* and *63*, in which he discussed the composition of the Senate, appeared on February 27 and March 1. These would be Madison's last essays as Publius. A few days later, he left New York City for Virginia to stand for election to his home state's ratifying convention.

The pressure on Madison to return to Virginia had been building for several months. On December 7, 1787, George Washington had written to him to warn him that Virginia was becoming increasingly Anti-Federalist: "I am sorry to inform you that the Constitution has lost ground so considerably that it is doubtful whether it has any longer a majority in its favor." In January, Madison received a letter from a worried friend, William Moore, urging him to leave New York and campaign for election to the ratifying convention: "I must therefore entreat and conjure you—nay command you, if it were in my power—to be here in February, or the first of March next. Pray don't disappoint the wishes of your friends, and many others, who are wavering on the Constitution. . . . I repeat again, come."

Many others joined in urging Madison to leave New York. At the end of January, his father wrote, "I think you had better come in as early in March as you can. Many of your friends wish it; there are some who suspend their opinion till they see you, & wish for an explanation, others wish you not to come, & will endeavor to shut you out of the Convention, the better to carry their point."

In February, as Madison continued to write his *Federalist* essays, Washington wrote to him again, imploring him to return to Virginia: "Many have asked me, with anxious solicitude, if you did not mean to get into the convention, conceiving it of indispensable importance." Madison finally acceded to these requests.

Before he left New York, Madison discussed with Hamilton the remaining topics to be covered. En route from New York to Virginia, Madison stopped in Philadelphia to mail Hamilton further suggestions. Madison's letter has not been found, but its influence can be seen in Hamilton's response. Hamilton wrote to Madison, thanking him for the comments. He stated, cryptically, "The remarks you made on a certain subject are important, and will be attended to. There is truly much embarrassment in the case."

After mailing his letter to Hamilton, Madison continued his trip to Virginia. He stopped for a few days to meet with Washington in Mount Vernon, and reached his home in Orange County on March 23, the day before the election. Prior to the vote, candidates addressed the crowd of voters outside a barn. Despite a "very strong wind," Madison spoke for two hours, standing atop a "hogshead of tobacco," explaining his support for the Constitution and answering questions from the assembled. When the votes were counted, Madison and his fellow Federalist, James Gordon, had easily won. This victory was both a critical event for the ratification of the Constitution and a personal triumph for Madison. One of the defeated Anti-Federalists was his former nemesis, the tavern-owning Charles Porter, who had defeated him in the election for Virginia Provincial Convention eleven years earlier by distributing alcohol to the voting population.

Back in New York, John Jay's final essay on the Senate's treaty power had been printed, leaving the remaining twenty-one essays for Hamilton. Interestingly, before Madison had left for Virginia, he and Hamilton had split the work evenly; each had written precisely twenty-nine essays. From March 7 on, Hamilton would be solely responsible for the essays covering impeachment, the presidency, and the judiciary.

At the same time, Hamilton was also in charge of overseeing the production of the book version of the essays. On March 22, John and Archibald McLean published an advertisement in the *New York Independent Journal,* announcing *"THIS DAY IS PUBLISHED . . . The FEDERALIST,* VOLUME FIRST." The volume, with the complete, if unwieldy, title of *The Federalist: A Collection of Essays, written in favour of the New Constitution, as agreed upon by the federal convention, September 17, 1787,* ran a total of 233 pages. The McLeans produced two different versions of the book. Most copies were printed on ordinary paper with regular board binding. A few, however, were quite ornate. Printed on "superfine Royal Writing Paper," they were bound in calfskin with gilt edging. When Hamilton sent one of these "finer" copies to George Washington, he wrote that it was "neatly enough bound to be honored with a place in your library."

The thirty-six essays in the McLean version of *The Federalist* were not identical to those that had appeared earlier in the newspapers. In addition to making several small editorial changes and adding a table of contents, Hamilton altered the order of some of the essays. The essay which had appeared in newspapers as *Federalist 35* discussed regulation of the militia, originally, but followed a discussion of taxation issues. Hamilton had it renumbered as *Federalist 29,* so that it could follow the essays addressing military matters. Hamilton also divided one large essay into two shorter ones. What had been *Federalist 31* in the newspapers thus appeared as *Federalist 32* and *33* in the book.

Hamilton also contributed a special unsigned preface, dated March 17, 1788. In this short introduction, after expressing the hope that the book would be found useful in "assisting the public judgment on the momentous question of the Constitution," he issued a peculiar apology. He expressed remorse that the essays had not been more carefully written and edited: "The particular circumstances under which these papers have been written, have rendered it impracticable to avoid violations of method and repetitions of ideas which cannot but displease a critical reader." Nonetheless, Hamilton concluded, he hoped the collection would "lead to a right judgment of the true interests of the community."

In his preface, Hamilton had promised his readers that the second volume would appear "as speedily as the Editor can get it ready for publication." Hamilton's attempt to complete the essays came to a sudden halt on April 2, with *Federalist 77*, which completed the discussion of the presidency. As Hamilton explained to Madison in a letter he sent the next day, the demands of his legal practice necessitated that he temporarily turn his attention away from the essays. Writing so as to preserve his anonymity from the possibly prying eyes of the postal carriers, Hamilton wrote of Publius, "If our suspicions of the author be right, he must be too much engaged to make a rapid progress in what remains. The Court of Chancery and a Circuit Court are now sitting."

Nothing further was heard from Publius for almost two months. Then, on May 28, the second volume of *The Federalist* was released. The book contained more than the essays which had appeared in the newspapers since the first volume had been released. Volume two also included the eight final essays, which had not been published previously, though they would appear in New York newspapers throughout the summer.

The first six of the new essays dealt with the judiciary and described federal courts as "the bulwarks of a limited constitution." In the subsequent essay, Hamilton attempted to address the one issue that seemed to be gaining traction for the Anti-Federalists: the Constitution's lack of a bill of rights.

The controversy over the lack of a bill of rights had caught most of the supporters of the Constitution by surprise. In Philadelphia, the issue had been raised only at the very end of the four-month session and was quickly voted down with virtually no discussion. As opposition to the Constitution developed, however, it became clear that the only thing that Anti-Federalists agreed upon was the need for some sort of bill of rights.

James Wilson of Pennsylvania was one of the first Federalists to recognize the volatility of the issue. On October 6, 1787, just weeks after the Constitution was presented to the public, Wilson delivered a speech outside the Pennsylvania State House. The text of his speech was reprinted throughout the nation and was, in fact, even more widely read than *The Federalist*. Historian Bernard Bailyn has concluded that Wilson's short speech became "the single most influential and most frequently cited document in the entire ratification debate."

Wilson's main argument was that a bill of rights was unnecessary because the federal government under the Constitution would have only the limited power which was given to it; everything not given was retained by the people. For example, Wilson said, Congress could never infringe "liberty of the press" because the Constitution did not give Congress any power to "regulate literary publications." Indeed, Wilson warned, a bill of rights would actually be a danger to the people's liberty because it might make Congress's powers appear more extensive than they were. Any declaration of rights might be used to imply that Congress had been given greater power than it actually had been given. Why declare that Congress was prohibited from doing something if it never had such power in the first place? He wrote, "That very declaration might have been construed to imply that some degree of power was given, since we undertook to define its extent."

The claim that rights were better protected without a specific bill of rights did not satisfy opponents of the Constitution. In November 1787, Brutus effectively demolished Wilson's argument. Brutus identified the fatal flaw in Wilson's claim that the omission of a bill of rights would prevent future claims of broadly implied federal power. He noted that the proposed Constitution as drafted would create that same danger, since other rights were declared to be protected even though they were included within Congress's express power. For example, Congress was barred from suspending the writ of habeas corpus, other than in times of rebellion or invasion, or from issuing titles of nobility; yet nowhere were such powers given. Brutus mockingly cited Wilson's argument and concluded, "If every thing which is not given is reserved, what propriety is there in these exceptions?"

Hamilton, when writing *Federalist 84* seven months after Wilson's speech, was unable to improve upon Wilson's argument. Indeed, he actually borrowed most of his analysis from the speech itself. Like Wilson, he stated that a bill of rights was "not only unnecessary in the proposed constitution, but would even be dangerous." Because the bill of rights would "contain various exceptions to powers which are not granted," Hamilton continued, they would "afford a colourable pretext to claim more than were granted."

In assessing Hamilton's weak showing on this issue, there are several reasons to be charitable. First, as with Madison's discussion on the slavery provisions of the Constitution, Hamilton may have been attempting to defend the indefensible. Publius, after all, could only advocate for the document as it had come out of Philadelphia. Second, by the time Hamilton was writing *Federalist 84*, he had reached the end of the process and was undoubtedly tired and rushed.

Most significant, Hamilton, like Madison and most of the rest of the Federalists, did not recognize the beginning of a major evolution in the nation's understanding of what a bill of rights signified. Historically, most declarations of rights lacked enforcement power. Any limitation they imposed on governments was based on their political and moral, rather than legal, authority. But by the time of the ratification debates, a more modern understanding of bills of rights was developing. The fact that the Constitution transcended ordinary legislation, and indeed controlled the legislature, made a reservation of rights appear far more meaningful. In the words of historian Jack Rakove, "Once the concept of the written constitution as supreme law had gained acceptance, as it had by 1787, the advantages of incorporating statements of rights within the constitutional text seemed evident." Thus, on this issue, *The Federalist* was on the wrong side of history.

With his discussion of the need for a bill of rights completed, Hamilton presented the final Publius essay, *Federalist 85*. He began by acknowledging that he had not yet written on two of his initial six topics, "the analogy of the proposed government to your own state constitution," and "the additional security which its adoption will afford to republican government, to liberty and to property." He would devote just a short paragraph to each because, he said, the subjects had been "so fully anticipated and exhausted in the progress of the work" that any further discussion would be redundant.

Hamilton then commenced his closing argument with a provocative concession. Not only did he not feel an "intire confidence" in all of his arguments, there was "real force" in the arguments of his opponents. But, Hamilton quickly added, that is not the relevant question: "I never expect to see a perfect work from imperfect man." Instead, the Constitution should be ratified because, as a negotiated compromise, it was "the best that the present views and circumstances of the country will permit" and would provide "every species of security which a reasonable people can desire."

Rather than conclude *The Federalist* with the civilized tone of reason that had characterized almost all of the essays, Hamilton chose to end on a negative, quarrelsome note that recalls his disastrous opening salvo against Governor Clinton nine months earlier. The final sentence of the last essay is an ominous warning that if ratification fails, the country might never get another chance to improve upon the Articles of Confederation due to the selfishness of certain people. Hamilton intoned, "I dread the more the consequences of new attempts, because I KNOW that POWERFUL INDIVIDUALS, in this and in other states, are enemies to a general national government, in every possible shape." With that unpleasant, anticlimactic declaration, Publius completed his labors.

Neither the fight for ratification nor the collaboration between Madison and Hamilton ended with the completion of the book. The Virginia convention began on June 2, 1788. The New York convention, to which both Hamilton and Jay had been elected, opened two weeks later, on June 17. Madison and Hamilton would play leading roles in their respective states, and their frequent letters to one another reveal both the coordination of strategy and the growing friendship that had developed between them.

In the era before telegrams and telephones, before faxes, e-mails, and text messages, letter writing was the primary means of communication. One of the clues to the status of a relationship was the writer's choice of how to close the letter. When Madison and Hamilton first wrote to each other in 1783, for example, they would conclude their letters formally with phrases such as "Your obedient servant." By the time the two men were coordinating strategy for their respective state conventions, their letters reveal a relationship that had evolved into true friendship. On June 9, for example, Madison ended his letter to Hamilton with words of affection, "Yrs Affely," which he used only for his friends. This letter is evidence of the closeness Madison felt for another reason. The normally very private Madison also discussed his health (a lifelong obsession for him) and told Hamilton that hot weather "has laid me up with a bilious attack."

Hamilton responded with solicitude for his friend. While expressing optimism over Madison's chances for success in Virginia, Hamilton added words of concern for Madison's health: "Yet I own I fear something from your indisposition." Hamilton ended his letter with the same sort of warm closing as had Madison: "Yrs Affecty."

Despite Hamilton's confidence, Virginia was far from certain to ratify. On June 13, Madison wrote to George Washington that the delegates seemed evenly divided and that "The business is in the most ticklish state that can be imagined." According to Madison, "The majority will certainly be very small on whatever side it may finally lie, and I dare not encourage much expectation that it will be on the favorable side."

Much of the difficulty Madison faced came from the strength of his leading opponent, Patrick Henry. Henry was not only a powerful political figure, he was widely considered the finest public speaker in the nation. Thomas Jefferson referred to him as "the greatest orator who ever lived." Madison certainly did not possess anything approaching Henry's verbal artistry. According to David Robertson, who took shorthand notes of the Virginia debates, when Madison rose to answer Henry, "he spoke so low" that his speech "could not be heard distinctly."

The main battle in Virginia was over "previous" versus "subsequent" amendments. As in Massachusetts, the Anti-Federalists wanted to delay ratification until after the Constitution had been amended. Federalists, on the other hand, wished to have the Constitution in place before amending the document. Madison viewed defeat on this issue as tantamount to losing the entire ratification battle. As he had written to fellow Virginian delegate George Nicholas, "Conditional amendments or a second general Convention, will be fatal."

The call of Anti-Federalists for previous amendments received an unexpected boost from Thomas Jefferson. In December, Jefferson had written a letter to Madison which, while generally supportive of the Constitution, criticized the absence of a bill of rights. Jefferson concluded his discussion by declaring that "a bill of rights is what the people are entitled to against every government on earth, general or particular, & what no just government should refuse, or rest on inferences."

Jefferson's opinion became part of the Virginia debate when a letter he had written to a Virginia merchant, Alexander Donald, was made public. In the letter, Jefferson wrote that to achieve both a constitution and a bill of rights, nine states should ratify the Constitution (making it effective) and the remainder of the states should refuse to ratify until a bill of rights was added: "I wish with all my soul, that the nine first conventions may accept the new constitution. . . . But I equally wish, that the four latest conventions, which ever they be, may refuse to accede to it, till a declaration of rights be annexed."

By mid-June, only eight states had ratified the Constitution, but Patrick Henry saw Jefferson's comments as a potentially powerful argument for delaying Virginia's ratification. Henry noted that New Hampshire was on the verge of becoming the ninth state to ratify. If Virginia were to follow Jefferson's advice, Henry argued, it must demand previous amendments before agreeing to ratify.

In combating Henry and his supporters, Madison possessed one particular advantage. Hoping to delay the procedures until he could gather more Anti-Federalist votes, George Mason had convinced the convention not to vote on ratification until the "Constitution shall have been discussed, clause by clause, through all its parts." At Madison's request, Hamilton had earlier sent fifty-two copies of *The Federalist* to Virginia Governor Randolph to distribute to supporters. Madison and his allies were now able to avail themselves of Publius's detailed analysis.

Throughout the month, this invaluable resource permitted Madison and his supporters "to coach specific speakers to talk on the various parts of the Constitution, and generally to organize and manage its defense in a systematic way."

The Federalist served a similar purpose in New York, although this time it was Hamilton who used the clause-by-clause analysis as a delaying tactic. The Anti-Federalists had won a significant victory in the election of delegates to the state ratifying convention. When the convention opened in Poughkeepsie, they outnumbered the Federalist delegates by more than two to one. Hamilton's plan was to keep his state from voting until either New Hampshire or Virginia ratified, thereby putting new pressure on delegates who would not want New York to be excluded from the new government. Governor Clinton was leading the Anti-Federalists, or, as he called them, "the friends to the rights of mankind," in the battle against those supporting ratification, whom he termed, "the advocates of despotism." Clinton mocked his opponents at the ratifying convention for relying almost exclusively on the analysis presented in *The Federalist*. As he wrote to his ally, John Lamb, "The most that has been said by the new government men has been a second edition of Publius, well delivered."

As the debate in New York continued, Hamilton nervously awaited news from Virginia and New Hampshire. Earlier, he had requested that Madison let him know if and when Virginia voted to ratify as quickly as possible: "I request you to dispatch an express to me with pointed orders to make all possible diligence, by changing horses, etc. All expences shall be thankfully and liberally paid."

Hamilton had made a similar request to John Sullivan, a supporter of the Constitution in New Hampshire. At one o'clock on June 21, New Hampshire voted to ratify. On June 24, within seventy-one hours of the vote, an express rider arrived in Poughkeepsie with the news that a ninth state had approved the Constitution, and the document was officially ratified. Hamilton immediately dispatched the rider, Colonel David Henley, to Virginia to share the good news with Madison. As Henley arrived in Alexandria en route to Richmond, he met a courier racing to New York with a message from Madison, informing Hamilton that on June 27, Virginia had voted 89–79 to ratify the Constitution.

Madison had been able to outlast Patrick Henry and convince a slim majority of delegates that Virginia's interests would be better protected under the Constitution than under the fragile system created by the Articles of Confederation. The price for this approval, though, was a long list of proposed changes to the Constitution. The delegates voted to recommend that it be amended by adding an extensive Declaration of Rights, plus twenty additional structural amendments, such as one requiring a two-thirds vote for any law regulating commerce.

Despite his apparent success, Madison was growing increasingly worried about the continued opposition of Anti-Federalists. His short note to Hamilton expressed his surprisingly dour assessment of the results in Virginia: "This day put an end to the existence of our Convention. The inclosed is a copy of the Act of Ratification. It has been followed by a number of recommendatory alterations; many of them highly objectionable."

Madison's news was carried back to New York by Colonel Henley, the same rider who had been racing down to Richmond. According to newspaper accounts, Henley "returned, with the same zealous expedition he went, to bring the tidings to the anxious expectants in New-York, and arrived here at THREE o'CLOCK" on the morning of July 2. By that afternoon, a celebration of New York City's Federalists had begun. The bells of the city rang out and "TEN guns were fired in honor of the ten states which have adopted the constitution."

To Hamilton's surprise, the votes of New Hampshire and Virginia seemed to have little effect on the Anti-Federalists in New York. They continued to insist that the Constitution be amended before they would consent to ratification. Hamilton, in despair, wrote to Madison with a proposed compromise. In a letter sent by an express courier to New York City, where Madison had gone to resume his seat in Congress, Hamilton asked whether Madison thought that Congress would permit New York State to ratify on the condition that amendments be passed. Essentially, New York would be voting to approve the Constitution but would retain the right to withdraw if it was not satisfied with the final amendments. Hamilton wrote that he thought such a compromise should be appealing: "If this can in the first instance be admitted as a ratification I do not fear any further consequences. Congress will I presume recommend certain amendments to render the structure of the governments more secure. This will satisfy the more considerate and honest opposers of the constitution, and with the aid of time will break up the party."

Madison was furious that Hamilton would consider supporting a proposal that would authorize anything less than complete ratification. He rushed his reply to Hamilton, admonishing him that "this idea of reserving right to withdraw was started in Richmond & considered as a conditional ratification which was itself considered as worse than a rejection." Madison explained that "The Constitution requires an adoption in toto, and for ever. . . . An adoption for a limited time would be as defective as an adoption of some of the articles only. In short any condition whatever must viciate the ratification." For the first time since *The Federalist* was completed, Madison did not conclude his letter to Hamilton with the warmth of a phrase such as "Yrs Affely."

That same day, Madison wrote to Washington and could barely contain his anger at Hamilton. After explaining Hamilton's proposal, Madison wrote, "It is not a little strange that [Hamilton] should hesitate in deciding that the expedient as effectually keeps the State for the present out of the New Union as the most unqualified rejection could do."

The next day, Hamilton read Madison's warning that Congress would not accept a conditional ratification on the floor of the convention. Madison's statement seemed to eliminate support for the proposal. As Hamilton wrote to Madison the next day, "Upon the whole however our fears diminish." Apparently not noticing Madison's undertone of anger, Hamilton closed his letter with his usual "Yrs Affecty A. Hamilton."

With the move for conditional ratification quashed, Hamilton, with assistance from John Jay, was able to negotiate a different compromise.

The convention would ratify unconditionally, but also draft a "Circular Letter" to be sent to all the governors, seeking support for a second constitutional convention. Among the amendments this second convention was to consider were restrictions on Congress's power to tax and borrow money and limitations on the power of the president and the Supreme Court. Even with this compromise, New York's ratification passed with the smallest margin of any state—three—in a vote of 30–27.

Madison continued to be disappointed with Hamilton. Rather than enjoy the fact that eleven states had ratified the Constitution, Madison viewed the circular letter as part of the ongoing struggle with the Anti-Federalists. He sent off another worried missive to Washington, complaining that "the circumstances involved in the ratification of New York will prove more injurious than a rejection would have done." Expressing regret that Hamilton and the other Federalists had supported the letter, Madison accused them of betraying their cause in order to improve New York's chances of serving as the nation's capital once the new Congress was seated. In order to achieve this goal, Madison declared, Hamilton and his New York supporters were determined "to purchase an immediate ratification in any form and at any price," and were willing "to risk and sacrifice every thing to it."

Madison's fears were greatly exaggerated. There was no mass call for another convention. Only one other state, ironically Madison's home state of Virginia, ever voted to support New York's proposal. The Constitution would indeed take effect unimpeded.

Unlike Madison, the citizens of New York City responded to the news from Poughkeepsie joyously. On July 23, three days before the final vote, a procession consisting of five thousand participants, and stretching for a mile and a half, made its way through the streets of New York. The highlight of the parade was a frigate which carried thirty-two guns and was pulled by thirteen horses. In honor of New York's strongest supporter for ratification, the ship bore the name *Hamilton*. On July 26, when news of New York's official ratification reached New York City, the guns of the *Hamilton* fired off several rounds in celebration.

5

"THE HEAD OF A FACTION DECIDEDLY HOSTILE TO ME"

THE DISINTEGRATION OF A RELATIONSHIP

*W*ith the Constitution ratified, the next task at hand was the creation of the new government, and Madison and Hamilton were again in the forefront. Despite his misgivings over Hamilton's actions during the New York ratifying convention, Madison continued to work closely with his former coauthor. In a remarkably brief period of time, however, their alliance degenerated into bitter enmity. The end of their friendship was not merely personal. The split also revealed deep legal and political fault lines that are still apparent in the nation today.

As plans for the new government were being formed, Hamilton considered Madison a friend as well as a political ally. Hamilton's letters to Madison were warm and cordial, and he spoke to others of his fondness for him. In late November 1788, for example, William Duer wrote to Madison that "our mutual Friend Hamilton" had shared the substance of one of Madison's letters concerning their strategy for selecting the first vice president.

Hamilton and Madison had decided that John Adams was the best choice to serve behind George Washington, but they realized that the

Constitution they had so vigorously defended posed a potential dilemma. Under the Constitution as originally approved, electors did not vote for a presidential/vice-presidential ticket. Instead each elector voted for two candidates, and the top two became president and vice president. If every elector voted for the same two candidates, however, there would be a tie, and the presidency would be determined by the House of Representatives. Hamilton wrote to Madison that because "it would be disagreeable to have a man treading close upon the heels of the person we wish as President," they needed to prevent "the possibility of rendering it doubtful who is appointed President." Together they devised a plan in which Hamilton would convince a small number of electors in several states not to vote for Adams.

The scheme worked. When the votes were counted on February 4, 1789, Washington received sixty-nine electoral votes and Adams came in second with thirty-four votes. There would be long-term repercussions from Hamilton's behind-the-scenes electioneering. Adams eventually learned that Hamilton had helped orchestrate the voting and never forgave him for the "scurvy manner in which it was done."

Hamilton also hoped that Madison would serve with him in Washington's cabinet, but Madison chose instead to join the legislative branch. Hamilton wrote that he would "console" himself with the realization that if Madison were not in the legislature, "the government may sincerely feel the want of men who unite to zeal all the requisite qualifications for parrying the machinations of its enemies." Hamilton ended the letter by advising Madison that he needed to actively campaign if he hoped to prevail, and that it would be best "that you bent your course to Virginia."

Hamilton's advice was well taken. Virginia Governor Patrick Henry, still resentful over Madison's victory at the ratifying convention, was determined to keep him out of the new federal government. During the Virginia assembly's debate over who should be selected to represent the state in the Senate, Henry led the opposition to Madison. On the floor of the assembly, Henry thundered that Madison was "unworthy of the confidence of the people" and that his "election would terminate in producing rivulets of blood throughout the land." On November 6, Madison was defeated in the vote for one of Virginia's two Senate seats by two allies of Henry, Richard Henry Lee and William Grayson.

Henry also tried to prevent Madison from winning a seat in the House of Representatives. In America's first case of gerrymandering—a term that would be coined twenty-four years later in honor of a similar tactic by a fellow Anti-Federalist, Elbridge Gerry—Henry designed Madison's home district so that it contained mostly counties that had opposed the ratification of the Constitution. Henry also convinced Madison's friend, James Monroe, to run against Madison.

Madison campaigned aggressively, but without any apparent ill will toward the man who later would serve as his secretary of state. During one outdoor debate on a cold day in January 1789, in the "face of a keen, north-easterly wind," Madison suffered frostbite on his nose and was left with a permanent scar. He would later joke that it was a "scar of a wound received in defense of his country." In an appeal to the numerous Anti-Federalist voters, Madison finally pledged to support what he had previously opposed so passionately: adding a bill of rights to the Constitution. Madison promised to seek amendments that would ensure "the most satisfactory provisions for all essential rights, particularly the rights of Conscience." On February 2, 1789, with his newly declared commitment for a bill of rights, Madison easily defeated Monroe to become a member of the first session of the House of Representatives.

Hamilton, meanwhile, was interested in only one job in the federal government: secretary of the treasury. In fact, in *Federalist 35*, Hamilton had practically written a job description for the post, which he, of course, met perfectly: "There is no part of the administration of government that requires extensive information and a thorough knowledge of the principles of political economy so much as the business of taxation." Hamilton added that the person who is placed in charge of the "power of taxation" must be "acquainted with the general genius, habits and modes of thinking of the people at large, and with the resources of the country."

Madison supported Hamilton in his quest for the Treasury position. On May 27, 1789, Madison wrote to Jefferson that Hamilton was the person who was "perhaps best qualified for that species of business and on that account would be preferred by those who know him personally." Washington agreed with Madison's assessment, and told Hamilton that he would nominate him for the job as soon as the position was created by Congress. On September 11, 1789, within minutes of his formal nomination, Hamilton was unanimously approved by the Senate as secretary of the treasury.

In the summer of 1789 as Hamilton awaited his nomination, Madison was in New York City for the first session of the House of Representatives. They were able to spend time together, with Madison apparently putting aside any ill feelings about Hamilton's actions in the New York ratification convention. A woman would later remark that she remembered "how Hamilton and Madison would talk together in the summer and then turn and laugh and play with a monkey that was climbing in a neighbor's yard."

In the fall, Hamilton turned to Madison for advice. Congress had authorized Hamilton to develop a plan for the "support of the public credit" and on October 12, 1789, he wrote Madison: "May I ask of your friendship, to put to paper and send me your thoughts on such objects as may have occurred to you, for an addition to our revenue, and also as to any modifications of the public debt, which could be made consistent with good faith." Hamilton closed by asking Madison, "What further taxes will be least unpopular?"

Hamilton was not so respectful of his friend's views on foreign policy. In explaining Madison's support for anti-British trade policies to George Beckwith, the unofficial British envoy to the United States, Hamilton said that while Madison was "a clever man, he is very little Acquainted with the world. That he is Uncorrupted and Incorruptible I have no doubt; he has the same End in view that I have."

Madison's tax suggestions came within a month of Hamilton's request, proposing taxes on "home distilleries," the importation of "spirituous liquors," and land. He added that he was opposed to a permanent national debt and hoped Hamilton would put the "debt in a manifest course of extinguishment." Madison ended with a warm closing: "With affect & regards." It was the last time Madison would use such amicable language in a letter to Hamilton.

On January 9, Hamilton released his "Report on Public Credit." It was the first step in the realization of his vision of a strong national government, one in control of its own economic destiny. Hamilton called for the repayment of the nation's debts. Countries, he wrote, "like individuals, who observe their engagements, are respected and trusted: while the reverse is the fate of those, who pursue an opposite conduct."

Under Hamilton's proposal, the government would repay its domestic creditors without "discrimination," that is, without differentiating between creditors who were the original holders of the government securities and those who had subsequently acquired them. This proved to be a highly controversial political issue because many of the original holders had been soldiers who, after the war had ended, were given government IOUs in lieu of payment. Deeply in debt, and not seeing a likelihood of immediate repayment, these soldiers had sold their securities to speculators at a tiny fraction of their face value. William Maclay, a senator from Pennsylvania, wrote that his servant had told him that he sold a war certificate with a face value "of eighty pounds for three pounds, and could get no more." Once the new government decided to back the securities, their value was certain to increase significantly.

On February 11, Madison rose to speak in the House of Representatives against Hamilton's plan and in favor of discrimination. In an emotional address, he proposed distributing most of the gain from the inevitable rise in the value of the securities to the original holders. Madison declared that the former soldiers "may appeal to humanity, for the sufferings of the military part of the creditors can never be forgotten while sympathy is an American virtue." Madison also stated that justice was on the side of the soldiers since "the value of the money, the service, or the property advanced by them, has never been really paid to them."

Hamilton was surprised and upset with Madison's opposition, as he had assumed that they were in agreement on this issue. They had, after all, joined together in 1783 to defeat a similar proposal to discriminate in favor of the creditor-soldiers. At that time, Madison had declared that such discrimination "would be a task equally unnecessary and invidious . . . the voice of policy, no less than justice pleads in favor of all."

When Hamilton heard rumors that Madison was now planning to speak against his plan, he went to confront him in person. Madison admitted that he had indeed changed his position, citing the great increase in speculation in securities that had occurred since 1783. Madison would later write that the class of soldier-creditor "was less in view" back then, and it was not until his return to Congress that "the outrageous speculations on the floating paper pressed on the attention."

Hamilton was easily able to convince both President Washington and a majority of the House that discrimination was unworkable, since many of the records of the original transactions had been destroyed or lost over time. Moreover, Hamilton argued, adopting a policy that failed to pay full value to the current holders of government securities was a "breach of faith" which threatened the value of the public debt. On February 22, 1790, Hamilton won his first victory over Madison, when the House voted to defeat Madison's proposal, 36–13.

At this point, a reservoir of good feelings between Madison and Hamilton remained. Even after losing the vote on discrimination, Madison wrote to a friend that Hamilton's funding program was "in general well digested . . . and supported by very able reasoning." When Elbridge Gerry discussed a motion to direct Hamilton to report to Congress concerning the revenues required to pay for assumption, Madison declared that he would "be the last" to favor the motion if it "carried with it any imputation that [Hamilton] was deficient in abilities or industry." Nonetheless, this first public dispute foreshadowed the greater battles to follow. As Hamilton wrote in 1795, it "laid the foundation of the great schism which has since prevailed."

The next confrontation between Madison and Hamilton arose over the most important aspect of the funding plan, the assumption by the federal government of state debts. Hamilton's proposal was designed to accomplish much of what he had unsuccessfully attempted to achieve when serving in the Confederation Congress. By having all loans centered in one place, he hoped to create a strong bond between the nation's creditors and the federal government. Additionally, Hamilton reasoned that assumption would protect the federal tax base. Without assumption, states desperate to pay off their debts would attempt to raise revenue by taxing the same resources that Hamilton was eyeing for federal revenue.

Madison, however, viewed assumption as a threat to Virginia's interests. His home state had paid off much of its war debt and would be required to pay to help debtor states such as Massachusetts and South Carolina. Madison delivered his longest speech against assumption on April 22, 1790, declaring that Virginia would not accept the assumption plan. With a swipe at Hamilton, Madison stated that the goal of strengthening the national government should not be achieved through assumption. If the national government was too weak, Madison maintained, "these defects [ought] to be remedied by additional constitutional powers, if they should be found necessary. This is the only proper, effectual, and permanent remedy."

Hamilton was again taken aback to see his former ally oppose his plan. He would later complain that he had discussed assumption with Madison during the Philadelphia convention and that they had both viewed it as a necessary part of any funding scheme. According to Hamilton, in the course of a long conversation during an afternoon's walk, "we were perfectly agreed in the expediency and propriety of such a measure; though we were both of opinion that it would be more advisable to make it a measure of administration than an article of Constitution."

Unlike the discrimination conflict, Hamilton was unable to defeat Madison on the question of assumption. On April 26, the House of Representatives voted to send the funding bill to the Senate without a provision for assumption.

Hamilton was despondent. His entire plan for restoring the national credit required the federal government to take responsibility for both the national and state debts. Help arrived from a most unexpected source, Secretary of State Thomas Jefferson.

According to Jefferson, one day in June 1790, he came upon Hamilton outside George Washington's residence. Hamilton appeared "somber, haggard, and dejected beyond description. Even his dress was uncouth and neglected." Hamilton tried to explain the necessity of assumption to the nation's economic and political well-being. If assumption was defeated, Hamilton said, he "could be of no use, and was determined to resign." Hamilton asked Jefferson to help convince his "friends from the South." Jefferson decided to "bring Mr. Madison and Colo. Hamilton to a friendly discussion on the subject," and invited them both to one of the most famous dinners in American history.

At this dinner, a deal was brokered. Madison would acquiesce on the question of assumption. He would still vote against it, but he would refrain from leading the opposition in the fight. In exchange, since "the pill would be a bitter one to the Southern states," Hamilton agreed to support Madison's long-term goal of situating the nation's capital on the Potomac River.

The battle to house the capital had raged since the Confederation Congress had evacuated Philadelphia in 1783. It had grown into a complicated struggle with three sides—New York City, Pennsylvania, and a coalition of Maryland and Virginia—fighting for two prizes: serving as the site for the temporary and for the permanent capital of the nation. Philadelphia wanted to regain its former place, and New York wanted to hold onto its current position. To those not intimately involved in the controversy, the battle seemed to be a distraction from Congress's more important work. Fisher Ames, a Massachusetts congressman, complained that "this despicable grog-shop contest, whether the taverns of New York or Philadelphia shall get the custom of Congress keeps us in discord, and covers us all with disgrace."

At Jefferson's dinner, in order to gain approval for his assumption plan, Hamilton essentially agreed to relinquish New York City's claim completely and to convince Robert Morris and the rest of the Pennsylvanian delegation to accept the consolation prize of a temporary, ten-year role as the nation's capital. Hamilton was not pleased with the deal, but considered it well worth the price. As he told New York Senator Rufus King, "the project of Philadelphia & Potomack is bad, but it will insure the funding system and the assumption."

It would be a mistake to assume that this dinner was the sole reason for the passage of assumption and the siting of the nation's capital on the Potomac. Several other negotiations were being conducted and many other compromises were being reached at the same time. Nonetheless, even if the political deals would have occurred anyway, Hamilton and Madison each seemed to have lived up to his part of the bargain. On July 9, the House of Representatives approved the bill locating the capital in Philadelphia until 1800, at which time it would be moved to land by the Potomac, "after Hamilton assured the New Englanders that assumption would pass."

Later that month, Madison convinced two Virginia and two Maryland legislators to vote for assumption. Madison had done well for his state. In addition to obtaining the nation's capital, Virginia also received an extra $500,000 in the assumption calculation. Some people, however, were disappointed that Madison had given up the fight against assumption. One New York newspaper mocked him for selling out his principles on assumption:

> Even the powers of Mr. M———n are to be silent on the subject, but to preserve a consistency of character, he must vote against it, his mouth is to be shut, his silent negative is to satisfy his new friends, and he is to prove "that every man may be purchased, if his price is offered"; his price is the Potowmack; he has accepted, and no doubt, he is a man of too much honor not to perform his part of the bargain.

Madison never wrote about his role in the deal, but we can suspect that he shared Jefferson's later misgivings. Assumption worked as Hamilton had conceived it. Concentrating the debt in the national government also concentrated political power. As the person in charge of the Treasury, Hamilton was the primary political beneficiary.

According to Jefferson, the assumption of state debts greatly "added to the number of votaries to the treasury and made its Chief the master of every vote in the legislature which might give to the government the direction suited to his political views." Jefferson would later complain to Washington that "of all the errors of my political life, this has occasioned me the deepest regret." It marked the last time that Madison or Jefferson made a political concession to Hamilton.

The next battle centered on Hamilton's plan to create a national bank and marked the first constitutional confrontation between *The Federalist* coauthors. Their legal disagreement focused on a question that remains of great contemporary importance: Does the Constitution give Congress broadly expansive or narrowly confined powers? Hamilton's proposal for the bank was presented to the House of Representatives on December 14, 1790. His plan was for the United States to create a bank similar to the Bank of England. The Bank of the United States would be capitalized at $10 million, which was four times the total capital of America's three existing banks, and it would be able to collect taxes and make commercial loans. Hamilton had long believed that a national bank was necessary for the country's economic growth. Now he was attempting to convince the House of Representatives that the bank would increase the flow of currency, facilitate the payment of taxes, and ensure a ready source of credit.

Much of the south was hostile to Hamilton's plan. Many feared that the bank would increase the power of the northern commercial interests. Madison led the opposition in the House, focusing his attention on what he saw as the highest ground for attacking the proposal: that chartering a bank was beyond the powers the Constitution had granted to Congress. On February 2, 1791, Madison laid out his argument for a narrow interpretation of the Constitution.

He began by noting that the Constitution provides "a grant of particular powers only." Congress can only do that which it is authorized to do and, he noted, there was no specific grant of power to incorporate a bank. More important, he added, such a power could not be implied simply from the Constitution's clause giving Congress the power to make all laws which shall be "necessary and proper" for carrying into execution its specified powers. This provision must be read narrowly, Madison warned, or else the Constitution would have the effect of granting "an unlimited discretion to Congress."

Despite Madison's argument, a bill authorizing the bank was approved by both houses and sent to President Washington for his signature. Washington was deeply troubled by Madison's argument and asked Secretary of State Jefferson and Attorney General Edmund Randolph for their opinions on the bill's constitutionality. In their analysis, the two Virginians generally followed Madison's constitutional reasoning, echoing the need for a narrow construction of the Constitution.

On Wednesday, February 16, Washington sent for Hamilton and told him that the arguments for the bill's unconstitutionality were convincing. Washington warned Hamilton, "You must answer them, or I cannot sign the bill." Hamilton was shocked. He would later say that he "had never dreamed of Washington's doubting" the constitutionality of the law. Hamilton spent the next week preparing his response. On Monday, February 21, he wrote a panicked note to Washington, apologizing for not yet having completed his report. He pleaded that ever since Washington's request he had been "sedulously engaged in it, but finds it will be impossible to complete it before Tuesday evening or Wednesday morning early." According to legend, on Monday evening Hamilton "told his wife to give him a cup of strong coffee, that he should not come to bed that night as he was to write all night."

The next day, Hamilton presented Washington with an eighty-page opinion which contained a detailed defense of the broadest plausible reading of Congress's power under the Constitution. Hamilton forcefully declared that limiting Congress's powers to those which were expressly specified in the Constitution would "be fatal to the just and indispensable authority of the United States." There could be no doubt, Hamilton said, "that there are implied, as well as express powers." A sovereign nation, he continued, had, by definition, the "right to employ all the means requisite and fairly applicable" to achieving its delegated purposes. The word "necessary" in the "necessary and proper" clause must, therefore, be understood to permit Congress to do that which was "needful, requisite, incidental, useful, or conducive to" accomplishing its purpose. The test for whether a proposal was within Congress's power, he said, "must be in this, as in every other case, whether the means to be employed, or, in this instance, the corporation to be erected, has a natural relation to any of the acknowledged objects or lawful ends of the government." Because the bank would be useful in collecting taxes, funding wars, and facilitating commerce, he concluded, it easily passed the test of constitutionality.

Hamilton's constitutional analysis was far closer than Madison's to the views which had been expressed in *The Federalist*. In fact, during the House debate, one of Hamilton's supporters, Elias Boudinot, quoted extensively from portions of Madison's own words from *Federalist 44* (though Boudinot did not know at the time that Madison had written this particular essay). Hamilton himself paraphrased, without attribution, that essay's conclusion that "wherever the end is required, the means are authorised; wherever a general power to do a thing is given, every particular power necessary for doing, it is included."

Hamilton sent his missive to Washington on February 23, just two days before the end of the ten-day period in which a president must decide whether to sign or veto legislation. With barely hours left in the deadline, George Washington decided to accept Hamilton's opinion and signed the bank bill into law.

Madison's battle with Hamilton now began in earnest. Madison and Jefferson had grown concerned with the effectiveness of a newspaper, John Fenno's *Gazette of the United States,* which consistently supported Hamilton's policies. Madison contacted an old classmate from his days at Princeton, Philip Freneau, to persuade him to start a rival newspaper, one that would espouse "republican principles" and serve as an "antidote to the doctrines and discourses circulated in favor of Monarchy and Aristocracy." To help support this venture, Madison suggested that Jefferson offer Freneau a part-time position as translator for the Department of State. As Jefferson wrote to Freneau, just three days after Washington signed the bank bill, the government job "gives so little to do, as not to interfere with any other calling the person may choose."

During the summer of 1791, as he was trying to persuade Freneau to accept the position, Madison also was attempting to convince Hamilton that he was not conspiring with Jefferson to "intermeddle with the Treasury Department." Hamilton had begun to complain that Jefferson had tried to get Washington to appoint an ally, Tench Coxe, to the position of comptroller of the treasury. As the comptroller was second in command to Hamilton, such an attempt by the secretary of state would have been "an obvious intrusion in Hamilton's domain."

The comptroller position became open on April 6, 1791, after the death of Nicholas Eveleigh, the first comptroller. Hamilton wrote to Washington, recommending that the president appoint Oliver Wolcott, then serving as an auditor in the Treasury Department. But Tench Coxe also wanted the job. He wrote to Jefferson, telling him that Hamilton was unable to support him publicly because of the competing application by Wolcott, but that Hamilton had given him permission to apply on his own. To improve his chances, Coxe asked Jefferson to forward his request to Washington. Jefferson passed along Coxe's request passively, without endorsing his application. Washington ultimately appointed Wolcott, but Hamilton, as his son would later write, suspected that Jefferson and Madison had tried to "encamp hostile officers within the very lines of the Government."

Madison encountered Hamilton at an evening function on July 23, and tried to impress upon him that their intentions had been entirely innocent. Madison explained that neither he nor Jefferson had lobbied for Coxe, and neither was trying to "thwart his purposes in his own department." The next day, Madison reported to Jefferson that his talk had been successful. Hamilton was "now satisfied that misrepresentations had been made to him" about the incident and, Madison concluded, Hamilton's present understanding was "the right one."

Madison was also successful in convincing Freneau to start his newspaper. The first issue of Freneau's *The National Gazette* appeared on October 31, 1791. Though the paper was based in Philadelphia, the nation's temporary capital, it was intended for national readership. Madison tried to increase its readership by soliciting subscriptions in both Culpepper and Fredericksburg, Virginia.

Freneau's attacks on Hamilton were often personal and vituperative. On May 3, 1792, Freneau blasted Hamilton's plan for an excise tax, declaring that "it is downright despotism when a public officer, drawing an arbitrary line of separation between his own interest, and those of the people, enriches and aggrandizes himself by cheating and betraying his employers."

Madison contributed nineteen anonymous articles to *The National Gazette,* many of which contained virulent attacks on Hamilton and his policies. On March 31, 1792, Madison wrote an essay entitled "The Union. Who Are Its Real Friends?" Without mentioning Hamilton by name, Madison recalled the battle over the bank bill and attacked "those who study, by arbitrary interpretation and insidious precedents, to pervert the limited government of the Union, into a government of unlimited discretion." Continuing his attack on the unnamed Hamilton, Madison decried "those who avow or betray principles of monarchy and aristocracy, in opposition to the republic principles of the Union."

Although Hamilton did not know at the time that Madison was writing articles for Freneau, he was aware that Madison had helped convince the publisher to begin his hostile opposition newspaper. Hamilton also knew that Madison was the driving force behind many of the congressional attacks on his role as secretary of the treasury. Hamilton was dismayed and hurt to find that Madison had so turned against him. He viewed Madison's opposition as a betrayal by a person he had considered "a personal and political friend." On May 26, 1792, Hamilton wrote one of the most extraordinary letters of his era. Having "concluded to unbosom myself" to his friend Edward Carrington, Hamilton expressed his anguish over the end of his relationship with Madison. The emotional letter was detailed and long; as long, in fact, as three of Hamilton's *Federalist* essays. Hamilton began by declaring that he had accepted the position of secretary of the treasury only because he felt assured, based on "similarity of thinking, conspiring with personal good-will, I should have the firm support of Mr. Madison." If he had known otherwise, Hamilton said, "I do not believe I should have accepted" the post.

Hamilton described "the variety of conversations [that] had taken place between him and myself," in which Madison had expressed clear agreement with Hamilton's positions on both assumption and discrimination. In bewilderment, Hamilton declared, "I cannot persuade myself that Mr. Madison and I, whose politics had formerly so much the same point of departure, should now diverge so widely in our opinions of the measures which are proper to be pursued."

Madison's role in helping Freneau start his newspaper also pained Hamilton. It proved, said Hamilton, that "Mr. Madison's true character is the reverse of that simple, fair, candid one which he has assumed."

Hamilton stated that he had no difficulty understanding Jefferson's animosity toward him. He attributed Jefferson's politics to his having spent the years from 1784 to 1789 in France. During that time, Hamilton claimed, Jefferson "drank freely of the French philosophy in religion, in science, in politics," and was "electrified" by the revolutionary "passions and feelings of which he shared both from temperament and situation." Hamilton added that he suspected that Jefferson was disappointed that he did not have more influence over Washington's administration. Jefferson arrived back in the country, Hamilton said, with "a too partial idea of his own powers; and with the expectation of a greater share in the direction of our councils than he has in reality enjoyed."

Madison's actions were more confusing to Hamilton. One possibility for his behavior, Hamilton said, was political expediency. Madison, he suggested, "seduced by the expectation of popularity, and possibly by the calculation of advantage to the State of Virginia, was led to change his own opinion." Hamilton's alternate hypothesis was that Madison was acquiescing to the views of Jefferson, as Madison "had always entertained an exalted opinion of the talents, knowledge, and virtues of Mr. Jefferson." Hamilton surmised that perhaps the "peculiar opinions of Mr. Jefferson's concerning the public debt wrought a change in the sentiments of Mr. Madison."

In any case, Hamilton concluded, there was no doubt that Madison had allied with Jefferson against him. He had become unequivocally convinced "that Mr. Madison, cooperating with Mr. Jefferson, is at the head of a faction decidedly hostile to me and my administration."

What Hamilton would describe as Madison's "perfidious desertion of the principles which he was solemnly pledged to defend" confounded both contemporaries and modern historians. Some have agreed with Hamilton's suggestion that Madison fell under the sway of Jefferson. A particularly acerbic political opponent, John Randolph, remarked that "Madison was always some great man's mistress—first Hamilton's, then Jefferson's." Similarly, historian Richard Brookhiser states that Madison changed his positions because he "was weak—susceptible to his constituents, and to the influence of stronger personalities."

Others believe that Madison changed his view of the meaning of the Constitution—but not his core beliefs—once he realized how the government would actually function and how the very character of the nation would be affected. He had not imagined that broad federal powers would be used in an attempt to create a commercial empire, a country run by people he described as "speculators and Tories." A narrow view of Congress's power was the only means he saw to preserve the country he had envisioned. Otherwise, not just its economic and social well-being, but "the nation's liberty was seriously at risk."

Historian Gordon Wood concluded that Madison idealistically expected the national government to serve "as a neutral disinterested umpire" rather than as a "modern European type of government with a bureaucracy, a standing army, and a powerful independent executive." Jack Rakove, the leading biographer of Madison, believes similarly that when the "emerging realities of national politics did not conform to his optimistic predictions of 1787 and 1788 . . . Madison adjusted his thinking accordingly."

Madison himself always claimed that he had remained consistent throughout his political career. Late in life, he described the rift in his relationship with Hamilton as based solely on their differing views of the Constitution: "I deserted Colonel Hamilton, or rather Colonel H. deserted me; in a word, the divergence between us took place from his wishing to administration, or rather to administer the Government . . . into what he thought it ought to be; while, on my part, I endeavored to make it conform to the Constitution as understood by the Convention that produced and recommended it, and particularly by the State conventions that adopted it." Madison considered his disagreements with Hamilton to be purely intellectual.

But Hamilton refused to see a difference between the public and private. Indeed, Hamilton had his friends spread the word so that Madison would learn that Hamilton "unequivocally declares" that Madison was "his personal and political enemy."

The next major head-to-head confrontation between Hamilton and Madison occurred in 1793, shortly after Washington began his second term in office. Foreign policy was now at the forefront, as France had declared war on England. This conflict raised the question of whether America was bound to side with France under their 1778 Treaty of Amity and Commerce.

One of the deepest dividing lines in American politics at that time was whether one viewed the English monarchy or the French revolutionaries as the greater threat. To Jefferson and Madison, England was not to be trusted, and they looked upon France as the embodiment of many of the principles of the American Revolution. Madison expressed the hope that France would "finally baffle all her enemies, who are in fact the enemies of human nature."

Hamilton, however, dismissed the foreign policy views of Madison and Jefferson, saying that they had "a womanish attachment to France and a womanish resentment against Great Britain." For Hamilton, closer ties to Great Britain were in America's interest. As he told George Beckwith, a British intelligence officer and unofficial envoy, "I have always preferred a Connexion with you to that of any other Country. We think in English, and have a similarity of prejudices and predilections."

At a heated cabinet meeting, Hamilton convinced Washington, over Jefferson's strong objections, that America's treaty with France was no longer operative because the French Revolution had resulted in a government different from the one which had signed the treaty. Moreover, Hamilton explained, it would be best for the United States if all the combatants understood that America intended to remain neutral in the European conflict.

Following Hamilton's advice, Washington, on April 23, 1793, issued a proclamation declaring that the United States would "pursue a conduct friendly and impartial toward the belligerent Powers." Washington also declared it unlawful for any American to commit acts of hostility against either England or France.

Although Washington never used the word "neutrality" in the statement, it is now universally known as Washington's "Proclamation of Neutrality." The significance of the title is that Jefferson, and later Madison, had argued that the president lacks constitutional power to declare unilaterally a state of neutrality. Such authority, they maintained, rests with Congress. Washington, while agreeing with Hamilton's foreign policy views, tried to minimize the internal political differences by avoiding using the word "neutrality" in his declaration.

Modern readers refer to this statement as the Proclamation of Neutrality because of Hamilton's vigorous defense of the president's power, in which he once again bested the constitutional analysis of James Madison. Writing as Pacificus in the *Gazette of the United States,* which favored the administration, Hamilton penned seven essays defending Washington's right to "make a declaration of neutrality." Hamilton began with a personal swipe at his opponents, declaring that their arguments were created "in a spirit of acrimony and invective," designed with the overall purpose of "weakening the confidence of the People" in President Washington. Hamilton's legal argument was more to the point. He did not deny that Congress had the power to declare war. The key point, according to Hamilton, was that it was "the duty of the executive to preserve peace, till the declaration is made." The president, who is constitutionally bound to faithfully execute the law, must "when the country is in a neutral position . . . avoid giving cause of war to foreign powers." In

Hamilton's view, the system of checks and balances gave each branch a distinct role, with the president charged with avoiding war whenever possible: "It is the province and duty of the executive to preserve to the nation the blessings of peace. The legislature alone can interrupt them by placing the nation in a state of war."

Jefferson was frustrated by the popularity of the Pacificus essays. On July 7, 1793, he wrote an urgent letter to Madison, pleading with him to answer Hamilton: "For God's sake, my dear Sir, take up your pen, select the most striking heresies, and cut him to pieces in the face of the public. There is nobody else who can and will enter the lists with him."

Madison reluctantly took up the challenge, with five essays under the name of Helvidius. Madison, like Hamilton, began with a personal attack, stating that the essays of Pacificus had been read "with singular pleasure and applause, by the foreigners and degenerate citizens among us, who hate our republican government. . . ." Madison's constitutional analysis presented a powerful case for limiting the president's war power, emphasizing the need for a legislative check on the president's authority as commander-in-chief: "Those who are to conduct a war cannot in the nature of things, be proper or safe judges, whether a war ought to be commenced, continued, or concluded. They are barred from the latter functions by a great principle in free government, analogous to that which separates the sword from the purse, or the power of executing from the power of enacting laws."

The problem for Madison was that Hamilton had crafted an argument that was perfectly consistent with this view of the separation of powers. Madison was never able to answer Hamilton's deeper point, that both the congressional authority to declare war, and the system of separation of powers in general, were best served by the president's taking an active role as peacekeeper.

Two years later, Madison opted to avoid a similar battle of essays with Hamilton altogether. The issue this time was the eponymous Jay treaty, which John Jay had negotiated with England. While many historians agree that it is "likely that no other American could have got anything nearly as good," many people believed that England had received the better of the bargain. Although England agreed to remove its soldiers from forts in the Northwest Territory, the treaty allowed England to keep its naval vessels in the Great Lakes. England also received "most favored nation" status for its imports to the United States, without granting similar status to American imports. Madison and Jefferson believed that despite the earlier pledge of neutrality, America was now favoring England over France.

Hamilton took it upon himself to become the treaty's most prominent defender, despite the fact that on January 31, 1795, he had resigned from the Treasury Department to resume his private law practice. On July 18, he attended an outdoor debate on the treaty in New York City. A crowd of five hundred turned hostile and began heckling the former secretary of the treasury, as he struggled to defend the treaty. In a short time the crowd became violent, throwing stones at the platform, one of which grazed Hamilton on his head. After burning a copy of the treaty, the crowd finally dispersed.

Just four days later, on July 22, 1795, Hamilton began an extensive series of essays, under the name Camillus, to defend the treaty. Over the next five months, Hamilton would produce twenty-eight essays, explicating both the commercial benefits and constitutionality of the treaty.

By mid-September, Jefferson was once more disheartened by Hamilton's effectiveness. He wrote to Madison, again pleading with him to respond to Hamilton's essays. Jefferson expressed anguished awe at Hamilton's literary prowess: "Hamilton is really a colossus to the anti-republican party. Without numbers, he is a host within himself." Looking over the political landscape, Jefferson saw only one person capable of defeating the colossus. "In truth," Jefferson wrote to Madison, "when he comes forward, there is nobody but yourself who can meet him." While we do not know Madison's exact response to Jefferson's beseeching, we do know that this time he declined the invitation.

It must have been particularly galling to Madison, then, when Hamilton concluded his final Camillus essay on January 9, 1796, by referencing Madison by name and quoting extensively from one of his *Federalist* essays. First, Hamilton said, the Constitutional Convention had intended the treaty power to include all manner of international compact, including those commercial matters that were covered by the Jay treaty. Hamilton challenged anyone who had attended that convention and was now a member of Congress, in particular, "Mr. Madison," to support his view. He added that he could deny what transpired in Philadelphia only if he were "utterly regardless of truth."

To further establish the accuracy of his interpretation of the treaty clause, Hamilton quoted from *Federalist 42*, which Madison had written, and noted how it specifically mentioned "treaties of commerce." To complete his assault on his former collaborator, Hamilton snidely implied that Madison was dishonest in his constitutional interpretation. Hamilton said that it was generally known that two of the authors of *The Federalist,* "from having been members of the convention, had a good opportunity of knowing its views—and were under no temptation at that time, in this particular, to misrepresent them."

In the House of Representatives, Madison lead the fight against the treaty, though he offered a constitutional argument that was more strained than even Hamilton had anticipated. Madison demanded that President Washington deliver to the House all of the papers relevant to the Jay treaty, so that the House could determine its merits. According to Madison, since the Constitution gave the House of Representatives, along with the Senate, the power to regulate foreign commerce, the House had the right to evaluate commercial treaties. The weakness in his argument was that the Constitution specifies that only the president and Senate are involved in the treaty-making process. Hence, Washington refused, on constitutional grounds, to hand over the papers. In many ways, Madison's constitutional argument was merely the weapon he chose to combat what he considered a major foreign policy mistake. Ultimately, both his constitutional and political analyses were rejected, when the House voted 51–48, on April 30, 1796, to fund the treaty.

Shortly after the conflict over the Jay treaty, American politics reached a milestone. The election of 1796 was the first under the Constitution in which neither Madison nor Washington would run for office.

Madison planned on returning to Virginia to begin a quiet life with his wife, Dolley. They had been married two years earlier, on September 15, 1794. Like Kitty Floyd, his first love, Dolley was a much younger woman; at the time of his marriage, he was forty-three and she, at twenty-six, was seventeen years his junior. Despite his hopes for a life of domestic peace, Madison was never to be far removed from the ongoing political battles of his day. He helped lead the fight against the Alien and Sedition Acts in 1798, and returned to national politics as secretary of state under newly elected President Jefferson in 1801.

For Washington, however, 1796 marked the end of his distinguished political career. In commemoration of this historic moment, on September 19, 1796, Philadelphia's largest newspaper, the *American Daily Advertiser,* published what would become known as Washington's Farewell Address. The address, which is read on the floor of the Senate every year on Washington's birthday, has become one of the classic writings in American history. The determination of the origin of the address has been almost as controversial as that surrounding *The Federalist.*

After Washington's death, his former allies were so intent that he should receive sole credit for writing the Farewell Address that they tried to hide an early draft written by Hamilton. One of the executors of Alexander Hamilton's estate, Nathaniel Pendleton, decided to give Hamilton's draft to Rufus King rather than to Hamilton's family. It was only when the family sued King in 1826 that Hamilton's role became public. But the story of the actual writing is even more complicated.

It began in 1792, four years before the address was published, when Washington was considering stepping down from the presidency at the end of his first term. He wrote to James Madison and asked him to prepare a "valedictory address from me to the public." Madison produced a relatively short address for Washington, stressing "the many ties by which the people of America are bound together."

Madison's draft was put aside when Washington decided to serve a second term. In February 1796, as he again contemplated leaving office, Washington told Hamilton that his help would be needed in drafting a new "valedictory." Washington's plan was to take Madison's draft and follow it with remarks relevant to the struggles in his second term, especially concerning what he considered the partisan assaults he had suffered over the Proclamation of Neutrality and the Jay treaty. Washington sent a draft to Hamilton on May 15, 1796, which contained early versions of what his Farewell Address is most remembered for, namely its calls for avoiding partisan attacks at home and for maintaining neutrality in international relations.

Washington told Hamilton that he could either edit the draft or "form one anew." Not surprisingly, Hamilton chose to create his own, building on what Washington had sent him, but stressing the points he valued most. On July 30, 1796, Hamilton sent his new draft to Washington. Hamilton's revision contained, in very close to their final form, most of the famous lines from the version that was ultimately published. The opening was still largely the section that Madison had written four years earlier. In both, for example, Washington declared that his leaving office was not due to a "diminution of zeal for your future interest," or from a "deficiency of grateful respect for your past kindness."

The heart of the final address, which Hamilton wrote from Washington's suggestions, can be found in Hamilton's draft. In his version, for example, one can read the final caution in the Farewell Address against excessive partisanship, as the nation is warned, "in the most solemn manner against the baneful effects of party spirit in general." The most quoted line from Washington's Farewell Address, "It is our true policy to steer clear of permanent alliances with any portion of the foreign world," appears in only slightly different form in Hamilton's draft: "Permanent alliance, intimate connection with any part of the foreign world is to be avoided."

Hamilton's language, now viewed as a symbol of American unity, was well understood at the time to be an attack on Madison, Jefferson, and their followers. Madison would write that the speech showed that Washington was "compleatly in the snares of the British faction."

As the time for release of the address drew near, Hamilton and

Washington sent versions of Hamilton's draft back and forth to one another, with small editorial suggestions. The version that was finally published on September 19 was essentially the draft that Hamilton had sent to Washington in August.

After both Hamilton and Washington had died, and the debate over who "really" wrote Washington's Farewell Address began, it was disclosed that Hamilton had sought advice from an old friend, John Jay. Jay revealed that Hamilton had asked him to review his nearly completed draft before it was sent to Washington. According to Jay, "We proceeded deliberately to discuss and consider it, paragraph by paragraph, until the whole met with our mutual approbation. Some amendments were made during the interview, but none of much importance."

What history now knows as Washington's Farewell Address turns out to have had an especially distinguished authorship. While the planning and ideology was largely that of George Washington, the address was written by James Madison and Alexander Hamilton, with some assistance from John Jay—an unlikely final collaboration by the authors of *The Federalist.*

PART II

Reading *The Federalist*

6

"THE MOST VALUABLE DISQUISITIONS OF GOVERNMENT"

WHY AND HOW TO READ *THE FEDERALIST*

The Federalist occupies a strangely contradictory position today. It is required reading not only for high school and college students but for lawyers arguing before the Supreme Court. The essays have been cited in over three hundred Supreme Court decisions and their use is ever increasing. While the Supreme Court first cited *The Federalist* in the 1798 case of *Calder v. Bull,* more than half of the decisions citing the essays have occurred in the last fifty years, with the number rising every decade. *The Federalist* has even been described as part of a holy trinity of founding-era documents. According to historian Clinton Rossiter, "It would not be stretching the truth more than a few inches to say that *The Federalist* stands third only to the Declaration of Independence and the Constitution itself among all the sacred writings of American political history."

Nonetheless, many respected scholars contend that *The Federalist* is of either little or no use in interpreting the Constitution. Many historians, legal theorists, and political scientists have disparaged not only the relevance but the quality of the essays and the role they played in the ratification process. *The Federalist* was, they say, "an almost total failure" when written, and today it "cannot be relied on for assistance in interpreting and applying legal rules."

Such hostility to the joint effort of Madison and Hamilton is surprising. After all, the two were intimately involved in every major event that led from the Revolutionary War to the ratification of the Constitution and to its initial implementation. At the barest minimum, Madison and Hamilton must be seen as having been uniquely educated by the experiences of the nation in the period leading up to the ratification of the Constitution, and as having understood as well as anyone, if not better than everyone else, the problems the Constitution was meant to address and the compromises necessary to bring the Constitution to fruition.

There is another aspect that should not be gainsaid: both principal authors were brilliant individuals who combined their experiences with extensive studies of history, economics, and political theory. In preparation for the Annapolis and Philadelphia conventions, Madison undertook a mammoth study of "ancient or modern foederal republics" and "the law of Nations," to produce "Ancient & Modern Confederacies" and the "Vices of the Political System of the United States." Hamilton, though not as studious as Madison, was an avid reader who understood the importance of history and theory in crafting and explaining policy. For example, in 1781, Hamilton prepared to write a letter introducing himself to the recently named superintendent of finance, Robert Morris, by engaging in his own intense study of economics and government. He wrote to his friend Timothy Pickering, requesting the loan of numerous books, including David Hume's *Political Discourses,* Malachy Postlethwayt's *The Universal Dictionary of Trade and Commerce,* and certain tracts which contained estimates of "the specie & current cash of Great Britain." The subsequent letter to Morris was a detailed, thirty-one-page dissertation elucidating the need for a national bank, describing how it should operate, and explaining that the bank would be "powerful cement of our union."

There can be little doubt that *The Federalist* was written by two extraordinarily intelligent, well-educated people who played pivotal roles in the creation of the Constitution and had firsthand experience with the problems the Constitution was meant to solve. But *The Federalist* is relevant to modern readers who wish to understand the Constitution for another reason: it performed a vitally important role in the ratification debates.

There is a trend among recent scholars to contend that *The Federalist* was actually unimportant and should be viewed as an ineffectual work whose readership was limited to, at most, New York. One commentator has argued that *The Federalist* should not be understood as reflecting any widespread understanding, since "it is now settled as a historical matter, for example, that the papers did not circulate widely outside New York." This conclusion is based on research showing that most of the newspapers which printed *The Federalist* were in New York City. As historian Elaine F. Crane has found, only twelve newspapers outside of New York State printed any of the letters of Publius, and most of them printed only a few of the essays. It would be incorrect, however, to conclude from this that "*The Federalist* was not widely circulated throughout the United States," or that "Publius did not reach an audience of any significant size in 1787–88." Simply relying on the number of newspapers reprinting *The Federalist* ignores the other ways that information in general, and *The Federalist* in particular, was disseminated in the 1780s. Readers in New York mailed copies of *The Federalist* throughout the country. Both Hamilton and Madison sent copies of essays to supporters in Pennsylvania. In November 1787, Hamilton sent several essays to Benjamin Rush to help him influence members of the Pennsylvania ratifying convention. On January 30, 1787, Madison sent essays 44 and 45 to Tench Coxe in Philadelphia so that he could respond to Anti-Federalist arguments. Pennsylvanian Anti-Federalists were also reading the essays. The Pennsylvanian writer called Centinel complained that the claim that the Anti-Federalists wanted to split up the country into several smaller confederacies "appears to have sprung from the deranged brain of Publius." While hardly a rave review, it proves that *The Federalist* had crossed the state border and was considered a major part of the ongoing national debate.

There is also significant evidence that many delegates to ratifying conventions throughout the nation were well aware of the writings of Publius and strove to obtain copies of *The Federalist*. On December 23, 1787, Christopher Gore, a delegate-elect to the Massachusetts ratifying convention, wrote to George Thacher, a member of the Massachusetts congressional delegation in New York, requesting that "if any thing new turns up let me hear it and whatever is written (viz., all Publius pieces at least) on the Constitution I will thank you to send me." William R. Davie, a delegate to the North Carolina convention, which met over the summer of 1788 but delayed ratification until the following year, pleaded with future Supreme Court Justice James Iredell to send him t he *Federalist* essays "as we are in greater want of its assistance here than you are in Edenton." A delegate to New Hampshire's ratifying convention, Samuel Tenney, even indulged in the guessing game as to the true identity of Publius, concluding that "we have christened him HAMILTON."

Others expressed their desire to collect all of the essays of *The Federalist*. Connecticut's Jeremiah Wadsworth wrote to both Rufus King and Henry Knox, asking them to send him *The Federalist* in book form. It was, indeed, as a two-volume book that *The Federalist* had its greatest impact. Advertisements for the book ran frequently in both New York and Virginia newspapers from January 2, 1788, to March 12, 1788. These advertisements, not surprisingly, proclaimed the excellence of the work: "[A]mongst the numerous publications that have issued from the press on the subject of Federal Government, none have attracted the public attention more than that intitled *The Federalist*, under the signature of PUBLIUS:—The justness of the reasoning, the force of the arguments, and the beauty of the language, which distinguish this performance, have justly recommended it to general applause."

Many copies of the book stayed in New York. Hamilton made sure that a considerable number of the delegates to New York's ratifying convention received a copy. It is impossible to know the whereabouts of the rest of the books, but there is solid evidence that copies were sent to Maryland, Pennsylvania, Delaware, North Carolina, and even the Northwest Territory.

Connecticut's Jeremiah Wadsworth was not the only state delegate interested in receiving the books. In Maryland, a delegate to the state ratifying convention, James McHenry, received his copy from the secretary of Congress, Charles Thomson, along with Thomson's wishes for the ratification of the Constitution. He wrote, "Enclosed I send you the first volume of the Foederalist. . . . The second volume is in the press and will, it is expected be out in the course of a week or two. As soon as it is published I will forward it to you."

The clearest impact of the bound version of *The Federalist* can be seen in Virginia. On April 5, 1788, George Nicholas, recently elected a delegate to the Virginia ratification convention, wrote a concerned letter to James Madison describing his desperate need for copies: "The greater part of the members of the convention will go to the meeting without information on the subject, it will be very important to give this as early as may be. . . . *Publius* or *the foederalist* if it is published in a pamphlet would do it better than any other work; if it is published can I get the favor of you to procure me thirty or forty copies of it, that I may distribute them." Madison responded three days later, promising to ship him the volumes as soon as they were available. Hamilton subsequently arranged to have more than fifty copies of each volume sent to Virginia Governor Randolph for distribution to those attending the ratifying convention.

Even if those seeking to minimize *The Federalist*'s modern-day relevance concede that it was widely read, they contend that the essays should be viewed as historically insignificant and unimportant to the ratification process. These critics argue that "there is no good evidence that anyone, even in New York, relied on *The Federalist* as the basis for voting to ratify." It is certainly true that the publication of *The Federalist* did not prevent New York from electing a majority of Anti-Federalist delegates to the state's ratifying convention. Hamilton's biographer, Forrest McDonald, wrote that "despite *The Federalist*, New Yorkers voted about sixteen thousand to seven thousand against ratification, electing forty-six anti-Federalists and only nineteen advocates of ratification." Linda Grant De Pauw, in her book on New York's ratification battle, concludes that "there is no evidence that Publius converted a single Antifederalist." The most quoted belittlement of *The Federalist*'s historical importance is from the editor of the popular 1961 edition of the essays, Clinton Rossiter, who wrote that they "worked only a small influence upon the course of events during the struggle over ratification. Promises, threats, bargains, and face-to-face debates, not eloquent words in even the most widely circulated newspapers, won hard-earned victories for the Constitution in the crucial states of Massachusetts, Virginia, and New York. . . . The chief usefulness of *The Federalist* in the events of 1788 was as a kind of debater's handbook in Virginia and New York."

This passive image of a largely meaningless debater's handbook belies the true significance of *The Federalist* to the ratification campaign. When the Constitution was first presented to the American public on September 19, 1787, in the *Pennsylvania Packet,* all that readers could see was its spare yet complicated language. It came with no owner's manual, no guide for the perplexed. The primary task for Publius was educational: to explain to those voting on the ratification question both the details of how the government would operate under the Constitution, as well as the theoretical justification for many of the decisions made in secret in Philadelphia.

The Federalist's deepest intellectual accomplishment may have been that, in describing how the Constitution would work, Publius made logical sense of the document as a whole. *The Federalist* was able to explain how this lean political document, created by fifty-five delegates after four months of negotiation and compromise, could be understood as a coherent whole—as an "expression not only of the popular will but of a rational will." Whether or not *The Federalist* was successful in changing people's minds, a sampling of their opinions shows that it clearly succeeded in educating a substantial portion of those involved in the ratification debates.

In August 1788, shortly after New York ratified the Constitution, George Washington wrote to Alexander Hamilton in praise of *The*

Federalist: "I have read every performance which has been printed on one side and the other of the great question lately agitated (so far as I have been able to obtain them) and, without an unmeaning compliment, I will say, that I have seen no other so well calculated (in my judgment) to produce conviction on an unbiased Mind, as the Production of your triumvirate."

Lest one think that Washington was simply flattering the author—a relatively unlikely possibility considering his well-known character—he had written similar praise in a letter to Pennsylvanian John Armstrong on April 25, 1788. In that letter Washington explained why he thought the opposition of the Anti-Federalists might actually prove to be beneficial in the long run. Supporters of the Constitution, he said, had been forced to articulate both a theory of government and an explanation of how the new Constitution would operate. According to Washington, those who had answered the Anti-Federalists "have thrown new light upon the science of Government [and] they have given the rights of man a full and fair discussion." Washington concluded by saying that the quality of these writings "cannot fail to make a lasting impression upon those who read the best publications on the subject, and particularly the pieces under the signature of Publius."

Others in the midst of the ratification battle shared Washington's view of the educational merits of *The Federalist*. In January 1788, Tench Coxe of Pennsylvania praised it as the "most valuable disquisitions of Government in its peculiar relations and connexions with this country." Samuel Tenney, of New Hampshire, in March 1788 similarly wrote that the "candor, ingenuity, depth of thought & force of argument" of Publius, ranked him first among the "numerous" writers on the Constitution. James Kent, who would later become chief judge of New York's Supreme Court and the author of the classic, four-volume "Commentaries of American Law," also recognized the exalted place of *The Federalist*, writing in December 1787, that it was "the best thing I have seen hitherto in print on the federal side." James Kent was not the only individual destined to become a dominating figure in the development of American law who bestowed praise upon it. James Iredell, a future justice of the

Supreme Court, wrote his own pro-ratification pamphlet in early 1788 in which he called *The Federalist* "a work which I hope will soon be in every body's hands."

The most important commentary may be that of future Chief Justice John Marshall. Marshall was intimately involved in the ratification debates and was an enthusiastic and eloquent defender of the Constitution at the Virginia ratifying convention. Looking back on the ratification battle, Marshall lauded *The Federalist* for its ability to "expose the real circumstances of America, and the dangers which hung over the republic; to detect the numerous misrepresentations of the constitution; to refute the arguments of its opponents; and to confirm, and increase, its friends, by a full and able development of its principles." *The Federalist,* Marshall concluded, "will be read and admired when the controversy in which that valuable treatise on government originated, shall be no longer remembered."

When the delegates to the ratifying conventions in New York and Virginia were given their own bound copies of *The Federalist,* they received far more than just a script or a mere "debater's handbook." The delegates read essays which shaped their very understanding of the document they were supporting. As Noah Webster wrote upon publication of the second volume of *The Federalist,* the letters of Publius are "well calculated . . . to impress upon candid minds, just ideas of the nature of republican governments, of the principles of civil liberty, and of the genius and probable operation of the proposed Federal Constitution."

The fact that *The Federalist* was praised enthusiastically by the most prominent supporters of ratification is not enough to satisfy modern critics who wish to diminish its importance. They argue that it should have limited modern relevance, since Hamilton and Madison's motivation was merely the pragmatic goal of obtaining votes for ratification. Thus, we are told, "its authors wrote it not as a learned treatise but as self-serving campaign literature." Readers seeking an understanding of the Constitution are warned to be skeptical because *The Federalist* is only "a piece of political advocacy, whose contents may at times reflect the exigencies of debate, rather than a dispassionate account of constitutional meaning."

There is no denying historian Douglass Adair's assertion that "*The Federalist* was at bottom an electioneering pamphlet written to persuade contemporary New Yorkers to vote right." But to thereby dismiss *The Federalist* out of hand disregards the thoughtful, reasoned means by which Madison and Hamilton attempted to accomplish this persuasion. They did not create an eighteenth-century version of a thirty-second television attack ad. While their essays were "designed to place the Constitution in the most desirable light possible," the manner in which they shone that light makes *The Federalist* an invaluable source for modern readers interested in understanding the thinking of many of those who voted to ratify the Constitution.

The Federalist was crafted to appeal to the reason of its readers, not their passions. Hamilton's earlier attempt to gain support for the Constitution through argument by personal invective had proven to be not only unsuccessful but counterproductive, and he consciously chose to try a radically different approach when planning *The Federalist*. As he stated in *Federalist 1*, Hamilton's goal was to influence readers to support the Constitution but not with "any impressions other than those which may result from the evidence of truth." He declared that his "arguments will be open to all, and may be judged of by all. They shall at least be offered in a spirit, which will not disgrace the cause of truth."

Madison similarly expressed disdain for those who disregarded rational argument, and he dismissed those who had prejudged the Constitution, either in support or opposition. "These papers," Madison wrote, "are not addressed to persons falling under either of these characters. They solicit the attention of those only, who add to a sincere zeal for the happiness of their country, a temper favorable to a just estimate of the means of promoting it."

Looking back at the work, in the final *Federalist* essay, Hamilton expressed satisfaction that he had accomplished the task he had set for himself: "I have not failed in the assurance I gave you respecting the spirit with which my endeavours should be conducted. I have addressed myself purely to your judgments, and have studiously avoided those asperities which are too apt to disgrace political disputants of all parties." He conceded that Publius had not maintained a tone of pure reason perfectly throughout and that there had been some "intemperances of expression." Still, Hamilton concluded, "it must be my excuse that it has been neither often nor much."

The spirit of reason which Hamilton and Madison sought was frequently recognized and appreciated by their readers. The deputy secretary of Congress, Roger Alden, sent copies of *The Federalist* to his brother-in-law, Samuel William Johnson, who was fighting for ratification in Connecticut, and declared, "A Writer under the signature of Publius takes up the matter upon the best grounds; and is a very fair, candid, sensible advocate upon the federal side. There is nothing personal or scurrilous in his writings; he only means to convince by plain reasoning; by arguments drawn from facts & experience."

To "convince by plain reasoning," Hamilton and Madison had to understand their readership. It was necessary for Publius to ascertain, and then to explain, how the Constitution reflected the hopes, ameliorated the concerns, and reduced the fears of those considering whether or not to vote for ratification. As Professor Dan Coenen has written, "Precisely because Publius's purpose was to gain support from a broad and diverse audience with arguments based on reason, the views set forth in the papers could be neither sloppy nor personal nor idiosyncratic. Rather, Publius's depiction of the Constitution needed to reflect a broadly acceptable view of the document's meaning."

This is not to say that one can read *The Federalist* and understand the individual mind-sets of those who voted to ratify the Constitution. Such a contention ignores the impossibility of reading the human mind, and the fact that thousands and thousands of different people were involved in the ratification debates, each coming to a decision by thought processes that were idiosyncratic and secret. Rather, *The Federalist* represents an intelligent attempt, by two brilliant and determined observers, to articulate a national consensus and express a generalized understanding of the concerns of the populace.

In addition, Madison and Hamilton's depiction of how the Constitution met these concerns had to be credible. Using their intimate knowledge of the drafting of the Constitution, Madison's deep understanding of the nature of government, and Hamilton's skill as one of the leading advocates of his day, they explained how their interpretation of each clause of every article was not only a logical reading of the language but served to address the fears and hopes of their readers.

The Federalist also represents a unique moment in American history. Almost immediately after the Constitution was ratified, a split developed between Madison and Hamilton as to not only the proper way to interpret the Constitution, but the very values which underlie the nation. While much has changed since the 1790s, their disagreements still resonate in the modern world. Proponents of supply-side economics battle those who urge a steep increase in the minimum wage. Politicians debate the conflicting values of urban voters versus those of small town America. *The Federalist,* in a sense, was the moment before the national big bang: a never-again-to-be-seen cohesiveness between competing visions for America.

But why should we care what the framers and ratifiers thought? Is there a role, besides historical curiosity, for using the insights from *The Federalist* in interpreting the Constitution? The answer cannot come directly from either Hamilton or Madison. Neither was a model of consistency in describing his approach for interpreting the Constitution. In 1791, while defending a broad reading of the "necessary and proper" clause to justify Congress's creation of the national bank, Hamilton argued that the framers' intent was irrelevant: "Whatever may have been the intentions of the framers of a constitution, or of a law, that intention is to be sought for in the instrument itself, according to the usual and established rules of construction." Just five years later, in 1796, in arguing that the Constitution denies the House of Representatives any role in making treaties, Hamilton reversed himself and emphasized the understanding of framers and ratifiers to support his position. He declared that he would analyze "the manner in which [the Constitution] was understood by the convention who framed it, and by the people who adopted it."

Madison, like Hamilton, was inconsistent in his approach to constitutional interpretation. During the 1791 debate on the national bank, Madison ignored the *Federalist* essays he had written (which largely refuted his immediate position) and relied instead on scattered comments from ratifying conventions. Later, when arguing that the Constitution provided the House of Representatives with a role in the treaty process, "[his] argument rested on text and inference alone, not history." Madison eventually arrived at the position that the only opinions that mattered were those of the people who had attended the state ratifying conventions. When the convention had finished its work, Madison declared the Constitution "was nothing more than the draft of a plan, nothing but a dead letter, until life and validity were breathed into it by the voice of the people, speaking through the several State Conventions." Thus, he explained, "the legitimate meaning of the Instrument must be derived from the text itself; or if a key is to be sought elsewhere, it must be not in the opinions or intentions of the Body which planned & proposed the Constitution, but in the sense attached to it by the people in their respective State Conventions where it recd. all the authority which it possesses."

The disappointing reality is that the methodologies used by Madison and Hamilton to interpret the Constitution after ratification did not reflect an objective mode of inquiry. They used temporary, mutable stratagems, adapted solely to support the political positions they were championing at the moment.

Can we do better? Is there a way to articulate a principled approach to interpreting the Constitution which is not a mask for reaching a set of desired political results? Before that question can be answered, it would be useful to understand why constitutional interpretation is so difficult.

Our thinking about interpretation may be helped by dividing constitutional questions into three categories:

1. Easy questions
2. The definition of words and phrases
3. The proper interpretation of silences

Words, as Chief Justice Marshall noted, especially those used in the Constitution, cannot be expected always to convey a set meaning to all readers. "Such is the character of human language," he wrote, "that no word conveys to the mind, in all situations, one single definite idea." According to Madison, human language is inherently incapable of accurately and precisely defining all aspects of complex and novel ideas: "No language is so copious as to supply words and phrases for every complex idea, or so correct as not to include many equivocally denoting different ideas." Imperfect language leads to imperfect understanding. In one of the most religious statements ever uttered by the public James Madison, he declared, "When the Almighty himself condescends to address mankind in their own language, his meaning, luminous as it must be, is rendered dim and doubtful by the cloudy medium through which it is communicated."

Nonetheless, many questions about the meaning of the Constitution can be resolved effortlessly. It is obvious that California Governor Arnold Schwarzenegger cannot become president because, according to Article II, Section 1 of the Constitution: "No person except a natural born citizen . . . shall be eligible to the office of President." There is no doubt here as to meaning and application. Because Schwarzenegger was born a citizen of Austria, the Constitution prohibits him from being elected president.

This is an "easy" case because the relevant language used is specific and unambiguous, lending itself to a "commonsense" understanding of its meaning. A significant number of other sections of the Constitution—the requirements that a senator be at least thirty years old and a president at least thirty-five, that a veto can only be overridden by a two-thirds vote of each house, or that members of the House of Representatives must run for election every two years, among many others—do not require any skill in or aids for interpretation.

By contrast, clauses that are open-ended frequently require judicial explication. Congress has the power to regulate "commerce . . . among the several states" and "to make all Laws which shall be necessary and proper" for "carrying into Execution" that power. While it is unmistakably clear that a bill to regulate nuclear wastes will not go into effect even if the Senate votes to override a presidential veto by a vote of 64–35, it is not self-evident that such a law, if validly enacted, would be a constitutional exercise of Congress's commerce-clause power. This is not to say that the law would be unconstitutional; rather, in order to decide if it is, the Supreme Court must supply nontrivial, working definitions of general terms such as "commerce" and "necessary." Similar questions, of course, arise over the meaning of such phrases as "due process of law," "equal protection of the laws," and "abridging the freedom of speech." In determining the content of these words and phrases, courts must also decide how broadly or narrowly to interpret them.

A related area in which constitutional interpretation is required is in determining the meaning of the silences in the Constitution; in particular, in ascertaining the significance, if any, of the omission by the drafters of a specific power or provision. For example, does the fact that the Constitution does not declare that courts can strike down acts of Congress preclude judicial review? Does the fact that the Constitution does not discuss a legislative veto of the decisions of administrative agencies establish that congressional exercise of such a veto would be unconstitutional? Does the omission of an explicit right to privacy lead to the conclusion that the Constitution has "nothing to say" about abortion and the right to die? In short, the Court must determine when an omission was deliberately intended to indicate an exclusion.

The task of constitutional interpretation, therefore, lies in defining the meaning and breadth of the language used in the Constitution and determining whether absent terms are to be interpreted as deliberate omissions.

Over the last half century, an especially heated debate has been waged over how to do this. Justices and scholars have divided themselves into antagonistic groups favoring differing methodologies, with the greatest divide appearing between the "originalists" and the "nonoriginalists."

One danger in attempting to discuss the role of *The Federalist* in interpreting the Constitution is the centrifugal force that seems to push any speaker on the subject into one or another of these warring camps. That is unfortunate. Such insistence upon labels carries with it several unnecessary costs. First, it masks significant disunity within a category. Not all who call themselves originalists think alike; neither is there uniformity of analysis among self-proclaimed non-originalists. Second, and ultimately most significant, the constraints of dichotomous thinking prevent us from gaining wisdom and insights from competing viewpoints and make it far more difficult to locate points of agreement and consensus. Our debates grow nastier, and our agreements are reached more begrudgingly.

The ready use of labels also permits people to be intellectually lazy. It takes no effort to discount opposing opinions simply by noting that they originated on the wrong side of the philosophical tracks. Responding to the strengths in the arguments of those with whom you disagree becomes a needless distraction. Transcending this attitude may be too much to ask in an age when political discourse frequently consists of putting "people in little boxes, yelling at each other." Nonetheless, I will try to use lessons gleaned from across the interpretive spectrum in considering why and how to use *The Federalist* in interpreting the Constitution.

"Originalism," when first used in 1985 by Attorney General Edwin Meese, referred to an attempt to rely on the framers' intent in interpreting the Constitution. After withering attacks based in part on the impossibility, first, of reading the minds of thousands of Americans who had been dead for two centuries, and then of combining those individual intents into a coherent collective intent, originalism evolved into a search for "original meaning."

According to the leading proponent of originalism, Justice Antonin Scalia, the modern version of the concept is not concerned with what any person involved in the drafting of the Constitution actually wanted in his heart of hearts; rather, the concern is what the language that was used meant: "What I look for in the Constitution is precisely what I look for in a statute: the original meaning of the text, not what the original draftsmen intended." The difference between intent and meaning is the difference between the subjective, what is inside a person's mind, and the objective, how a reasonable person would understand what has transpired. Proponents of this style of interpretation often use a technique termed "textualism" to determine how the words in the Constitution "would have been understood by a hypothetical, objective, reasonably well-informed reader of those words and phrases in context, at the time they were adopted, and within the political and linguistic community in which they were adopted."

A classic example of originalist analysis can be seen in Justice Clarence Thomas's concurring opinion in *McIntyre v. Ohio Elections Commission.* The Supreme Court, in an opinion written by Justice Stevens, found an Ohio statute that prohibited the distribution of anonymous campaign literature to be unconstitutional. The Court's majority opinion cited the works of authors such as Mark Twain and George Eliot to demonstrate that anonymity can encourage authors to disseminate their works and to explain why the right to publish anonymously is an aspect of freedom of speech. While Thomas agreed that the law was unconstitutional, he strongly objected to the analysis by Stevens. According to Thomas, the only relevant inquiry is whether those who wrote and ratified the First Amendment understood that the phrase "freedom of speech, or of the press," protected anonymous political leafleting. Noting the "outpouring of anonymous political writing that occurred during the ratification of the Constitution," including, of course, *The Federalist,* and the fact that "Founding-era Americans opposed attempts to require that anonymous authors reveal their identities on the ground that forced disclosure violated the 'freedom of the press,'" Thomas concluded that the Ohio law was unconstitutional because "the Framers shared the belief that [anonymous publication] was firmly part of the freedom of the press."

Justice Stevens's opinion for the Court in *McIntyre* reflects what might well be called a non-originalist approach to interpreting the Constitution. Some non-originalists have argued that, on all constitutional questions, judges must take current values and understandings directly into account. Under this approach, courts would "give meaning to all constitutional provisions on the basis of contemporary values that the justices regard as worthy of constitutional protection."

One of the most striking examples of a non-originalist opinion was the Supreme Court's 1954 decision in *Bolling v. Sharpe,* declaring unconstitutional the congressionally authorized racial discrimination in District of Columbia public schools. Decided the same day as *Brown v. Board of Education, Bolling* posed a difficult problem for the Court. While state-mandated segregation could be prohibited under the equal protection clause of the Fourteenth Amendment, that clause, which reads, "No State shall . . . deny to any person within its jurisdiction the equal protection of the laws," does not cover the federal government. The Court relied instead on the Fifth Amendment's language, which prohibits the federal government from depriving individuals of "life, liberty, or property, without due process of law." Under an originalist approach, the Fifth Amendment, which was written and ratified in the 1790s while slavery still existed in most of the country, could hardly be used to mandate racial equality. Nonetheless, the Court in *Bolling* so interpreted its language, saying, "In view of our decision that the Constitution prohibits the states from maintaining racially segregated public schools, it would be unthinkable that the same Constitution would impose a lesser duty on the Federal Government."

The gap between originalists and non-originalists need not be as wide as the strongest partisans believe. Many so-called moderate non-originalists are also committed to understanding the historical background for constitutional language. They look to "the most fundamental original intention of the Framers themselves" as the starting point for their constitutional interpretation. One such non-originalist, Justice Stephen Breyer, has argued that constitutional language should be interpreted to fulfill the original goal of the Constitution, which he terms "Active Liberty," or "the right of individuals to participate in democratic self-government." Others use the original meaning of the Constitution to establish an "historical baseline" which can serve as the starting point for their inquiry, and sometimes can limit the range of permissible interpretations.

Some who are considered moderate originalists have begun to argue that fidelity to the original meaning of constitutional language does not preclude considering the purposes behind its clauses at a "relatively high level of generality." They look to the more general purpose behind constitutional language rather than the narrow expectation of how a given clause would work. Under this approach, the fact that those who adopted the Fourteenth Amendment had a general desire for racial equality justifies *Brown,* even if those same people would not have supported desegregating schools themselves.

The attempt of both moderate originalists and moderate non-originalists to borrow the strengths of each other's traditional mode of inquiry reflects the fact that there is wisdom to be found in each of the various approaches. On the one hand, the history of the drafting and ratification of a document such as the Constitution simply cannot be irrelevant in understanding the meaning of unclear terms and enigmatic omissions. The strongest rationale for an originalist approach is that it helps justify treating the Constitution as an "authoritative" source for answering the crucial questions of our time. A convincing originalist opinion gives particular legitimacy to a decision resolving contemporary constitutional questions by declaring, in effect, that "The Constitution is supreme law because it rests on the direct imprimatur of a sovereign people, expressed through the extraordinary procedures required for ratification; and its original meaning, whenever it can be recovered, should accordingly prevail over the lesser acts of legislators and the preferences of jurists."

Ignoring the text of the Constitution and its history risks permitting justices to implement their own values, without having to answer to any other branch of government or to the people in general. This allows judges, according to Justice Scalia, to "mistake their own predilections for the law. . . . It is very difficult for a person to discern a difference between those political values that he personally thinks most important, and those political values that are 'fundamental to our society.'"

On the other hand, those who are skeptical about originalism are correct on two important points. First, despite the claims of some of its proponents, originalism does not eliminate judicial discretion. As Professor Erwin Chemerinsky has noted, "History is inevitably ambiguous, requiring judges to make value judgments in interpreting the historical record." It is often impossible to uncover an original meaning when there was not clear agreement at the time when the language was originally used. Justice Scalia's own originalist analysis in the *McIntyre* case led him to conclude that the right to publish anonymously was not protected by the First Amendment, exactly the opposite decision reached by his fellow originalist, Justice Thomas.

Second, we as a society may not, and perhaps should not, be willing to accept a method of interpreting the Constitution which leads to results that contradict our more evolved understanding of such issues as equality, freedom, and justice, particularly when there are plausible alternatives to reading our founding document. Critics of originalism argue that the adoption of an eighteenth-century mindset leads to an unnecessarily crimped and narrow view of the most fundamental issues of our time. They fear that such a worldview permits, if not requires, those interpreting the Constitution to ignore the hard-won lessons of the civil rights and the women's movements, as well as the strides made toward the democratization of America over the last two centuries. The late Justice William Brennan argued that "those who would restrict claims of right to the values of 1789 specifically articulated in the Constitution turn a blind eye to social progress and eschew adaptation of overarching principles to changes of social circumstance." He also expressed the widely held suspicion that some originalists had a political agenda since, "A position that upholds constitutional claims only if they were within the specific contemplation of the Framers in effect establishes a presumption of resolving textual ambiguities against the claim of constitutional right." Many have argued that originalism leads to the conclusion that *Brown v. Board of Education* was incorrectly decided. And Justice Scalia has written that any honest application of originalism leads one to oppose Court decisions which interpret the Constitution to prohibit abortion and outlaw single-sex state schools.

Even if we could feel completely confident that the original, generally understood meaning of the equal protection clause consigned women to second-class citizenship and permitted the criminalization of interracial marriage, it is not self-evident that the open, imprecise phrase "equal protection of the laws" should be so interpreted. Similarly, we may not want to utilize a method of constitutional interpretation that would result in the government being permitted to imprison critics unless they can convince a jury of the literal truth of their charges, even were we convinced that the phrase "make no law abridging freedom of speech" was understood to permit such censorial practices in the early 1790s.

There are some people who argue that similar concerns render *The Federalist* hopelessly outdated: "Because it was written 200 years ago, and because the Constitution and the nation have decisively evolved in ways the authors did not anticipate, *The Federalist* operates upon assumptions that long ago died." Thus, they ask, why should we seek guidance from *The Federalist* when "the nature of government has changed so much"?

The nature of government, with its enormous administrative bureaucracy, two dominant political parties, and large corporations financing candidates and lobbying elected officials, has undoubtedly changed since the eighteenth century. Nonetheless, what remains unchanged is its overall structure. Power is still separated both horizontally, between the legislative, executive, and judicial branches, and vertically, between the federal and state governments.

Moreover, the existence of emergencies is not a twenty-first-century phenomenon. The framers experienced frequent emergency situations which necessitated speedy and decisive actions. Unlike today, because their communications and transportation systems were so slow, it would take weeks, if not months, to bring together members of Congress who had gone home at the end of a session. Yet, as Supreme Court Justice Robert Jackson wrote in 1952, those who wrote the Constitution knew that emergencies could always create a pretext for those in government to usurp power: "We may also suspect that they suspected that emergency powers would tend to kindle emergencies." Those with power today are still liable to abuse it. As historian Bernard Bailyn noted, "The Federalist papers remain relevant, and acutely relevant, because they address masterfully our permanent concerns with political power." If the Constitution is to be a "machine that would go of itself," there surely is some utility in reading its original instruction manual.

A study of the history and teachings of *The Federalist* may also provide an intriguing way to obtain many of the benefits of both the originalist and non-originalist schools of interpretation, while avoiding many of the pitfalls of each. The key is for both to agree to "split the atom" and treat the interpretation of the original Constitution differently from the interpretation of its later amendments. Thus, there would be one mode of interpreting issues involving the separation of powers and the relationship between the federal and state governments, which generally derive from the Constitution framed in Philadelphia, and a different approach for dealing with questions such as freedom of speech and religion, equality, and privacy, which generally derive from either the Bill of Rights or the Fourteenth Amendment. This difference is premised on the historical fact that none of the latter amendments was drafted through a method similar to the painstaking manner of the original Constitution, and none was explained to its ratifiers with anything approaching the clarity of *The Federalist.*

The drafting and ratification of the Bill of Rights occurred with far less attention to detail than the original Constitution. In large measure it was proposed by Madison in response to complaints of the Anti-Federalists and his friend Thomas Jefferson. When Madison finally introduced his version of the Bill of Rights in the House, the notes for his June 8, 1789, speech contained the following unenthusiastic notation: "Bill of Rights—useful—not essential." Many of his fellow representatives were even less interested, complaining that the time taken up with its drafting would detract from more important items. Representative Aedanus Burke of South Carolina suspected that the proposed amendments were designed to distract former opponents of the Constitution without giving them the substantive change in the form of government that really motivated their opposition. The proposed Bill of Rights, Burke declared, was "merely a tub to the whale."

Once proposed, the amendments underwent many changes, but usually without any clear public statement as to the reason for the alteration. When a House committee significantly altered a proposal, its reasoning was never announced. And when the amendments went to the Senate, the opacity of the process worsened; the Senate meetings were not open to the public and there is no record of their debates. By the time the Bill of Rights was sent to the states for ratification, the public learned how a few issues had been discussed, such as whether there should be a right to "instruct" legislators, but no definition of the critical terms was provided.

If the understanding which matters for modern interpreters is that of the ratifiers, it is unclear that there was any understanding at all. The debates in the state legislatures, when they did occur, centered not on the Bill of Rights, which George Mason dismissed as "milk & water propositions," but on amendments not proposed, those that Anti-Federalists had wanted to strengthen states' rights, such as a limitation of the federal government's ability to tax. When a controversy over ratification of the Bill of Rights did arise, as in Virginia, it was focused on whether approval would preclude the opportunity to amend the Constitution further so as to change the structure of the government; there was little, if any, discussion of what the Bill of Rights actually covered.

Significantly, there was no Publius for the Bill of Rights. While *The Federalist* had examined "the conformity of the proposed constitution to the true principles of republican government," there was no one to explain "the conformity of the proposed amendments to the true principles of republican government."

The modern interpreter cannot know, with anything approaching the same level of confidence, what the drafters and ratifiers of the Bill of Rights understood their words to mean and whether they intended those words to be interpreted in a narrow or broad way, to be applied only to those concerns that motivated them in 1789, or whether these words were designed to evolve as new situations presented themselves and society gained new understandings of general principles. Lacking a *Federalist* for the Bill of Rights, it is more difficult, if not impossible, for us today to know the reason particular words were chosen or the significance of the silences therein.

An analogous problem arises when interpreting the Fourteenth Amendment. Whereas the Bill of Rights was first drafted by James Madison, the Fourteenth Amendment was drafted by a far lesser luminary, Ohio Representative John Bingham. Many who look to the original understanding of the rest of the Constitution blanch at relying on Bingham. In the words of legal historian Raoul Berger, Bingham was a "muddled thinker, given to the florid windy rhetoric of a stump orator, liberally interspersed with invocations to the Deity." It is fair to say that Bingham was known to misstate the law. For example, despite the fact that neither the original Constitution nor the Bill of Rights requires "equal protection," Bingham declared that, prior to his amendment, "every word" of the Fourteenth Amendment was already in the Constitution.

If we look to the ratifiers of the Fourteenth Amendment, there is even less clarity as to how it was understood. As the Supreme Court has stated, its ratification debates are "at best . . . inconclusive"; some speakers evince a desire to remove all legal distinctions among citizens while others want the amendment to have the most limited effect possible. Because ratification was required before the southern states could be readmitted to the Union, any analysis of how those states reasonably understood the amendment's meaning is particularly problematic. And again, there was no Publius to articulate the national consensus of the purposes to be served by the very broad language of equal protection and due process of law and to reveal whether the meaning of these phrases was meant to be determined by a nineteenth-century vision of equality and liberty.

Some language in the Fourteenth Amendment is specific enough to avoid causing serious interpretive problems. The first sentence of the first section simply states that "all persons born or naturalized in the United States . . . are citizens of the United States and of the State wherein they reside." Courts have been able to apply this reasonably clear language without having to wade through interminable discussions of understanding and intent. For the broad phrases of the

Fourteenth Amendment, equal protection and due process, however, we modern interpreters can hardly feel confident that we can ascertain a clear, objective, generally agreed upon meaning shared by those who wrote and voted for the amendment. Unlike the original Constitution, there is no guide.

Thus, a study of the history of *The Federalist* reveals an unexpected paradox: While interpretation of the Bill of Rights and the Fourteenth Amendment may require substantially more reference to modern understandings of the values implicit in their constitutional guarantees, there are compelling reasons to focus more on the original understanding for interpreting the original Constitution. And for that task, there is no more useful resource than the papers of Publius.

But once we conclude that *The Federalist* can be useful for constitutional interpretation, we still must determine precisely how it should be used. It would be both dangerous and foolish to treat *The Federalist* as "holy writ," and mechanically accept every word as definitive. Some statements made by Publius are simply incorrect. In *Federalist 69*, Hamilton wrote, "In the national government, if the Senate should be divided, no appointment could be made: in the government of New-York, if the Council should be divided the Governor can turn the scale and confirm his own nomination." It is not accurate that no appointment can be made with a divided Senate. Since Article I, Section 3 of the Constitution expressly provides that the vice president shall vote if the Senate "be equally divided," the appointment will be effective when the Senate is divided, so long as the vice president supports the president.

In addition to technical errors, modern readers might well be unsettled by *The Federalist*'s defense of two troubling aspects of the original Constitution. First, the justification for the lack of a bill of rights was not convincing to many of its initial readers and appears to have even less validity now. Second, we must confront Madison's uncomfortable defense of the constitutional provision which declared that slaves were to be regarded as three-fifths of a person for purposes of representation and taxation. While he did not express support for slavery, many a modern reader would have preferred Madison to have expressed outrage at this constitutional compromise.

Another argument against unquestioning reliance on *The Federalist* is that the authors themselves never treated the work with such reverence. Several members of the first Congress argued that, because the Constitution gives the Senate approval power over the president's appointments of certain officers, it should be implied that the Senate also should play a role in removing those officers. To bolster this argument, Representative William Smith of South Carolina quoted this statement in *Federalist 77*: "One of the advantages to be expected from the co-operation of the senate, in the business of appointments, [is] that it would contribute to the stability of the administration. The consent of that body would be necessary to displace as well as to appoint." This did not turn out to be the trump card that Smith had anticipated. The next day, he received a note from Hamilton's friend, Egbert Benson, on the floor of the House stating that "Publius had informed him since the preceding day's debate, that upon mature reflection he had changed his opinion & was now convinced that the President alone should have the power of removal at pleasure."

In retirement, Madison described his own complex feelings about *The Federalist*. When Thomas Jefferson asked Madison for his opinion on including it as part of the curriculum for law students at the University of Virginia, Madison responded that "*The Federalist* may fairly enough be regarded as the most authentic exposition of the text of the federal Constitution, as understood by the Body which prepared & the Authority which accepted it." Madison explained, however, that it was not a perfect book, as "it did not foresee all the misconstructions which have occurred; nor prevent some that it did foresee." He also noted that, while *The Federalist* was respected, the details within it had not been universally accepted: "Neither of the great rival Parties have acquiesced in all its comments."

Conceding that *The Federalist* is not the final oracle, however, does not mean that it should not be, in the words of Chief Justice Marshall, "considered as of great authority" on questions regarding the meaning of the Constitution. As Marshall wrote in the 1819 landmark case, *McCulloch v. Maryland,* the opinions expressed in *The Federalist* "have been justly supposed to be entitled to great respect in expounding the constitution." But, he added, "in applying their opinions to the cases which may arise in the progress of our government, a right to judge of their correctness must be retained."

Therein lies the best way to make use of *The Federalist.* We should treat it as an invaluable yet fallible book. Following Chief Justice Marshall, we should accord the essays great respect in their expounding of the Constitution but never relinquish our "right to judge of their correctness." Such a respectful reading would treat *The Federalist* as presumptively correct. The analysis by Publius of specific sections of the Constitution should be scrutinized to ensure both that they were correct at the time they were made and that they remain relevant in our modern world. The broader, time- less principles of human nature enunciated in *The Federalist,* which form the foundation for much of the Constitution, should likewise serve as the foundation for constitutional analysis. Inevitably, it will not be determinative in many cases; even those who agree to use it may reach different conclusions. But we will all be wiser for the effort.

Those interpreting the Constitution will gain a heightened respect for the care with which it was crafted. A reading of *The Federalist* helps identify which words in the Constitution were chosen to convey narrow, generally agreed upon, and reasonably identifiable meanings, and which were selected for their broader meaning. Similarly, the essays can help a modern interpreter ascertain when, in Hamilton's words, "common sense" indicates that a particular omission reflected a deliberate choice of one method to accomplish a particular task and the rejection of all alternative methods.

Before looking at the ways in which specific constitutional questions are illuminated by *The Federalist,* one final criticism of such use should be addressed. Some commentators concerned with issues of modern so- cial justice question the appropriateness of any reliance on the views of Madison and Hamilton. They see the authors of *The Federalist* as emblematic of a narrow group of men who represented the elite of the eighteenth century and were opposed to the blossoming democratic yearnings of postrevolutionary America. These modern scholars believe that we should not be bound by those who "wished to erect a political system that would guarantee the liberties of certain minorities whose advantages of status, power, and wealth would . . . probably not be tolerated indefinitely by a constitutionally untrammeled majority." A careful reading of history certainly raises extreme doubt over whether that is an accurate appraisal of Madison's and Hamilton's opinions. More fundamentally, this objection mistakes the authors for their words. Regardless of the personal motivations of Madison and Hamilton, as the remainder of this book will demonstrate, *The Federalist* is a work which contains wisdom that is both moral and timeless.

7

"The Diseases Most Incident to Republican Government"

APPRECIATING *FEDERALIST 10*

James Madison's *Federalist 10* holds a unique place in the annals of American thought. It is easily the best known of all of the essays by Publius and arguably the most famous writing in the field of American political science. It appears in countless high school and college textbooks in such diverse subjects as history, law, and rhetoric. It has been called the "most often anthologized, taught, studied, and remembered" of all American political writing. As historian Gary Wills has noted, many people, when reading *The Federalist* "turn first to No. 10. As they should." I will also begin my exploration of the lessons of *The Federalist* by considering what makes this essay so extraordinary.

For all its contemporary acclaim, *Federalist 10* has a peculiarly checkered history. Despite the fact that *The Federalist* has been intensely scrutinized and discussed since its initial publication, this particular essay was essentially ignored for more than a century after its publication. For all that time, it is never mentioned in any book discussing the essays, and was scarcely referred to in any of Madison's biographies. Professor Larry Kramer has raised an intriguing possibility for the essay's early disappearance: The insights contained in

Madison's essay were so novel and so profound that most people, including those at the Constitutional Convention, those in state ratifying conventions, and the general readership in the nineteenth century, simply "failed to comprehend the argument."

One of the few contemporaries of Madison who seems to have clearly understood his message was his coauthor, Alexander Hamilton. Several of Hamilton's later *Federalist* essays support, paraphrase, and build on the arguments of *Federalist 10*. But Hamilton was the exception, and *Federalist 10* lay hidden in plain sight until it was rescued from obscurity by a most unlikely source. In 1913, Charles A. Beard, a Progressive-era historian and political scientist, wrote a book, *An Economic Interpretation of the Constitution of the United States,* which sought to prove that the Constitution was primarily drafted to protect the economic interests of the wealthy men who wrote it. Beard called the Constitution "an economic document drawn with superb skill by men whose property interests were immediately at stake." He centered his conclusion on *Federalist 10*. According to Beard, Madison used this essay to enunciate "in no uncertain language, the principle that the first and elemental concern of every government is economic."

Later historians have discredited Beard's primary thesis by showing that the economic data of the time do not support his conclusions. While Beard's accompanying interpretation of *Federalist 10* also is no longer considered valid, it had the fortuitous effect of awakening interest in the essay. As *Federalist 10* became more widely read, it evoked an extraordinary array of competing interpretations. In the words of one of Madison's biographers, "The history of modern scholarly analysis of *Federalist* no.10 has been notorious for the repeated overthrow of one compelling misinterpretation by another."

Federalist 10, which appeared on November 22, 1787, in the *Daily Advertiser,* was Madison's first essay as Publius. It was designed to confront one of the major arguments of the Anti-Federalists: that nothing "short of despotism" could govern an area as large and as populous as the United States. Madison was especially concerned with answering Brutus, whom he considered a particularly effective advocate "with considerable address & plausibility." In the first of his essays, Brutus articulated the argument that freedom could only flourish if the governed society consisted of a small, homogeneous population in a localized area: "A free republic cannot succeed over a country of such immense extent, containing such a number of inhabitants." To answer Brutus, Madison expanded upon a theory he had been developing since he wrote "Vices of the Political System of the United States" when preparing for the convention earlier in the year. Madison had further refined his thoughts in a long letter to Thomas Jefferson on October 24, 1787, and presented his vision to the world a month later when *Federalist 10* was published.

One of the most distinctive features of *Federalist 10* is the elegant, logical structure of Madison's analysis. He began by stating that one of the major advantages of a "well constructed Union" is its ability to control the problem of "factions." Next, he presented a definition of a faction as a group consisting of "a number of citizens, whether amounting to a majority or a minority of the whole, who are united and actuated by some common impulse of passion, or of interest, adverse to the rights of other citizens, or to the permanent and aggregate interests of the community." The heart of Madison's description is his depiction of a faction as any group whose goals and interests are opposed, or "adverse," to either the rights of others or the public good. We still have factions today; we just call them special interest groups.

Note that there is something elusive about Madison's definition. It implies that there are identifiable "permanent and aggregate interests of the community." Of course, there is no objective measure of community interest, no societal arbiter who can make such a determination. Instead, people tend to categorize a group as a special interest if its objectives conflict with their own. To Democrats, special interest groups such as the tobacco lobby and "big oil" are willing to destroy lives and the environment in order to advance their own narrow economic interests. To Republicans, it is "big labor" and trial lawyers who are willing to bankrupt the nation to protect their undeserved bounty. If you believe that you are on the side of justice and the public good, your opponents are nothing but destructive factions.

Even without universal agreement as to which group is a faction and which is serving the interests of the community, Madison's definition is meaningful. All that is needed is assent to the simple notion that when government is faced with serious problems, some proposed solutions will serve the overall general interest more effectively than others. Those pursuing alternate proposals which would benefit only a segment of the society, while injuring the rest, constitute a faction. And factions—which by definition oppose the public welfare—are dangerous.

Madison reinforced the point that factions are an evil that threatens all free governments by declaring that the "instability, injustice and confusion" created by factions "have in truth been the mortal diseases under which popular governments have every where perished." Thus, regardless of which partisans a reader perceived as being part of a destructive faction, it could not be disputed that governments must be designed so that they are able to confront the evils of faction.

At this point in *Federalist 10*, Madison began the essay's signature rhetorical technique. He set up a simple dichotomy, declaring that there are only two ways "of curing the mischiefs of faction: the one, by removing its causes; the other, by controlling its effects." In other words, society must either prevent factions from arising or ameliorate their consequences when they do appear.

Madison's technique of dividing a topic, such as how to deal with the problem of factions, into two smaller classifications can be linked directly to a methodology for reasoning first introduced by Plato. In his dialogues *The Sophist* and *The Statesman,* Plato creates an analytical system that uses what has been described as "an elaborate tree-like system of roads. The inquirers travel down these branching roads; at each fork they must choose which branch to take."

After Madison introduced the two roads to consider for coping with factions, he turned his attention to the first approach: preventing the causes of factions. For this topic he created another division, this time informing his reader that there are only two means possible for those who want to prevent factions from arising: "the one by destroying the liberty which is essential to its existence; the other, by giving to every citizen the same opinions, the same passions, and the same interests." Obviously either of these approaches would prevent factions. Without liberty, people could not discuss their common interests and plot the formation of a faction to advance their goals. Similarly, if everyone shared the same goals and views on how to achieve them, there would be no factions, since each individual's interests would be identical to those of the larger society. Either method, therefore, would eliminate the problem of factions. Madison quickly dismissed the option of destroying liberty, calling it a remedy that is "worse than the disease." It would be as unthinkable, he added, as eliminating the air because it contributes to the harm caused by fire.

With the first option refuted, Madison turned to the second choice of creating a uniformity of interests and immediately rejected it as "impracticable." Madison's explication as to why such a society cannot be created is one of the major intellectual breakthroughs of the essay. He declared that "the latent causes of faction are . . . sown in the nature of man." His proof that factions are inevitable is a breathtaking discourse on psychology, economics, politics, and history.

For Madison, the most "common and durable" reason that society will ever be segmented is economic—"the various and unequal distribution of property." People's interests vary depending on whether or not they have property, if they are debtors or creditors, and how they make their money. Farmers, manufacturers, and bankers would be affected differently by various tax and trade policies, and thus will always be at odds over the proper path for the government to follow. It was this section of *Federalist 10* that led Charles Beard to his conclusion that Madison was strictly concerned with class warfare. Some commentators still describe Madison's concern as centering on the improper political motives of the "great mass of the little propertied and the unpropertied." But this obsessive focus on the economic causes reveals the interests of the reader, not of Madison.

In his discussion of the causes of factions, Madison explored many aspects of the human condition apart from the merely financial. In fact, he began his analysis with the simple observation that mortal man is "fallible." Since fallible people will inevitably make errors sooner or later, he said, subsequent disagreements with others as to wisdom and truth are equally inevitable. He observed that people do not consider public issues in an intellectual vacuum; there will always be a deep connection between a person's reasoning and "his self-love." In other words, our seemingly objective intellectual analysis will always be affected by our personal desires and self-interest. This distortion of the reasoning process will also lead to inevitable differences in opinion, reflecting the differences in our individual self-interests.

Madison further noted that external forces can lead to a lack of uniformity. People, we are told, have always been divided by their "zeal" for opposing charismatic leaders or different religions. It was, indeed, Madison's own experience fighting for religious freedom in Virginia which provided most of the emotional power for his discussion of the abuses that can be inflicted by factions. Even when no obvious cause for disagreement exists, Madison concluded, there is such a strong natural tendency for people to split into antagonistic groups that they will make up excuses for fostering division. Absent any real reason to fight, he said, "the most frivolous and fanciful distinctions have been sufficient to kindle their unfriendly passions and excite their most violent conflicts."

Because factions are an inherent part of the human condition, society can never prevent the formation of factions by assuring that every citizen has "the same opinions, the same passions, and the same interests." Having already rejected the option of destroying liberty, Madison declares that "the *causes* of faction cannot be removed; and that relief is only to be sought in the means of controlling its *effects*."

In analyzing the means of controlling the harmful effects of factions, Madison presented another division, this time splitting factions into two categories: those which consist of only a minority of the population and those which include a majority. Madison spent less than a paragraph on his first category. In a free nation one need not worry about a minority faction; even if it gains power, it can hold its power only temporarily. Eventually the majority will be able "to defeat its sinister views by regular vote." In other words, the voters, upon realizing that the interests of a minority faction are harmful to the welfare of the majority, are able to "throw the rascals out" in the next regularly scheduled election.

With his next sentence came the critical element of Madison's argument. The ability of a free people to govern themselves not only fails to prevent the problem of majority factions but actually empowers the majority to work its evil: "When a majority is included in a faction, the form of popular government on the other hand enables it to sacrifice to its ruling passion or interest, both the public good and the rights of other citizens."

The key to this argument is the understanding that the people who make up a ruling majority are still human, and hence subject to the same greed, passions, and prejudices as other mortals. When there is opportunity for oppression or economic gain, Madison warned, "we well know that neither moral nor religious motives can be relied on as an adequate control."

To appreciate the evils that can be perpetrated by a majority faction, one need only consider the bleak reality of slavery to see how readily a majority can, in the words of Madison, "sacrifice the weaker party." In his essay, Madison alluded to the problem of slavery when he stated that "the most frivolous and fanciful distinctions" have led to the violence of factions. He did not give any example of a fanciful distinction in *Federalist 10*, which is unfortunate, because he had been much more forthcoming behind the closed doors of the Constitutional Convention. In Philadelphia, Madison had made a similar argument on the danger of factions. In a statement that was not to be made public until after his death, he observed that, in America, the ability of the white majority to impose the institution of slavery was a prime example of the destructive power of factions. As he said, "We have seen the mere distinction of colour made in the most enlightened period of time, a ground of the most oppressive dominion ever exercised by man over man."

This is a remarkable statement to be made in 1787, and it is even more remarkable when made by the slave-owning Madison. It reflects his ambivalence about the institution from which he derived a major source of income. He could own slaves and simultaneously recognize the evil of the institution of slavery. In *The Federalist,* however, this understanding was withheld. Madison the politician chose not to repeat his insight that slaveholders were, in common with other self-ish factions, defending a practice which was "adversed to the rights of other citizens," and of "the permanent and aggregate interests of the community."

Even without this most concrete and compelling of examples, *Federalist 10* presents a clear warning that no just government can rely entirely on the goodwill of the majority. There is always the danger that majorities can abuse the power they obtain in a democracy. Madison would later write that "wherever the real power in a government lies, there is the danger of oppression. In our government, the real power lies in the majority of the community, and the invasion of private rights is *chiefly* to be apprehended. . . from acts in which the government is the mere instrument of the major number of the constituents." As Justice Louis Brandeis wrote in 1927, the Constitution was designed to prevent "the occasional tyrannies of governing majorities."

The crucial question for anyone trying to design a free government is to figure out how to allow the people to rule while restraining majority factions. The only means, according to Madison, can be seen in yet another division: either prevent a majority from having a common interest or ensure that such it is unable to carry out its "schemes of oppression."

Madison approached the question of how to accomplish these seemingly impossible tasks with another dichotomous division. Free governments, he said, can be divided into pure democracies and republics. Madison's definition of democracy brings to mind a simple Vermont town meeting, which is "a Society, consisting of a small number of citizens, who assemble and administer the Government in person." By contrast, according to Madison, a "republic" means "a Government in which the scheme of representation takes place." This definition today would more likely fit the term "representative democracy."

Madison's definition of a republic has always been seen as idiosyncratic at best. As legal historian Mortimer Sellers has noted, the general understanding of the word "republic" when the Constitution was being debated was based on the Roman ideal of a sovereign people, pursuing justice and the common good through the rule of law. In other essays, Madison employed a more orthodox definition. In *Federalist 39*, for example, he defined a republic as "a government which derives all its powers directly or indirectly from the great body of the people; and is administered by persons holding their offices during pleasure, for a limited period, or during good behavior."

The mystery as to why Madison defined republic so differently in *Federalist 10* is resolved when one recalls that his prime target in the essay was Brutus. In his opening Anti-Federalist essay, Brutus had distinguished between "pure democracy" where the citizens all "come together to deliberate, and decide" and a "free republic" in which "the people do not declare their consent by themselves in person, but by representatives, chosen by them." This is the source of Madison's peculiar definition. To counter the arguments Brutus made, Madison apparently decided that it would be best to use the definitions Brutus supplied.

When dealing with majority factions, Madison wrote, Brutus's republic possessed two advantages over a pure democracy. First, the people may choose the best, the wisest, and the most just among them to be their representatives. Such an assembly might well seek out and find the public good. But, Madison conceded, we cannot count on only the good being elected: "Men of factious tempers, of local prejudices, or of sinister designs, may by intrigue by corruption, or by other means, first obtain the suffrages, and then betray the interests, of the people." Even when enlightened representatives are elected, Madison said, they may not be able to convince the electorate to forego "the immediate interest which one party may find in disregarding the rights of another or the good of the whole." If a faithful representative pursues the selfish goals of the majority faction, it will only make matters worse.

Acknowledging that we cannot rely on a system of representation to prevent majority factions, Madison revealed a critical second advantage that a representative democracy holds over a pure democracy. Any system in which citizens meet in person to decide political questions must consist of only a limited area, while a republic can encompass both a larger population and a larger geographic territory. With a smaller population, Madison wrote, there will be fewer distinct parties and interests, and thus it will be much easier for a few groups to turn an alliance into a permanent governing majority. Moreover, because this all takes place in a discrete geographic area, it will be easier (especially in the days before automobiles, computers, and telephones) for the leaders of these groups to get together and plot their misdeeds.

A republic, with its larger size, alleviates these problems. "Extend the sphere," wrote Madison, and you suddenly have many more groups with many more competing interests. There are farmers, manufacturers, and bankers. There are different cultures and different religions. It is much more difficult to discover a common interest and create the sort of ongoing majority coalition that can continually oppress the weaker segments of society. Temporary alliances will occur, but maintaining a permanent governing majority across a large and diverse spectrum of interests will never be easy. While the persistence of slavery shows that long-term majoritarian oppression is possible, the civil rights movement of the 1950s and 1960s demonstrated the power of Madison's insight. It was primarily pressure from the national government—from the Supreme Court's decision in *Brown v. Board of Education* and from the Civil Rights Act of 1964—that forced the southern states to end racial segregation.

Having established that a republic is better than a pure democracy for combating majority factions, Madison made one final division to complete his analysis. He divided republics into two categories, large and small. He noted that the same advantage that size gives to republics over pure democracies—a more diverse population and larger geographic area—is enjoyed by large republics over smaller ones. Moreover, Madison added, one is more likely to find virtuous representatives if one can choose from a larger pool of applicants. Since the union of the states is obviously much larger than the individual states,

this union presents the best opportunity for alleviating the problem of majority factions. A strong national government, as envisioned by the Constitution, creates the "greater obstacles opposed to the concert and accomplishment of the secret wishes of an unjust and interested majority."

Madison stressed that his ideal republic would not be of unlimited size. If a nation were too large, representation would be less effective, as "you render the representatives too little acquainted with all their local circumstances and lesser interests." In *Federalist 14*, he described as the "natural limit" of a republic the largest area which would permit the representatives to meet "as often as may be necessary." The United States, according to Madison, was well within that "natural" limit.

Madison never claimed that he had discovered a mechanism for preventing all majority factions. His more modest assertion was that the extended sphere makes their creation "more difficult" and "less probable." He thus can conclude confidently that "we behold a Republican remedy for the diseases most incident to Republican Government."

But it is only a partial remedy. Liberty requires even more protection. Indeed, Publius devoted most of his essays to demonstrating how the Constitution provides such protection through its systems of separation of powers and federalism.

8

"AMBITION MUST BE MADE TO COUNTERACT AMBITION"

LESSONS ON THE SEPARATION OF POWERS

One of the fundamental themes of *The Federalist* is that a governmental structure which preserves liberty must be premised on the understanding that all power can be abused. In every system of government imaginable, the "power to advance the public happiness involves a discretion which may be misapplied and abused." Or, as Madison put it more simply in the debates during the Constitutional Convention, "all men having power ought to be distrusted to a certain degree." In explaining the complex constitutional system of the separation of powers, *The Federalist* provides us with an understanding of the underlying principles which permit an eighteenth-century document created in a time of sailing ships and single-shot muskets to be applied to a twenty-first-century world of stealth aircraft and dirty bombs.

The starting point, which is frequently overlooked by constitutional commentators, is that all power begins and ends with the people. America was not meant to be a monarchy or a dictatorship. The most universally accepted lesson of the American Revolution was that "the people are the only legitimate fountain of power." The new

Constitution, therefore, would be premised on "the capacity of mankind for self-government."

Paradoxically, while the people would govern themselves, they would play no direct role in their governance. In fact, according to Madison, "the total exclusion of the people, in their collective capacity," from any role in the administration of government, is one of the virtues of the American system. It would be left to the representatives to govern. But, if representation is to fulfill the promise of self-government, the representatives must be sufficiently connected to the people.

According to Madison, the Constitution accomplished that task. The House of Representatives was elected directly by the people. The Senate (at least until the Seventeenth Amendment in 1913) was selected by state legislatures, but that also was consistent with the theory of republican government, since the state legislators were all elected by the people. This sort of indirect relationship similarly applied to the president, who was selected through the Electoral College. In just a bit of a stretch, Madison argued that even the courts were, through "a remote choice," selected by the people, since the president, who nominated federal judges, and the Senate, which confirmed them, were both selected, albeit indirectly, by the people.

The earliest, so-called republican theories of government presupposed that a system of representative government could succeed only if its leaders were virtuous. According to historian Gordon Wood, "The eighteenth-century mind was thoroughly convinced that a popularly based government 'cannot be supported without Virtue.'" One aim of the Constitution was indeed, according to Madison, "to obtain for rulers, men who possess most wisdom to discern, and most virtue to pursue the common good of the society."

But both Madison and Hamilton understood that virtue, while desirable and possible, could scarcely be guaranteed. It would be foolhardy to build a governmental structure that ignored the fallibility of mortals. This insight was described in what is perhaps the best-known quote from *The Federalist*: "If men were angels, no government would be necessary. If angels were to govern men, neither external nor internal controuls on government would be necessary." The United States was not destined to be ruled by angels.

The Federalist describes two types of decidedly nonangelic sorts who can be elected to positions of power. First, evil people may gain the people's favor: "Men of factious tempers, of local prejudices, or of sinister designs, may by intrigue, by corruption or by other means, first obtain the suffrages, and then betray the interests of the people." Second, even well-meaning representatives may be corrupted, and "may forget their obligations to their constituents, and prove unfaithful to their important trust."

The most obvious mechanism for dealing with those who betray the public trust is the electoral process. Since the people retain ultimate control, it is within their power to police their representatives: "The natural cure for an ill administration, in a popular or representative constitution, is a change of men." In the final analysis, it is the ballot box that must keep us free.

But the ability of the people to vote is not enough. According to *The Federalist*, the people may, in moments of weakness or panic, elect demagogues and permit them to remain in power. A leader, upon winning election, may improperly maintain power. This, in fact, is how many a modern dictatorship has been born. Accordingly, Madison explained, "A dependence on the people is no doubt the primary controul on the government; but experience has taught mankind the necessity of auxiliary precautions."

The design of these "auxiliary precautions" lies at the heart of the constitutional separation of powers. To prevent its abuse, power must be divided. No single individual or group, however selected or monitored, can be entrusted with the authority to write laws, enforce them, and then decide on the guilt or innocence of the accused. As Madison wrote in *Federalist 47*, "The accumulation of all powers, legislative, executive and judiciary in the same hands, whether of one, a few or many, and whether hereditary, self appointed, or elective, may justly be pronounced the very definition of tyranny."

The first step in avoiding tyranny, then, is to separate power. The British system of separation of power reflected that nation's obsession with rank, class, and status. Its version of mixed government provided a place for royalty, aristocracy, and the common people. The king served as ruler, the House of Lords provided a base for the titled elite, and the House of Commons represented the voice of the commoner. Such a system was unacceptable to an America which had struggled to free itself from the tyranny of the crown. All power needed to be retained and divided amongst entities whose authority could be traced to the people. To design these separate entities, the natural breaking point was based on a division of labor, creating discrete branches for what had become accepted as the three major tasks of government: legislative, executive, and judicial.

Americans in the 1780s traced their understanding of the concept of the separation of powers to the French philosopher, Baron de Montesquieu. Montesquieu had asserted that "there would be an end of every thing were the same man, or the same body, whether of the nobles or of the people to exercise those three powers: that of enacting laws, that of executing the public resolutions, and that of judging the crimes or differences of individuals." Anti-Federalists frequently invoked his maxim to criticize the Constitution for not providing a "compleat separation of the great distinctions of power."

Madison responded to these criticisms in *Federalist 48*. Merely assigning specific tasks does not prevent one branch from usurping the power of another.

Those who possess power tend to lust for more, or, in the prophetic words of Publius, "power is of an encroaching nature." A mere constitutional demarcation of allotted roles would be nothing but a "parchment barrier," incapable of defeating those seeking self-aggrandizement.

The genius of the Constitution, according to *The Federalist*, is that it empowers each branch to defend itself and relies not on the uncertain virtue of our character but on the instincts of our lesser angels. The plan is elegantly summarized thus: "Ambition must be made to counteract ambition." Recognizing human weakness, the structure of government will remedy "by opposite and rival interests, the defect of better motives." Thus is created one of the deepest ironies in the constitutional structure—we must allow an intermixture of power to maintain a separation of power. Each branch must be independent enough to perform its assigned tasks effectively but remain connected with the other branches to prevent the misuse of power. *The Federalist* explained that each branch has a different structure with characteristic strengths and weaknesses that are counterbalanced by the structure of the other branches.

The legislature, the branch closest to the people, is meant to be the strongest. Not only is it empowered to write laws and impose taxes, it is the only branch with the ability to remove officials from the other two. The power of impeachment gives Congress the means to evict judges and presidents from their posts. Congress is also the only branch of the federal government which can propose an amendment to the Constitution; the president and judiciary were deliberately omitted from the amendment-making process.

Madison considered the legislative branch the most dangerous of the three. He warned, "The legislative department is every where extending the sphere of its activity, and drawing all power into its impetuous vortex." The people's branch should be the strongest, Madison reasoned, but such power requires the most careful protections. To counterbalance its power, the legislative branch is divided into two houses, necessitating the "concurrence of two distinct bodies in schemes of usurpation or perfidy." To·render conspiracies even more unlikely, the two houses have different constituencies. Members of the House of Representatives are drawn from relatively small districts. Senators represent entire states. Under the original Constitution, the Senate was chosen by state legislators, rather than by popular vote, so senators could be viewed as representatives of the states themselves. Thus, no legislative action could be taken without the assent of at least a majority of those speaking on behalf of the states. Today, even with the direct election of senators, statewide election serves an analogous function.

Neither the House nor the Senate can do anything by itself. To remove a member of another branch, for instance, the two bodies must act in concert. In fact, successful impeachment and removal requires both a majority of the House of Representatives and a two-thirds, super-majority vote of the Senate. As the enemies of President Bill Clinton—who remained in office when the Senate could muster no more than fifty votes to convict him—learned, it takes a very strong consensus to remove a president.

Another advantage of the two-house legislature is that it makes it more difficult to create laws. While recognizing the obvious need for some legislation to pass, *The Federalist* expressed deep skepticism about the wisdom of most legislation: "The injury which may possibly be done by defeating a few good laws will be amply compensated by the advantage of preventing a number of bad ones." Sometimes, Madison warned, we the people, through our "own temporary errors and delusions" will push for legislation that we "will afterwards be the most ready to lament and condemn." The need for both houses to approve legislation slows down the process, and permits cooler heads to prevail. Put another way, gridlock can be good.

The presidential veto furnishes "an additional security against the enaction of improper laws." Even with the two-house process, the "love of power" or "spirit of faction" may lead to unwise laws. As every law requires either a majority of both houses plus the approval of the president, or a two-thirds super-majority vote to override a presidential veto, the path from proposal to law is deliberately designed to foster delay, dialogue, and careful review. The advantage of such a complicated system is that it is "far less probable, that culpable views of any kind should infect all the parts of the government, at the same moment and in relation to the same object."

The presidency was designed to avoid many of the obstructions set up to slow Congress but was never intended to be free from effective checks and balances. Hamilton expressed strong support for putting a single person in charge of the executive branch, as opposed to alternate proposals for either a hydra-headed, multi-person executive or a single executive who required the approval of a governing "council" to operate. The fact that the executive power was to be carried out by a single individual would permit the president to act with "energy" to provide "protection . . . against foreign attacks" and to ensure "the steady administration of the laws." The advantages of unity seemed obvious to Hamilton: "Decision, activity, secrecy, and dispatch will generally characterise the proceedings of one man."

Taken out of context, this would be a dangerous doctrine. Limitless power is always subject to abuse. For example, in 2005, Vice President Cheney, in justifying President Bush's program of warrantless wiretapping, declared that "the President of the United States needs to have his constitutional powers unimpaired, if you will, in terms of the conduct of national security policy." *The Federalist* teaches us that such a philosophy is misguided and that the power of the federal government, even in matters of national security, was meant to be divided and shared. We must not confuse the granting of power with the question of who will yield that power. As Madison noted, there are two distinct issues involving national authority in the Constitution: "The FIRST relates to the sum or quantity of power which it vests in the Government... The SECOND, to the particular structure of the Government, and the distribution of this power, among its several branches."

Publius was well aware that the national government would be confronted frequently with the dangers of war, because the "causes of hostility among nations are innumerable." Whether for power, commerce, or revenge, "nations in general will make war whenever they have a prospect of getting anything by it." The primary task of government is to ensure the safety of its people. As James Madison noted, "Security against foreign danger is . . . an avowed and essential object of the American Union." In explaining why the Constitution did not place restrictions on the national government's power to create, support, and direct the armed forces, Hamilton proclaimed that "there can be no limitation of that authority, which is to provide for the defence and protection of the community, in any matter essential to its efficacy." Accordingly, Hamilton wrote, that government "ought to be cloathed with all the powers requisite to complete execution of its trust."

In *Federalist 23*, Hamilton described the components of the national power to provide for the common defense: "to raise armies; to build and equip fleets; to prescribe rules for the government of both; to direct their operations; to provide for their support." The Constitution specifies that it is the role of Congress to perform each of these functions but one, the direction of the "operations" of the army and navy.

The president was given the power to serve as "commander-in-chief of the army and navy of the United States." In explaining why the president's power is far less extensive than that of the king of England, Hamilton wrote that the presidential power, "would amount to nothing more than the supreme command and direction of the military and naval forces . . . while that of the British king extends to the *declaring* of war and to the *raising* and *regulating* of fleets and armies—all which by the Constitution under consideration, would appertain to the Legislature."

Publius thus envisioned a bifurcated approach to military matters. While significant overlap exists between the powers of the two branches, the constitutional scheme of separation of powers grants each branch primary responsibility over different aspects. Since the time of President Washington, the two branches have battled over supremacy in this area. The Helvidius-Pacificus debates over the Proclamation of Neutrality, the Cooper-Church amendment of 1971, which denied funding for the introduction of ground troops into Cambodia, and the 1984 Boland Amendment, which prohibited U.S. aid to the contras fighting in Nicaragua (and which led to the Iran-Contra scandal), are just a few of the skirmishes over the respective war powers of Congress and the president.

The Federalist cannot provide a complete answer to the question of where we should draw the line today, but it does indicate the extremes that should be avoided. A strong argument can be made that, according to *The Federalist*, Congress should not claim unlimited authority to micromanage the president's conduct of an ongoing war. Those in Congress who disapprove of a war can vote to rescind an authorization for it, but a resolution which delimits the precise number of troops that can be deployed on the field of battle comes perilously close to infringing on the president's "supreme command and direction of the military and naval forces."

It would be a grave mistake, however, to assume, as Vice President Cheney did, that the president's unitary status somehow equates to a conclusion that the president has essentially unlimited and nonreviewable power over all issues of national security. Justice Clarence Thomas made a similar error when he cited *The Federalist*'s endorsement of an energetic chief executive as support for his position that the Supreme Court should not "second guess" the president's decisions in national security matters. In his dissent in the 2004 case, *Hamdi v. Rumsfeld*, Thomas argued that the Court should not review the president's determination that an American citizen could be held indefinitely as an "enemy combatant" and quoted Hamilton's observation that the "direction of war most peculiarly demands those qualities which distinguish the exercise of power by a single hand."

The Court ultimately rejected his analysis. In holding that the president lacked the power to make his own rules for determining which American citizens were "enemy combatants," the Court declared that "a state of war is not a blank check for the President when it comes to the rights of the Nation's citizens."

Thomas's analysis ignores *The Federalist*'s painstaking depiction of the complex intertwining between the branches, and Publius's overarching concern that no single branch be left unchecked. As Justice Souter noted in his own *Hamdi* opinion, Madison's *Federalist 51* set forth the fundamental constitutional principle that "the constant aim is to divide and arrange the several offices in such a manner as that each may be a check on the other; that the private interest of every individual, may be a sentinel over the public rights."

The opinion of Justice Scalia, which was joined by Justice Stevens, presented a particularly careful and persuasive use of *The Federalist*. They used the work to support their contention that the president "lacks indefinite wartime detention authority over citizens." Scalia relied on several different essays of *The Federalist* to emphasize that the constitutional separation of powers divides authority over military power and does not grant unlimited power to the president. As he concluded, "The proposition that the Executive lacks indefinite wartime detention authority over citizens is consistent with the Founders' general mistrust of military power permanently at the Executive's disposal."

Scalia also employed *The Federalist* to demonstrate the constitutional commitment to eliminate "the practice of arbitrary imprisonments" by enshrining the "establishment of the writ of *habeas corpus.*" Scalia concluded that until Congress declared that there was a "rebellion or insurrection" necessitating the suspension of the writ of habeas corpus, American citizens on American soil needed to be either tried in courts or set free.

Scalia's analysis draws on far more than just a few catchphrases to dress up a judicial opinion. Rather, he uses *The Federalist* to illustrate the common fears of those who ratified the Constitution about a concentration of military power, and to explicate the manner in which it avoids that concentration by dividing governmental responsibility. To do this successfully, of course, the entirety of *The Federalist* had to be considered.

Regrettably, justices sometimes cherry-pick *The Federalist*, citing as gospel the sections which support their conclusions while ignoring the inconvenient essays which point in the opposite direction. Justice Souter fell victim to this problem in another case which presented important separation of powers issues, *American Insurance Ass'n v. Garamendi*. This case involved a challenge to California's Holocaust Victim Insurance Relief Act, which required companies doing business in the state to disclose information about insurance policies they had issued in Europe from 1920 to 1945. The purpose of the law was to determine what had happened to the insurance proceeds that were owed to the victims of the Holocaust. An association of insurance companies challenged the state law, asserting that it was preempted by an agreement signed by President Clinton and German Chancellor Gerhard Schroeder which established a separate procedure to compensate Holocaust victims. This agreement was not a treaty; it went into effect without the approval of two-thirds of the Senate.

There were two distinct questions faced by the Court in *Garamendi*. First, whether an executive agreement made without the approval of the Senate is valid; second, whether such an agreement can preempt state law. In finding such preemption, Justice Souter cited several sections of *The Federalist* for the proposition that individual states should not be permitted to contradict the country's relations with foreign nations: "If we are to be one nation in any respect, it clearly ought to be in respect to other nations."

When discussing the validity of the executive agreement, though, Justice Souter did not mention any of the *Federalist* essays which declare, or at least strongly imply, that the treaty provision—with its requirement of approval by two-thirds of the Senate—was meant to be the exclusive means for making binding agreements between the United States and other nations. The Constitution states that a treaty is created only when the president submits it to the Senate and "two thirds of the Senators present concur." In the past seventy-five years, however, presidents have taken to using agreements rather than treaties to make binding commitments with other nations.

There are two types of executive agreements, neither of which is mentioned in the Constitution. The first, called a congressional-executive agreement, is like NAFTA (the North America Free Trade Agreement), which became effective upon the approval of both houses of Congress in 1993. The second, a sole-executive agreement, like the one in the *Garamendi* case, becomes effective simply upon the president's signature, without any congressional involvement at all. These two types of executive agreements have virtually replaced treaties. In fact, since 1960, fewer than 5 percent of all American foreign commitments have been formalized by treaty. The appeal of the agreement process is obvious: it is simpler than obtaining a two-thirds vote in the Senate. Indeed, NAFTA in all likelihood never could have been ratified as a treaty; it received only sixty-one votes in the Senate, significantly less than the sixty-seven which would have constituted the requisite two-thirds super-majority.

Despite, or perhaps because of, the greater ease of putting agreements into place, the fact that they are not mentioned in the Constitution is troubling. A reading of *The Federalist* leads to the strong conclusion that the decision by the drafters of the Constitution to include treaties but not executive agreements in the text was meant to indicate that treaties were to be the exclusive way to bind our nation to another; omission was meant to indicate exclusion.

First, the House of Representatives was deliberately excluded from this process. Hamilton wrote that the size of the House was not conducive to making delicate foreign policy decisions: "The multitudinous composition of that body, forbid us to expect in it those qualities which are essential to the proper execution of such a trust." He also expressed concern as to whether the locally elected representatives would have "a nice and uniform sensibility to national character."

Next, to ensure a national consensus reflecting this "national character," the Constitution requires that two-thirds of the Senate, meaning two-thirds of the body charged with representing the states, approves. Hamilton refers to this as "the advantage of numbers in the formation of treaties." To those Anti-Federalists who argued that, under the Constitution, foreign intrigue would lead to corruption in the creation of treaties, John Jay wrote that the two-thirds mandate provided powerful insurance against such malfeasance: "He must either have been very unfortunate in his intercourse with the world, or possess a heart very susceptible of such impressions, who can think it probable that the president and two thirds of the senate will ever be capable of such unworthy conduct. The idea is too gross and too invidious to be entertained."

While permitting the majority votes of congressional-executive agreements such as NAFTA to bypass the security meant to be provided by the two-thirds constitutional requirement is worrisome, it is even more dangerous to permit the president to act unilaterally. Hamilton explained that the reason for requiring Senate involvement was to prevent the president from "betraying the interests of the nation in a ruinous treaty." The Constitution provides security against ill-considered or ill-motivated treaties by preventing one person, the president, from acting alone. As delineated in *Federalist 66*, "The security essentially intended by the constitution against corruption and treachery in the formation of treaties, is to be sought for in the numbers and characters of those who are to make them. The JOINT AGENCY of the chief magistrate of the union, and of two thirds [of the Senate] is designed to be the pledge for the fidelity of the national councils in this particular."

Hamilton demonstrated, as he did with the chief executive's power over the military, that the limited power of the president under the Constitution can be appreciated by comparing it with the far greater autonomy of the English monarchy: "The President is to have power with the advice and consent of the Senate to make treaties; provided two thirds of the Senators present concur. The King of Great-Britain is the sole and absolute representative of the nation in all foreign transactions. He can of his own accord make treaties of peace, commerce, alliance, and of every other description." It should be impossible, in other words, for the president to act like a king and "on his own accord" make binding international agreements. As Hamilton concluded, "The history of human conduct does not warrant that exalted opinion of human virtue which would make it wise in a nation to commit interests of so delicate and momentous a kind as those which concern its intercourse with the rest of the world to the sole disposal of a magistrate created and circumstanced, as would be a president of the United States."

In *Garamendi*, Justice Souter, writing for the majority, upheld the constitutionality of sole-executive agreements, based on the "historical practice" of upholding similar agreements. Such reasoning may explain why, despite the express language of the Constitution and the teaching of *The Federalist*, an executive agreement is constitutional. But if Justice Souter respected *The Federalist* enough to cite it for support of his preemption analysis, he ought at least to have responded to Publius on the issue of executive agreements.

One possible concern for the Court in a case such as *Garamendi* is whether the justices are overstepping their constitutionally assigned role and interfering with issues which are better left to the other branches. As it does with so many other questions, *The Federalist* can provide useful insights into the proper workings of the judicial branch.

According to Hamilton, federal judges are charged with a critical responsibility in our constitutional system. They are entrusted with ensuring that both the legislative and executive branches stay within constitutional limits. Judges serve as an "excellent barrier to the encroachments and oppressions of the representative body" and act to "secure a steady, upright and impartial administration of the laws." Presaging the 1803 ruling of Chief Justice John Marshall in *Marbury v. Madison*, which upheld the principle of judicial review, Hamilton wrote that "whenever a particular statute contravenes the constitution, it will be the duty of the judicial tribunals to adhere to the latter and disregard the former."

To perform this task, judges must be independent of the other branches. To create this independence, Publius reasoned, federal judges must be appointed for life. According to Hamilton, the "permanent tenure of judicial offices" is the single most important factor for creating an "independent spirit" in the judiciary. Madison agreed, stating that "the permanent tenure by which the appointments are held in that department, must soon destroy all sense of dependence on the authority conferring them." The accuracy of this prediction can be seen in a simple review of the careers of Justices Sandra Day O'Connor, Anthony Kennedy, and David Souter, all of whom were appointed by presidents pledged to oppose abortion, and all of whom voted to reaffirm the holding of *Roe v. Wade*. Recently, much more care has been taken to scour the past speeches, writings, and opinions of Supreme Court nominees to make sure that their future votes will be consistent with the political views of the president who appointed them. Time will tell whether the freedom of permanent tenure will result in more judicial surprises.

Anti-Federalists argued, as do many critics of decisions such as *Roe*, that the power of judicial review, coupled with judicial independence, renders the judicial branch superior to all the other branches. The most articulate Anti-Federalist proponent of this view was Brutus. In the course of five essays, Brutus warned that the Supreme Court would be dangerous because its rulings were final and irreversible: "There is no power above them that can correct their errors or controul their decisions." Brutus argued that because the Court had final say over the meaning of the Constitution, Congress would have no choice but to obey the command of the Court: "If, therefore, the legislature pass any laws, inconsistent with the sense the judges put upon the constitution, they will declare it void; and therefore in this respect their power is superior to that of the legislature."

Brutus also voiced the concern that the Constitution did not limit the methodology by which the Court would interpret it. The greatest fear Brutus expressed was that judges would be free not only to evaluate laws based on the literal language of the Constitution but on the Court's understanding of its more general purpose: "In their decisions they will not confine themselves to any fixed or established rules, but will determine, according to what appears to them, the reason and spirit of the constitution."

Hamilton, without mentioning Brutus by name, attempted to provide "a point-by-point rejoinder" to his argument. Significantly, this is one of the few times in *The Federalist* in which Publius was unsuccessful in rebutting the arguments of his opponents. Hamilton tried to finesse the issue of judicial supremacy by arguing that the power to strike down laws did not mean that judges were superior to legislators, but that the Constitution was superior to all. It was the people, Hamilton declared, who spoke through the constitutional process to create a supreme law. The courts, then, were to function as "an intermediate body between the people and the legislature, in order, among other things, to keep the latter within the limits assigned to their authority."

The power of judicial review was designed not merely to protect the people from rogue legislators, but also to guard "the rights of individuals" against abuse from the majority. Judges are obliged to step in, Hamilton argued, whenever the legislature passes a law that embodies "a momentary inclination [that] happens to lay hold of a majority of their constituents incompatible with the provisions in the existing constitution." The majority of the people, acting in unison, do not have the right to violate the Constitution, and it is the courts that are charged with preventing "serious oppressions of the minor party in the community."

Hamilton recognized the strength of the argument that the courts could misuse their power to strike down laws and "substitute their own pleasure to the constitutional intentions of the legislature." In response, Hamilton agreed that it would be wrong for judges to make constitutional rulings based on their personal preferences rather than their "sense of the law." If judges were, instead, "to exercise WILL instead of JUDGMENT, the consequence would equally be the substitution of their pleasure to that of the legislative body." Put differently, it is the job of the legislature, not the courts, to make policy decisions.

Hamilton did not, however, consider judges interpreting the Constitution according to its "spirit" to be the same as judges substituting their will for the legislative branch. He did not directly refute the claim Brutus made that judges were free to interpret the Constitution according to its spirit, but he made the significantly different point that "there is not a syllable in the plan under consideration, which *directly* empowers the national courts to construe the laws according to the spirit of the constitution." Note the careful use of the phrase "directly empowers." Hamilton did not contend that judges will not interpret the Constitution beyond its letters, but according to its more general spirit; he merely asserted that this is not required.

So how are judges to be controlled? Here, Hamilton offered a peculiarly weak argument, one that Brutus previously had successfully debunked. Hamilton claimed that the continual threat of impeachment provided "a complete security" against judges overstepping their power. "There never can be danger that the judges, by a series of deliberate usurpations on the authority of the legislature, would hazard the united resentment of the body entrusted with it, while this body was possessed of the means of punishing their presumption by degrading them from their stations."

More than two months before this essay was published, Brutus had explained why impeachment could not serve as an effective mechanism for policing the courts. Noting that the only constitutional grounds for impeachment were "treason, bribery, or other high crimes and misdemeanors," Brutus stated that judges could only be removed from office if their errors were committed from "wicked and corrupt motives." Simple ineptitude would not amount to an impeachable offense: "A man may mistake a case in giving judgment, or manifest that he is incompetent to the discharge of the duties of a judge, and yet give no evidence of corruption or want of integrity." To this well-reasoned logic, Publius had no successful rejoinder.

Hamilton also tried to argue that the discretion of judges would be limited by their obligation to follow precedent. Under the English common law system, judges were required to "abide by former precedents, where the same points come again in litigation." Of course, precedent could be overruled if it "may happen that the judge may mistake the law." Nonetheless, Hamilton claimed that the reliance on precedent would control judges by limiting their freedom to rule at whim: "To avoid an arbitrary discretion in the courts, it is indispensable that they should be bound down by strict rules and precedents, which serve to define and point out their duty in every particular case that comes before them."

There is a weakness in this argument, however. As Brutus noted, the pull of precedent can just as well lead to an ever-increasing accretion of power. Brutus warned that by slowly building one case at a time, the courts will be able to reach any result they choose: "They will be able to extend the limits of the general government gradually, and by insensible degrees, and to accommodate themselves to the temper of the people . . . one adjudication will form a precedent to the next, and this to a following one." Thus, rather than reining in the judiciary, the use of precedent permits the courts to empower themselves in slow but steady steps.

A reading of Hamilton's six essays on the judiciary leaves one suspecting that he was aware that there was no easy answer to the charge that the judiciary was the branch for which the Constitution had provided the fewest checks. One possible response he did not raise was that the greatest corrector for the Court was time; new justices, selected and confirmed by the political branches, would replace the former justices. Moreover, Congress had the power to increase the number of justices, though admittedly this plan did not work well when Franklin Roosevelt tried to pack the Court in 1937.

Hamilton's strongest arguments came when he acknowledged the reality of judicial power. He contended that judicial autonomy is ultimately the price we pay for a Constitution which limits the power of the elected branches of government. If we are to avoid having a system in which the legislature is uncontrollable, the courts must have the power to strike down legislative acts which violate the fundamental charter of government. To criticize the Constitution for empowering courts to declare acts of Congress unconstitutional, Hamilton said, is "to condemn every constitution that attempts to set bounds to the legislative discretion."

Hamilton's ultimate attempt to deal with the power of the courts contains one of his most misunderstood statements. Since some entity must be empowered to serve as the final arbiter of the meaning of the Constitution, he wrote, it is best that such power be placed in the judiciary's hands because they are the "least dangerous" branch. Some today mistakenly think that the lack of danger refers to judges deferring to the political branches and avoiding "policymaking" and "deciding issues no more broadly than the legal dispute needing resolution." Others claim the "least dangerous" branch meant that the Court was the branch "least responsive to opinion," and therefore least affected by the fads and impulses of contemporary politics.

In reality, Hamilton was comparing worst-case scenarios and saying that an errant Court, by nature of its role in the governmental structure, could inflict less harm than would result if either of the other two branches were permitted to wield their power unchecked. The complete Hamiltonian quote is that, compared to the other two branches of government, "the judiciary, from the nature of its functions, will always be the least dangerous to the political rights of the Constitution; because it will be least in a capacity to annoy or injure them." The legislative branch, Hamilton noted, controls taxes and makes the law; it both "commands the purse" and "prescribes the rules by which the duties and rights of every citizen are to be regulated." The president is in charge of the military. He "holds the sword of the community." The courts, in contrast, lack control of either "the strength or of the wealth of the society." Even in the courts' area of greatest authority, deciding individual cases, the rulings are mere words unless the executive branch agrees to enforce their judgments.

Thus, even when the courts go wrong, the harm is limited: "Particular misconstructions and contraventions of the will of the legislature may now and then happen; but they can never be so extensive as to amount to an inconvenience, or in any sensible degree to affect the order of the political system."

And Hamilton was correct. Both the president, as commander-in-chief of the army and navy, and Congress, with its ability to regulate the most minute detail of human existence and impose even the harshest taxes, possess the means of destroying all semblance of freedom. It may be cold comfort to those who are angered by decisions of the Court, but Publius was willing to accept the possibility of the judiciary occasionally overstepping its bounds as being preferable to any alternative. Since someone must be the final arbiter of the constitutionality of governmental action, let it be the branch lacking any other real power. As Hamilton concluded, while "individual oppression may now and then proceed from the courts of justice, the general liberty of the people can never be endangered."

9

"A DOUBLE SECURITY"

LESSONS ON FEDERALISM

*S*tates' rights is a loaded term. During the civil rights movement, it was the battle cry of segregationists determined to prevent the federal government from creating a society of racial equality. At the 1948 convention of the States Rights Party, presidential nominee Strom Thurmond articulated the group's underlying philosophy: "I want to tell you that there's not enough troops in the army to force the Southern people to break down segregation and admit the Negro Race into our theatres, into our swimming pools, into our homes and into our churches."

During his 1980 presidential campaign, Ronald Reagan visited Philadelphia, Mississippi, the site of the savage murders of three civil rights workers in 1964 and declared, "I believe in states' rights." Some saw his use of the term in such a setting as insensitive, if not implied support for those who retained a racist ideology, but there was another philosophy at work as well. By the end of the decade, conservatives were embracing states' rights as the vehicle for limiting the size and reach of the federal bureaucracy. In 1987 President Reagan declared that "federalism"—a word with a less inflammatory heritage than states' rights—was "rooted in the knowledge that our political liberties are best assured by limiting the size and scope of the national government." According to this view of federalism, regulation of a wide range of issues, including poverty, the environment, and consumer protection, should lie within the purview of state, not federal, government. Opponents of the Reagan administration claimed that federalism was merely an excuse for those who wanted to do away with most federal regulation. It was seen by "many liberals as a smoke screen for a conservative political agenda."

Ironically, liberals began taking up the banner of states' rights a quarter century later. When the federal government acted to stop California from legalizing medical marijuana and when a national constitutional amendment was proposed to prevent states from recognizing gay marriage, the potential virtues of state sovereignty became apparent to the other side of the political spectrum.

Viewed over the vast canvas of time, federalism is neither a conservative nor a liberal issue. If the politicians in control in Washington are conservative, increasing the power of the states will lead to a more liberal agenda; if liberals are in control of the national government, the reverse is true. According to *The Federalist*, such flexibility is a virtue. Although Madison fought in Philadelphia to grant the new national government the ability to veto any state law, and Hamilton had stated that he would have preferred a consolidated union, Publius enthusiastically expounded on the virtues of limiting federal power to maintain some level of state sovereignty.

The line between state and federal power, as Madison noted, cannot be precisely drawn. He cautioned that "in delineating the boundary between the Federal and State jurisdictions" it was to be expected that the best the delegates at the Philadelphia convention could produce would be "vague and incorrect definitions." Not only are the lines between the two levels of government complex and difficult to ascertain precisely, he said, but our political vocabulary may be unable to find "words distinctly and exclusively appropriated to them." Even were we able to understand the distinctions perfectly, Madison wrote, "the definition of them may be rendered inaccurate by the inaccuracy of the terms in which it is delivered."

Much of *The Federalist* is devoted to trying to delineate the competing roles of the national and state governments. In the course of his discussion, Publius uttered statements that, if taken out of context, would lead to extreme and contradictory positions. Some language reflects a very nationalistic viewpoint, seemingly permitting the federal government to assume almost any power it wants. Other essays depict an extraordinarily limited national authority, with the overwhelming portion of governmental authority residing with the states. Commentators, and even Supreme Court justices, have been known to quote only those statements which support the outcome they desire, while ignoring or discounting those which point in the opposite direction.

A particularly glaring example of this partisan invocation of *The Federalist* can be seen in the 1997 case, *Printz v. United States,* in which the Court held that Congress could not require state police officials to help enforce federal gun control laws. In his dissenting opinion, arguing that Congress has the power to enlist state employees to enforce federal law, Justice Souter cited Hamilton's statement in *Federalist 27* that "the Legislatures Courts and Magistrates, of the respective members will be incorporated into the operations of the national government *as far as its just and constitutional authority extends*; and will be rendered auxiliary to the enforcement of its laws." Souter concluded that by requiring state police to enforce federal gun laws, the state employees were serving as "auxiliary to the enforcement" of federal laws.

Justice Scalia, writing for the majority, attempted to discount *Federalist 27* with a strange array of attacks. First, he said, the essay was not reliable since it was written by Hamilton, and was thus from "the pen of the most expansive expositor of federal power." Scalia also argued that Hamilton's Publius essays were at odds with Madison's since "it is widely recognized that '*The Federalist* reads with a split personality' on matters of federalism." Presupposing a conflict between the coauthors, Scalia concluded that it would be wrong for the Court to follow Hamilton's viewpoint, and "turn a blind eye to the fact that it was Madison's—not Hamilton's—that prevailed . . . at the Constitutional Convention."

It is especially disconcerting to see Justice Scalia, who so frequently quotes *The Federalist*, strain so mightily to discount it when it leads to a conclusion he does not like. First, it certainly is not clear that Madison's view on federalism prevailed over Hamilton's at the Constitutional Convention. In fact, the two men did not present competing proposals on the issue at Philadelphia, both were keenly disappointed in much of the final document, and neither was able to convince the convention to incorporate his personally preferred plans into the Constitution. Second, as the rest of this chapter demonstrates, the essays of Madison and Hamilton do not reflect a split personality and are generally quite consistent in matters of states' rights. Many, if not most, modern scholars agree that Publius represents "a remarkably 'whole personality'" so that it appears sometimes as if Madison and Hamilton had "interchanged their minds" when writing these essays.

Finally, it seems disingenuous to quote an author when you agree with him yet declare him inconsequential when his teachings do not lead to the conclusion you desire. *The Federalist* should be read in its entirety, not cherry-picked for small extracts. A full reading reveals the underlying eternal principles which Publius saw embodied in the structure established by the Constitution, even though it may not resolve the question of how those principles should apply today.

According to *The Federalist*, the relationship between federal and state government is guided by three fundamental but not entirely consistent considerations. First, in addition to their responsibility for "local" concerns, the states also provide security against the abuse of power on the national level. Second, the national government must be "energetic" enough to accomplish its assigned tasks. Finally, the division of powers between the federal and state governments is intended to be fluid. As opposed to the separation of powers between the three branches of the federal government, a certain amount of "encroaching" is not only inevitable but desirable.

The Federalist maintained that America's system providing multiple levels of government preserves liberty. It may seem counterintuitive that we are more free when there are two governments with which we must contend, but, as Madison repeatedly noted, governmental power which is controlled by a single person or entity is always subject to abuse. The underlying theory that Madison had applied to the separation of powers, namely that "ambition must be made to counteract ambition," applies to the differing levels of government as well. Hamilton noted that the federal government and the states would counteract one another and stand guard to ensure that neither exceeded its authority: "Power being almost always the rival of power; the General Government will at all times stand ready to check the usurpations of the state governments; and these will have the same disposition towards the General Government." Because each level of government can police the other, Madison said, "a double security arises to the rights of the people."

For the security to be effective, power must be shared between the two levels of governments. The national government was not given all governmental authority and was not made responsible for regulating all aspects of public life. The scope of state power was defined in the negative; the states were intended to possess that power which was not allotted to the federal government. The Constitution lists, or "enumerates," the power for the federal government and "the States in all unenumerated cases, are left in the enjoyment of their sovereign and independent jurisdiction." Hamilton agreed that the Constitution preserved for the states "certain exclusive and very important portions of sovereign power."

The key question, of course, is how much of the sovereign power was given to the federal government and how much was left to the states. Justice Clarence Thomas has taken the most extreme position on this issue, contending that most of America's economy should be off limits to federal regulation. To appreciate the extent of Thomas's argument, one need only look at a long-discarded case from the late nineteenth century, which he refers to as illustrating his view of the law. In *United States v. E. C. Knight Co.*, the American Sugar Refining Company, through a series of mergers and acquisitions, had gained control of 98 percent of the manufacturing of all refined sugar produced in the entire country. The federal government sued, claiming that this market domination violated antitrust laws. The Court ruled that the company's monopolistic behavior was beyond the reach of Congress, since manufacturing was not included in the definition of commerce.

Thomas agrees with this definition. He has stated that while Congress can regulate interstate commerce, the meaning of "commerce" is limited to the buying and selling of goods and services "trafficked across state lines." Pursuant to this view, manufacturing and agriculture are not commerce but are activities that precede commerce; they only produce items which will later be sold in commerce. Thus, according to Thomas, Congress cannot regulate "productive activities like manufacturing and agriculture." Under his definition, federal minimum wage and child labor laws also would be unconstitutional.

The Federalist does in some essays describe the regulatory authority of the federal government in similarly restrictive language. In *Federalist 45*, Madison declared that "The powers delegated by the proposed Constitution to the Federal Government, are few and defined. Those which are to remain in the State Governments are numerous and indefinite." According to Madison, while national power is generally concerned with international military and commercial relations, "The powers reserved to the several States will extend to all the objects, which, in the ordinary course of affairs, concern the lives, liberties and properties of the people; and the internal order, improvement, and prosperity of the State." Hamilton presented a similar picture of state authority, stressing that "the ordinary administration of criminal and civil justice" would be an essential part of state, not federal, responsibility.

These statements, which imply a severely limited power for the federal government, do not present the full view of *The Federalist*. Many other essays indicate that Congress's powers were meant to be expansive enough to permit it to accomplish all of its assigned tasks. According to Hamilton, since the national government is responsible for regulating commerce between the states, it "must be empowered to pass all laws, and to make all regulations which have relation to them." Madison similarly asserted that the Constitution assigned to Congress responsibility for "maintenance of harmony and proper intercourse among the States," and provided "provisions for giving due efficacy to all these powers."

One reason that Congress is not limited by a literal, eighteenth-century definition of commerce is that the Constitution's "necessary and proper clause" expands the enumeration beyond its literal language. Both Hamilton and Madison said that the granting of power to the national government to accomplish a general task implies the authority to do what is necessary for success. According to Hamilton, this was as obvious as an axiom of logic: "the *means* ought to be proportioned to the *end*; the persons, from whose agency the attainment of any *end* is expected, ought to possess the *means* by which it is to be attained." Since Congress is empowered to regulate commerce, Hamilton explained that "the government of the Union must be empowered to pass all laws, and to make all regulations which have relation. . . to commerce."

Though Madison would later regret his comments on this subject, he echoed Hamilton's belief that the Constitution conferred implied powers on Congress. He wrote that "wherever the end is required, the means are authorised; wherever a general power to do a thing is given, every particular power necessary for doing it, is included."

In agreement with this position, the Supreme Court has rejected Thomas's restrictive view of the commerce clause and has held that Congress's power over commerce extends to include the regulation of local economic activity such as manufacturing, labor, and agriculture. In the words of Justice Kennedy, Congress can regulate "in the commercial sphere on the assumption that we have a single market and a unified purpose to build a stable national economy." Such an assumption recognizes both the result-oriented approach to federalism in *The Federalist* as well as the extraordinary economic, political, and social changes that have occurred since the essays were written. The Civil War and the Fourteenth Amendment forever altered the relationship between the states and the federal government. Changes in transportation and communication have united the country in ways truly unimaginable at a time when it could take weeks to travel from New York to Virginia. America's twenty-first-century economy is based on interstate and international commerce in ways in which Publius never would have anticipated.

The details of what type of economic activities Madison and Hamilton considered local, therefore, are not as important for us today as understanding why those activities were considered then to be outside Congress's authority. Madison stated that Congress was empowered to regulate those areas "which concern all the members of the republic, but which are not to be attained by the separate provisions of any." From the time *The Federalist* was written to the present, the range of issues which "concern all the members of the republic" has increased dramatically. Merely because an activity was local in the eighteenth century, should not necessarily define the status of its modern counterpart. While Thomas Jefferson had a grand total of forty-three hogs on his farm in the 1780s, Smithfield Foods in 2006 controlled more than fifteen million. Though agriculture was undoubtedly local when *The Federalist* was written, modern agribusiness would certainly seem to affect "all the members of the republic" today.

While they could not envision the changes wrought by modern technology and business structures, both Madison and Hamilton recognized that the line dividing the regulatory authorities of state and federal government might need to change over time. Whether one would be "able to enlarge its sphere of jurisdiction at the expense of the other," wrote Madison, will "depend on the sentiments and sanction of their common constituents"—that is, the people. In determining "the constitutional equilibrium between the General and the State Governments," Hamilton wrote, the people "will hold the scales in their own hands." The Constitution permits the people, "by throwing themselves into either scale," to make one side or the other "preponderate."

Both Madison and Hamilton expected that the American people's initial allegiance would be to those serving in state government, who were likely to be both better known on a personal level and more concerned with local issues. The people's loyalties would change, however, should they find that the national government was better able to serve their needs. If, Madison wrote, "the people should in [the] future become more partial to the federal than to the State governments, the change can only result from such manifest and irresistible proofs of a better administration, as will overcome all their antecedent propensities." If either the federal or the state government proves more worthy, Madison concluded, "the people ought not surely to be precluded from giving most of their confidence where they may discover it to be most due."

The Federalist envisioned a fluid relationship between the federal and state governments. As political scientists John Dinan and Dale Krane have noted, "The structures, finances, and policies of a federal system are not permanently fixed; rather federal arrangements are 'elastic,' and citizens and officials can take advantage of this flexibility as they strive to achieve their policy goals."

But is there a limit to the elasticity? Is there a way to prevent the federal government from obliterating the states? While it may seem difficult to imagine today, both Madison and Hamilton believed that the state militias would enable the effective "exertion of that original right of self-defense" in case the federal legislators ever acted to "betray their constituents."

The image of armed uprisings was very much part of the American consciousness when *The Federalist* was written, less than five years after the end of the War of Independence. Hamilton could expect his readers to understand why, in response to the fear that the national government would establish a standing army, he would be able to assert confidently that no army supported by the federal government could be "formidable to the liberties of the people while there is a large body of citizens, little, if at all, inferior to them in discipline and the use of arms, who stand ready to defend their own rights and those of their fellow-citizens." Madison agreed, citing "the advantage of being armed, which the Americans possess over the people of almost every other nation." Madison stated that if a national army attempted to subvert the people's liberty, it would be defeated by "a militia amounting to near half a million of citizens with arms in their hands," run by their own state governments.

Of course, Madison and Hamilton expected more peaceful resolution of disputes over governmental power. The most obvious remedy in a democracy is that voters, in their election of members of the federal legislature, can remove those who overreach and, as Madison wrote, "by the election of more faithful representatives, annul the acts of the usurpers." The electoral process, while the primary means of controlling government, was always seen by Publius as requiring "auxiliary precautions." To protect the states, the most important precaution was the very structure of the federal government. Madison noted that federal officials were beholden to the states in that "each of the principal branches of the federal government will owe its existence more or less to the favor of the State governments." Under the original Constitution, senators were selected by state legislatures; presidential electors were chosen "in such manner" as each state legislature decides; similarly, the "time, places and manner" of holding elections for members of the House of Representatives was to be prescribed by state legislatures.

While the popular election of senators has decreased the power of state legislatures over the Senate, they can still exert enormous influence over Congress. Members of the House of Representatives are elected from districts drawn by the state legislature, and representatives must remain sensitive to the desires of those who hold the power to carve either a favorable or hostile district for them. Madison's observation is still valid; federally elected officials "feel a dependence" on the state legislature, "which is much more likely to beget a disposition too obsequious than too overbearing towards them."

The Supreme Court has agreed that in certain cases the political process will be able to protect the states from the federal government. In a 1985 case, *Garcia v. San Antonio Metropolitan Transit Authority*, the Court had to decide whether federal minimum wage and overtime laws could be applied to state employees. Put differently, the constitutional question was whether it violated state sovereignty for Congress to tell a state how much to pay its own janitors and bus drivers. The Court upheld the federal law and stated that it was "the structure of the federal government itself," rather than the Court, which was designed to protect state interests. The Court quoted Madison's statement in *Federalist 46* that the federal government "will partake sufficiently of the spirit [of the states], to be disinclined to invade the rights of the individual States, or the prerogatives of their governments." Thus the Supreme Court stated that any protection of state autonomy must stem from the political rather than the legal process.

This turned out to be a rather limited holding. The Court will step in when Congress attempts to regulate areas which have no relation to commerce at all. According to *The Federalist*, federal courts are responsible for ensuring that Congress does not invade the "residuary authorities" of the states. Hamilton said that acts of Congress which exceeded its constitutional authority were "merely acts of usurpation" which "deserve to be treated as such." In Madison's words, it is the job of the judiciary to prevent the "success of the usurpation" if Congress were to exercise power which the Constitution reserved for the states. Madison maintained that "in controversies relating to the boundary between the two jurisdictions, the tribunal which is ultimately to decide, is to be established under the general government."

Starting in 1995, the Supreme Court began to articulate the location of the boundary marking the limits of congressional power under the commerce clause. The first case, *United States v. Lopez*, involved a federal law banning the possession of guns near schools. The issue for the Court was not whether it is a good idea to keep guns away from schools but whether the responsibility for such a law fell to the federal government. In a second case five years later, *United States v. Morrison*, the Court was faced with a federal law prohibiting violence based on gender. The Court struck down both laws, saying that the regulation of intrastate, noneconomic, criminal conduct was a local responsibility of the states and not of Congress. Limiting the powers of Congress, the Court declared, was the only way to preserve "a distinction between what is truly national and what is truly local."

This distinction is consistent with the teachings of *The Federalist*. The federal government can continue to claim what Publius termed "an unconfined authority" to regulate economic activity which affects interstate commerce. At the same time, the Court has reaffirmed the principle that "the general government is not to be charged with the whole power of making and administering laws. . . The subordinate governments, which can extend their care to all those other subjects which can be separately provided for, will retain their due authority and activity."

There is a danger, though, that the Supreme Court will use this principle to limit the ability of the federal government to deal with localized threats to the national environment. In 2001 the Court expressed doubts as to whether the Constitution permits the federal Clean Water Act to regulate activities such as draining or filling a pond in an isolated part of a single state, even when necessary to preserve the habitat of migratory birds which fly across state lines. To determine the constitutionality of environmental laws the Court must appreciate several important changes which have occurred since 1788. Not only were concerns such as endangered species and global warming beyond the imagination of Madison, Hamilton, and the other framers, we now have substantial scientific knowledge on the far-reaching effect that so-called local activities can have. While it may have been true that when this nation began the environment could be "separately provided for" by individual states, the Court will need to recognize that is no longer the case.

While doubting Congress's ability to regulate intrastate activity in the cause of environmental protection, the Court permitted Congress to squelch California's attempt to "extend its care" for its own citizens. California had enacted the Compassionate Use Act, which permitted state residents with certain serious medical conditions to grow small amounts of marijuana for their personal medical use. The Court, in *Gonzales v. Raich,* upheld a federal law prohibiting such use, accepting the federal government's assertion that criminalizing the state-approved use of medical marijuana was an "essential" part of the greater congressional goal of preventing the interstate sale of illegal drugs.

This case actually presented the issue of the rights of the "subordinate governments" even more directly than earlier cases, since California was directly regulating the health and medical care of its citizens, an area traditionally reserved for state supervision. As Justice O'Connor argued in dissent, the state was "concerned for the lives and liberties of their people" and had decided the "difficult and sensitive question of whether marijuana should be available to relieve severe pain and suffering." This appears to be a matter best left to the states. There was no commerce involved, let alone interstate commerce, and no evidence that homegrown medicinal marijuana use would have any significant impact on the national drug market. The Court, in permitting Congress to overrule this local decision, may well have acquiesced in what Publius would have termed "a usurpation of power not granted by the Constitution."

An interesting, related question of power over commerce concerns the role of the federal courts in preventing states from favoring local business by interrupting the flow of interstate commerce. In 2005 the Supreme Court struck down Michigan's attempt to permit only wineries in the state to sell their products directly to state consumers. The Court's ruling was based on the theory that implicit in the Constitution's grant of power to Congress to regulate interstate commerce is a ban on states interfering with interstate commerce. Under the so-called dormant commerce clause, the Court has struck down many state laws which harm out-of-state businesses while favoring local enterprises. Justices Scalia and Thomas have strongly opposed many of these rulings and have argued that the Court should not have the power to strike down state laws simply because they interfere with interstate commerce. Justice Scalia, noting that the actual text of the commerce clause grants power to Congress, declared that the provision "is a charter for Congress, not the courts." Justice Thomas concluded that the dormant commerce clause "has no basis in the text of the Constitution," and "makes little sense," and therefore "cannot serve as a basis for striking down a state statute."

The Federalist indicates that, notwithstanding the lack of clear constitutional language, the current state of the law in which the Court can prevent state protectionist legislation may well be correct. One of the benefits of the Constitution which Hamilton foresaw was the creation of an "unrestrained intercourse between the States themselves" which would "advance the trade of each by an interchange of their respective productions." Madison defended the Constitution by warning that federal regulation of international trade would be imperiled were coastal states "at liberty to regulate the trade between State and State" since they could place duties on goods passing through them on their way to the interior states.

The Federalist envisioned a special role for the federal courts in preventing any individual state from regulating "trade between State and State." When describing the power of the judiciary, Hamilton explained that it was "essential to the peace of the Union" that federal courts have the authority to resolve disputes between a state and a citizen of another state. Hamilton said that under the Articles of Confederation, states had unfairly burdened outsiders and that "fraudulent laws . . . have been passed in too many of the States." He noted that the Constitution specifically barred states from these historic practices, such as issuing paper money for the easy payment of debts or impairing rights under existing contracts. But, he warned, new oppressive laws were likely, because "the spirit which produced them will assume new shapes that could not be foreseen nor specifically provided against." When such state laws do arise, Hamilton concluded, the federal courts must be able to intervene: "Whatever practices may have a tendency to disturb the harmony between the States, are proper objects of federal superintendence and control." To the extent that protectionist legislation disrupts interstate harmony and has the potential to trigger retaliation or the equivalent of trade wars between the states, *The Federalist* supports a role for the federal courts in policing the dormant commerce clause.

It is not as clear that *The Federalist* supports the Court's doctrine in a final area of federalism: the ability of Congress to permit private individuals to sue states for monetary damages. To illustrate this topic, consider the case of Patricia Garrett. She was the director of nursing for the University of Alabama in Birmingham Hospital in 1994, when she was diagnosed with breast cancer. After her subsequent radiation treatment required her to take substantial leave from work, Garrett was demoted. She then sued her employer for lost wages under the federal Americans with Disabilities Act. The Supreme Court ruled that because Garrett's employer was a state hospital, the Constitution barred her from suing for damages under the federal law.

A similar fate befell state probation officers in Maine. When the state government refused to pay its workers overtime required by

the federal Fair Labor Standards Act, the Court held that the probation officers could not sue the state for their back pay.

In holding that the states are protected from these lawsuits by a
doctrine known as sovereign immunity, the Court has relied heavily
on one particular *Federalist* essay. In *Federalist 81*, Hamilton appears
to present a strong argument that states would not be liable to lawsuits in federal court:

> It is inherent in the nature of sovereignty not to be amenable to
> the suit of an individual without its consent. This is the general
> sense, and the general practice of mankind; and the exemption,
> as one of the attributes of sovereignty, is now enjoyed by the
> government of every State in the Union. Unless therefore, there
> is a surrender of this immunity in the plan of the convention, it
> will remain with the States, and the danger intimated must be
> merely ideal. . . . . There is no color to pretend that the State gov-
> ernments would, by the adoption of that plan, be divested of the
> privilege of paying their own debts in their own way, free from
> every constraint but that which flows from the obligations of
> good faith.

In recent years, the Supreme Court has repeatedly quoted this
statement to establish the principle that "federal jurisdiction over
suits against unconsenting states was not contemplated by the
Constitution when establishing the judicial power of the United
States." Hamilton, we are told, "assured the people in no uncertain
terms that the Constitution would not strip the States of sovereign
immunity." Thus, the Court has concluded, Congress cannot use
its commerce clause power to authorize private lawsuits for damages against individual states.

There are two critical problems with the Court's reliance on
Hamilton's essay to reach this conclusion. First, the full context of the
quoted passage reveals that Hamilton was not speaking about congressional power at all; he was solely concerned with states being
forced to pay their contractual debts. Hamilton was responding to the

Anti-Federalist Brutus, who had written a few months earlier that it was "humiliating and degrading" for state governments to have to face private individuals in "suits at law, for the recovery of the debts they have contracted."

When Hamilton asserted that a state is "not to be amenable to the suit of an individual without its consent," he referenced the payment of contractual debts. His language clearly reflects the narrow focus of his comment: "It has been suggested that an assignment of the public securities of one State to the citizens of another, would enable them to prosecute that State in the federal courts for the amount of those securities; a suggestion which the following considerations prove to be without foundation." Thus, the quote that follows, the one the Court repeatedly cites, addresses only the traditional enforcement of a contract by a creditor of the state government; it does not reveal what Hamilton thought would happen were Congress to pass legislation authorizing a private lawsuit.

We can glean a clue, though, from the essay that Hamilton wrote immediately preceding this one, in which he indicated that individuals could indeed sue states in federal courts. Hamilton wrote that the federal courts would hear claims by individuals against states alleging violation of the "privileges and immunity clause," which guarantees that a state treat noncitizens equally with its own. According to Hamilton, to ensure the "equality of privileges and immunities to which the citizens of the Union will be entitled, the national judiciary ought to preside in all cases in which one State or its citizens are opposed to another State or its citizens." A reading of the complete *Federalist* "rather clearly assumes that states are subject to suits by another state's citizens."

A second problem with the Court's reliance on *Federalist 81* is that the essay contains a serious misstatement of history. Much of the power of Hamilton's analysis derives from his statement that the exemption from private lawsuits was "now enjoyed by the government of every State in the Union." As a factual matter, this blanket statement was incorrect. Several states, including Connecticut and Rhode Island, expressly permitted such lawsuits at the time *The Federalist* was written. As the editors of the *Documentary History of the Supreme Court* have concluded, "suits against sovereigns were far from unknown in the eighteenth century."

Despite the Supreme Court's assertions, *The Federalist* cannot provide significant support for the Court's sovereign immunity opinions. The Court's reliance on *The Federalist* for these rulings thus provides a useful reminder of the perils that may arise from using the essays to interpret the Constitution. *The Federalist* is a superb source of constitutional insight, but the modern reader must always strive to understand the context in which it was written. Those who wish to rely on the wisdom of a historical work such as *The Federalist* often must conduct substantially more historical research in order to ensure the accuracy of the propositions they assert.

10

"THE GREATEST OF ALL REFLECTIONS ON HUMAN NATURE"

LASTING LESSONS

*I*n explaining the need for a system of checks and balances, Madison conceded that such protection was based on the assumption that people in general were ambitious and unprincipled in their pursuit of power. "But," he asked rhetorically, "what is government itself, but the greatest of all reflections on human nature?" Most of *The Federalist*'s reasoning is, in fact, based on a conception of the universality of certain human traits and characteristics.

According to Publius, the motivations for people's differing beliefs and conduct can be divided into three broad categories. The most powerful and most destructive of these is "passion," whereby a person's intellect is dominated by prejudice and emotion. Next is "interest," which arises from rational but selfish considerations. Both passion and interest can be harmful to civilized society; when Madison defined faction in *Federalist 10*, he described citizens who were united "by some common impulse of passion, or of interest" which was opposed to either the rights of others or to the interests of the community at large. In contrast to passion and interest is reason, which according to Madison is "timid and cautious." Reason represents the culmination of logical thought combined with either a concern for the needs of others or, at minimum, the recognition that one's own long-term interest requires such concern.

According to Publius, under normal circumstances people act according to their passions and interests rather than their reason. In Hamilton's view, "momentary passions and immediate interest have a more active and imperious control over human conduct than general or remote considerations of policy, utility or justice." That is why, he added, government was instituted at all: "Because the passions of men will not conform to the dictates of reason and justice, without constraint." In the most negative assessment of the human character expressed in *The Federalist,* Hamilton, in predicting violent confrontations should the nation ever be disunited, declared that "men are ambitious, vindictive and rapacious." And, Madison added, we should expect that injustice and violence will arise whenever "the impulse and the opportunity" coincide and "that neither moral nor religious motives can be relied on as an adequate control."

This view of humanity poses an obvious problem for anyone trying to design a government of the people. A country, after all, is nothing more than a collection of individuals, each ruled by his or her passions and interests. Madison observed that "a nation of philosophers is as little to be expected as the philosophical race of kings wished for by Plato." If the government responds to the passions of the people, untold harm may result.

Failure to grasp this fundamental lesson of *The Federalist* may lead to disastrous consequences. In defending the war in Iraq, President Bush declared that democracy is the "best antidote" to extremism. His administration has asserted that the spread of democracy will prevent the "ideologies of hatred" that feed terrorism. Such misplaced faith in democracy ignores the central teaching of *The Federalist* that majoritarian control in and of itself is not a panacea. A truly democratic system empowers the majority "to sacrifice to its ruling passion or interest both the public good and the rights of other citizens." In the words of Madison, "If a majority be united by a common interest, the rights of the minority will be insecure." The democratic principle of "majority rules" provides no check on abuses by the majority. As the victory of extremists such as Hamas in the 2006 Palestinian elections demonstrates, the mere fact that a country is democratic will not protect it from the forces of intolerance, hatred, and violence.

Publius further recognized that some societal situations are so volatile that these destructive forces simply cannot be contained. There may be "mortal feuds," Hamilton wrote, which are caused by either "weighty causes of discontent" or "the contagion of some violent popular paroxysm." These "conflagrations" fueled by widespread hatred and violence can destroy a nation, and "no form of government" can control them. Such situations, according to Madison, are "without the compass of human remedies" and create a risk "for which no possible constitution can provide a cure." It would not take much effort to find situations in the world today that prove the wisdom of this observation.

The Federalist teaches that in addition to a proper form of government, a nation must have a population willing to live together in peace. Americans, according to *The Federalist,* were fortunate to be "one united people" who had just prevailed in their shared revolution by fighting "side by side." There was a common national culture with "each individual citizen everywhere enjoying the same national rights, privileges, and protection," and, perhaps most importantly, each was "enamoured of liberty."

But even a nation so blessed, *The Federalist* repeatedly reminded its readers, will still have to deal with its rapacious neighbors. According to Hamilton, those who predicted an idyllic, peaceful existence for the nation should first consider "that peace or war, will not always be left to our option; that however moderate or unambitious we may be, we cannot count upon the moderation, or hope to extinguish the ambition of others." Accordingly, said Hamilton, "to model our political systems upon speculations of lasting tranquility, is to calculate on the weaker springs of the human character."

Once war arrives, the passions of the people are quickly inflamed. "When the sword is once drawn," Hamilton observed, "the passions of men observe no bounds of moderation." In a warning that has particular resonance for American civil liberties and the war on terrorism, Hamilton described how even a freedom-loving people may be willing to sacrifice their liberties in response to "the continual effort and alarm attendant on a state of continual danger." Such fears, Hamilton concluded, will compel people to support proposals that "have a tendency to destroy their civil and political rights. To be more safe they at length become willing to run the risk of being less free."

If the people have indeed lost their way, if they have been overtaken by what Hamilton termed a "sudden breese of passion," it becomes the task of their servants, the elected officials, to moderate those passions. The obvious problem is that the government is also supposed to represent the people's will. Madison provided an interesting explanation of this seeming contradiction: "It is the reason, alone, of the public that ought to controul and regulate the government. The passions ought to be controuled and regulated by the government."

According to Madison, the people's representatives must pursue what they believe is the best course for society, even if their constituents disagree. Back in the Confederation Congress, Madison himself had demonstrated this principle when he continued fighting for the national impost after the Virginia legislature, which had appointed him, explicitly rejected it. As Publius, he argued similarly that a good representative should be prepared to "suspend the blow meditated by the people against themselves, until reason, justice, and truth can regain their authority over the public mind." Noting the "bitter anguish," felt by a population when they finally come to the realization that they had acted under "the tyranny of their own passions," Madison stated that proper representative government would have prevented "the indelible reproach of decreeing to the same citizens the hemlock on one day and statues on the next." Hamilton agreed that "it is the duty of the persons whom they have appointed to be the guardians . . . to withstand the temporary delusion, in order to give them time and opportunity for more cool and sedate reflection."

But these guardians, like the citizenry itself, are but fallible individuals. Hamilton and Madison knew that society was destined to be ruled by decidedly nonangelic people who were subject to every source of human fallibility. While Madison hoped for representatives who possessed the "wisdom . . . patriotism and love of justice" to discern the true interest of their country, he was well aware that "enlightened statesmen will not always be at the helm." In the first place, he noted, the people may be "misled by the artful misrepresentations of interested men," and put evil people into power. Hamilton voiced similar concern that despotism can come from those who proclaim their concern for the rights of the people most emphatically, whose political trajectory is "commencing Demagogues and ending tyrants."

Hamilton identified yet another problem with elected representatives. Once cloaked with the title of representative, these officials can become overawed at their own sense of self-importance. According to Hamilton, "The representatives of the people, in a popular assembly, seem sometimes to fancy that they are the people themselves; and betray strong symptoms of impatience and disgust at the least sign of opposition from any other quarter."

The lust for power or economic gain can also corrupt elected officials. Madison warned that there was always the likelihood that those in charge of administering any government "may forget their obligations to their constituents, and prove unfaithful to their important trust." It was to remedy "the defect of better motives" that so many constitutional safeguards were implemented.

Along with the intellectual and moral limitations of the individual representative, an additional problem for representative government is the dangers that can flow whenever people gather together. Hamilton declared that it was foolish to expect groups to "act with more rectitude or greater disinterestedness than individuals." Madison warned that it was not difficult for "factious leaders" to incite "sudden and violent passions." The response to such passions is often excessive, Hamilton added, since one of the major restraints on personal misconduct, "regard to reputation," has far less influence "when the infamy of a bad action is to be divided among a number, than when it is to fall singly upon one." Accordingly, he concluded, people in groups all too willingly engage in "improprieties and excesses, for which they would blush in a private capacity."

Madison also was suspicious of "the confusion and intemperance of a multitude." He agreed that it was especially difficult to control the passions of a large group. Madison noted that "the mild voice of reason, pleading the cause of an enlarged and permanent interest, is but too often drowned, before public bodies." A group mentality can lead to evil, regardless of the personal character of the individuals who compose the group. In Madison's arch phraseology, "Had every Athenian citizen been a Socrates; every Athenian assembly would still have been a mob." According to *The Federalist,* much of the constitutional structure was designed to ensure "personal responsibility," that is, to provide a mechanism to hold individual officials "justly and effectually answerable" for their actions. It is perhaps particularly appropriate, then, that according to the *Oxford English Dictionary* the first time in the history of the English language that the word "responsibility" appeared in print is in *The Federalist.*

Yet despite its constant focus on human fallibility, *The Federalist* does not present a pessimistic or fatalistic view. Not all those who govern society will fall victim to the litany of weaknesses Publius has described. Hamilton predicted that, as in the British House of Commons, the American legislature would see a significant number of "independent and public spirited men." Madison, too, believed that there would be people who, when elected to public office, would have the wisdom to "discern the true interest of their country" and the "virtue to pursue, the common good of the society." Heroic leaders, while rare, do exist: "There are men who, under any circumstances will have the courage to do their duty at every hazard."

In a frequently overlooked statement, *The Federalist* refuted the notion that people should be regarded as innately selfish and evil. Hamilton declared that it would be a mistake to attempt to construct a political system on the basis that all people are crooks and thieves: "This supposition of universal venality in human nature is little less an error in political reasoning than the supposition of universal rectitude." Madison agreed that the only proper way to understand people was to appreciate not only the evil, but the virtue they possessed as well: "As there is a degree of depravity in mankind which requires a certain degree of circumspection and distrust, so there are other qualities in human nature which justify a certain portion of esteem and confidence."

Both Hamilton and Madison knew that these positive qualities are what make self-government possible. The fact that the people are permitted to govern themselves, said Hamilton, implied a degree of "virtue and honor among mankind, which may be a reasonable foundation of confidence. And experience justifies the theory." Without such virtue in the people, Madison stated, we would need to assume that "nothing less than the chains of despotism can restrain them from destroying and devouring one another."

The ability to appreciate the contradictions inherent in human nature is essential for those fighting for freedom. This wisdom was well understood by the Philippine opposition leader Benigno Aquino, who was assassinated in 1983. When he departed the United States to return to his homeland to fight the dictatorial rule of Ferdinand Marcos, Aquino declared, "Man's sense of justice makes democracy possible; man's injustice makes it necessary." This duality reflects one of the underlying themes of *The Federalist*. The nature of mankind does not permit flawlessness, but it does allow for excellence. Life's unavoidable defects mean that the quest on which we are embarked when we engage in a political discussion is to find "the GREATER, not the PERFECT, good."

Accordingly, Hamilton and Madison repeatedly urged their readers not to demand perfection of the Constitution. Emphasizing both the difficulty of the task of writing it and the inevitable limitations of the human mind, Madison warned that "a faultless plan was not to be expected." Hamilton explained that he was not surprised that he found some "real force" in the arguments of those opposed to the Constitution since he would "never expect to see a perfect work from imperfect man." It is futile to demand perfection from mere mortals, Madison said, stressing "the necessity of moderating still farther our expectations and hopes from the efforts of human sagacity."

Accepting the inevitable limitation of the human animal leads to several important corollaries about the nature of political debates. Disagreements are a natural outgrowth of both the uniqueness and the fallibility of the individual: "When men exercise their reason, coolly and freely on a variety of distinct questions, they inevitably fall into different opinions, on some of them." The fact that people are imperfect should also lead an honest person to recognize the possibility that he or she might be the one who is wrong. Each of us can be in error, since, in Madison's memorable phrase, "the reason of man continues fallible."

It is not only our reasoning we should question, but our motives. Both Madison and Hamilton cautioned that people may be on the right side for the wrong reason. Hamilton said that even people who advocate the truth may well be inspired by "ambition, avarice, personal animosity, party opposition, and many other motives, not more laudable than these." To Madison, links between selfish motives and intellectual reasoning are to be expected from any person, "as long as the connection subsists between his reason and his self-love." It might well reduce the sense of moral superiority that infects so many modern political debates if advocates for each side recognized that their own supporters, if not the individual advocate, could also be as influenced by greed and self-interested motivations as their opponents.

In the current climate of partisan bickering, it is all too easy to attribute the disagreement of our political opponents to their foolishness or venality. How different was Hamilton's approach in the very first *Federalist* essay, where he acknowledged that there are "wise and good men on the wrong as well as on the right side of questions, of the first magnitude to society." The recognition that even intelligent and decent people can be wrong and that the most rational thought process can be perverted by self-interest should lead, ideally, to a dose of healthy humility in the course of the most heated debates. "This circumstance," Hamilton explained, can "furnish a lesson of moderation to those, who are ever so much persuaded of their being in the right, in any controversy." Antagonists would be far less arrogant if they could remember, as Madison noted, "they themselves also are but men, and ought not to assume an infallibility in rejudging the fallible opinions of others." Such a concession permits a far more reasoned and respectful discussion than is common today.

The Federalist also points the way to more intelligent discussion. One important paradox presented in *The Federalist* is the need to consult the past while planning for the future. Madison and Hamilton were part of a generation of revolutionaries. As Madison wrote, they were the beneficiaries of a nation which had "accomplished a revolution which has no parallel in the annals of human society." The United States was born a country unafraid of the novel and experimental. In one of his more impassioned passages, Madison extolled this national spirit: "Is it not the glory of the people of America, that whilst they have paid a decent regard to the opinions of former times and other nations, they have not suffered a blind veneration for antiquity, for custom, or for names, to overrule the suggestions of their own good sense, the knowledge of their own situation, and the lessons of their own experience?" Yet both Madison and Hamilton believed that the study of history was indispensable. In the second of his *Federalist* essays, Hamilton attempted to establish that republics can be as "addicted to war" as monarchies. For proof, he said, "Let experience the least fallible guide of human opinions be appealed to for an answer." A quick review of the military experiences of Sparta, Athens, Rome, and Carthage provided all the evidence he needed.

To answer the Anti-Federalist attack on the biennial election of members of the House of Representatives—summed up in the maxim "Where annual elections end, tyranny begins"—Madison also turned to historical analysis. "Let us consult experience, the guide that ought always to be followed, whenever it can be found," he declared. For Madison, the fact that elections in England had been held at frequencies ranging from every three to every seven years, and in the colonies from one to seven years, served as "proof, and I conceive it to be a very substantial proof, that the liberties of the people can be in no danger from *biennial* elections."

Historical references fill the pages of *The Federalist,* with the most extensive discussion occurring in essays *18* through *20,* for which

Madison largely reworked his "Ancient and Modern Confederacies."
In page after page, Madison described the governmental structure of
earlier confederacies and how their weaknesses portended similar harm
for the United States if the Constitution was not ratified. Had but the
ancient Greeks been wiser and formed a closer union, Madison wrote,
they would have averted their fate in which "mutual jealousies, fears,
hatreds, and injuries ended in the celebrated Peloponnesian war;
which itself ended in the ruin and slavery of the Athenians, who had
begun it."

At the end of his three essays on historical analysis, Madison
declared that he would "make no apology for having dwelt so long
on the contemplation of these federal precedents." He wanted his
readers to be aware of what had happened in other places at other
times. "Experience is the oracle of truth," Madison said, "and where
its responses are unequivocal, they ought to be conclusive and
sacred." Despite the unqualified nature of this statement, Madison
understood that there were important limitations on the use of history. Sometimes the best that a review of the past can reveal is what
path to avoid. Just because one can ascertain what has previously
failed, does not mean that a more successful approach is obvious.
Such a study can "furnish no other light than that of beacons, which
give warning of the course to be shunned, without pointing out that
which ought to be pursued."

An even more serious constraint on the use of history is that modern
circumstances might be so different from those in the past that a perfect
analogy may be impossible. Madison admitted that the American government and experience differed from his historical examples and that
these differences "render extreme circumspection necessary in reasoning
from the one case to the other." Still, he concluded, "after allowing due
weight to this consideration" there were "many points of similitude
which render these examples not unworthy of our attention."

Madison provided one final thought about why history merited
attention when he explained his opposition to a proposal that would
make it easy to call for constitutional conventions. Repeated changes
in the Constitution, he said, would lead the people to assume that

their founding document was fundamentally flawed and thus to question whether the most current iteration was destined to be replaced. Constantly altering the Constitution, he said, would "deprive the government of that veneration which time bestows on every thing."

One benefit of a study of history, then, is that it reveals those items that time has shown deserve our respect and reverence. Perhaps that is why *The Federalist* is still read, consulted, and relied on two hundred and twenty years after its initial publication.

ACKNOWLEDGMENTS

There are many, many people to whom I am deeply indebted for their help with this book. First, I want to thank my extraordinary agent Geri Thoma, of the Elaine Markson Agency, who, among many other vital lessons, taught me how to write a book proposal which someone would want to read. I also want to thank my editor at Basic Books, Bill Frucht, who had a vision of this book that was substantially sharper than my own. His editorial assistant, Courtney Miller, provided endless amounts of wise comments, creative suggestions, supportive encouragement, and, when needed, astute criticism. Sandra Beris, my project editor, and Tom Lacey, my copyeditor, have worked tirelessly on the production end of the project.

There were also many people who gave me information and advice throughout my writing of the book. From the University of Baltimore School of Law, I want to thank both my former dean, Gil Holmes, and my current dean, Phil Closius, for their support and encouragement. I also want to thank Eric Easton, Tim Sellers, and Charles Tiefer for their valued comments.

I also want to acknowledge the many people at George Washington University Law School who helped me in my research: Michael Abramowicz, Jerry Barron, Naomi Cahn, Bradford Clark, Bob Cottroll, Thomas Dienes, Ira Lupu, Maeva Marcus, Lawrence Mitchell, Todd Peterson, Peter Smith, Dalia Tsuk Mitchell, and Art Wilmarth. I also benefited greatly from discussing my book with the following members of the faculty of the University of Maryland School of Law: Danny Citron, Mark Graber, Helen Norton, Peter Quint, Meredith Render, and Max Stearns.

Among the many others who took the time to share their expertise, I would like to single out Robert Frankel, David Mattern, and Calvin Johnson for particular thanks.

This project could not have been completed without the strong support of the library staff at the University of Baltimore School of Law. I want to give my special thanks to the queen of interlibrary loans, Bijal Shah, as well as Harvey Morrell, Bob Pool, Elizabeth Rhodes, and Will Tress.

I have also been fortunate to have had a cadre of wonderful research assistants from both George Washington University Law School and the University of Baltimore School of Law: Cynthia Brougher, Katherine Doyle, Itta Englander, Talley Kovacs, and Cheryl Lyons. To each of you, I want to thank you for both the help you provided and the enthusiasm which you brought to your work.

Many people also provided me with emotional support and encouragement throughout this long process. I want to thank Professors Jerry Barron, Bob Cottroll, Roger Fairfax, Michal Higginbotham, and Max Stearns, as well Bob and Adrienne Berger and the RPM Discussion Group. I also want to thank my parents, Jack and Marian, for all the support they have always shown me, as well as for teaching me the importance of reading and the value of virtue.

My sons, William and Andrew, have not only served as invaluable sounding boards, but as continual sources of inspiration and joy. Finally I want to thank my wife, Lesly Berger, for everything.

WORKS FREQUENTLY CITED

DHRC: *The Documentary History of the Ratification of the Constitution* (Merrill Jensen, John P. Kaminski, and John P. Saladino, et al., eds. Wisconsin Historical Society, 1976–2005).

JCC: *Journals of the Continental Congress, 1774–1789* (Government Printing Office, 1904–1937).

LDC: *Letters of Delegates to Congress, 1774–1789* (Paul H. Smith et al., eds. Library of Congress, 1976–2000).

LMCC: *Letters of Members of the Continental Congress* (Edmund C. Burnett, ed. Carnegie Institution of Washington, 1921–1936).

PAH: *The Papers of Alexander Hamilton* (Harold Syrett, ed. Columbia University Press, 1961–1987).

PGW-CS: *The Papers of George Washington—Confederation Series* (Dorothy Twohig, ed. University of Virginia Press, 1992–1997).

PJM: *The Papers of James Madison* (William T. Hutchinson, Robert A. Rutland, and Charles F. Hobson et al., eds. University of Chicago Press, 1962–1977; University of Virginia Press, 1977–1991).

PTJ: *The Papers of Thomas Jefferson* (Julian Boyd and John Catanzariti, eds. Princeton University Press, 1950–1990).

RDC: *The Revolutionary Diplomatic Correspondence of the United States* (Francis Wharton, ed. Government Printing Office, 1889).

Storing: *The Complete Anti-Federalist* (Herbert J. Storing and Murray Dry, eds. University of Chicago Press, 1981).

WJM: *The Writings of James Madison* (Gaillard Hunt, ed. G. P. Putnam's Sons, 1900).

NOTEWORTHY EDITIONS
OF *THE FEDERALIST*

The Federalist has been republished hundreds of times since its initial publication in book form in 1788. What follows is a list of the editors and publishers of some noteworthy, easy-to-find editions. Note that when the book is published under a name other than *The Federalist*, I have place the title in brackets.

Bailyn, Bernard. Washington: Library of Congress, 1998.

Cooke, Jacob E. Middletown, Conn.: Wesleyan University Press, 1961.

Earle, Edward Meade. New York: Modern Library, 1941.

Gideon, Jacob. (1818). Reprinted and edited by George W. Carey and James McClellan. Indianapolis: Liberty Fund, 2001.

Hamilton, John C. Philadelphia: J. B. Lippincott & Co., 1866. Full text available online through Google book search.

Pole, J. R. Indianapolis: Hackett, 2005.

Rakove, Jack N. [The Federalist: The Essential Essays] Boston: Bedford/St. Martin's, 2003.

Rossiter, Clinton L. [The Federalist Papers] New York: New American Library, 1961.

Rossiter, Clinton L., and Charles R. Kesler. [The Federalist Papers] New York: Mentor, 1999.

Scigliano, Robert. New York: Modern Library, 2000.

Wills, Garry. New York: Bantam Books, 1982.

Notes on the Title

Although the essays which Madison and Hamilton wrote were actually called *The Federalist,* their work has been most commonly referred to as the Federalist Papers. While this title had been used periodically since the nineteenth century, it entered the general American vocabulary in 1961 when Clinton Rossiter used it as the title for his edition of the essays. Since even the Library of Congress refers to them as the Federalist Papers, I chose to use that name in my subtitle.

The title for this book had already been chosen when I came across an essay by one of the great political scientists, Martin Diamond, in which he stated that Madison and Hamilton undertook to "make democracy safe for the world" ("The Federalist," in William Schambra, ed., *As Far as Republican Principles Will Admit,* 44). With deep respect to Dr. Diamond, I decided to keep the phrase in my subtitle.

NOTES

PREFACE

x   **When Thomas Jefferson recommended:** Thomas Jefferson, "Minutes of the Board of Visitors, University of Virginia" (Mar. 4, 1825), in Merrill D. Peterson, ed., *Thomas Jefferson, Writings* (1984), 479.

x   **Chief Justice John Marshall wrote:** *Cohens v. Virginia*, 19 U.S. 264, 418 (1821).

x   **Theodore Roosevelt would praise:** Theodore Roosevelt, "Speech before the Liberal Club" (Sept. 10, 1895), in Albert B. Hart and Herbert R. Ferleger, *Theodore Roosevelt Cyclopedia*, 2nd ed. (1989), 179.

xiv   **"his personal and political enemy":** John Beckley to James Madison, Sept. 2, 1792, *PJM* 14:355–356.

INTRODUCTION

1   **"Pray, if it is not a secret":** George Washington to Henry Knox, Feb. 5, 1788, *PGW-CS* 6:88.

1   **"greatness is acknowledged":** Archibald Stuart to James Madison, Jan. 14, 1788, *WJM* 5:54. At the time of this letter, Stuart did not know he was writing to one of the authors.

1   **Thomas Jefferson would declare:** Thomas Jefferson to James Madison, Nov. 18, 1788, *PTJ* 14:188.

2   **"If our suspicions of the author":** Alexander Hamilton to James Madison, Apr. 3, 1788, *PAH* 4:644.

2   **"the Author must be Hamilton":** James Kent to Nathaniel Lawrence, Dec. 21, 1787, *DHRC* 14:363.

2   **"Madison has the principal hand":** Walter Rutherfurd to James Rutherfurd, Jan. 22, 1788, *DHRC* 13:489.

2   **"attributed to the joint efforts":** Henry Knox to George Washington, Feb. 20, 1788, *PGW-CS* 6:150.

2   **"The inclosed is the first number":** Alexander Hamilton to George Washington, Oct. 30, 1787, *PAH* 4:306.

3   **"I will not conceal from you":** James Madison to George Washington, Nov. 18, 1787, *PJM* 10:253–254.

3   **publishers John and Archibald McLean:** "Advertisement," *New York Independent Journal*, Mar. 22, 1788, in *DHRC* 20:880–881.

3   **"there were probably not a dozen":** Douglass Adair, "The Authorship of the Disputed Federalist Papers," in Trevor Colbourn, ed., *Fame and the Founding Fathers* (New York: W. W. Norton, 1974), 73.

3   **"brought reason to its present maturity":** Robert Palmer, *The Age of the Democratic Revolution: A Political History of Europe and America, 1760–1800* (Princeton, N.J.: Princeton University Press, 1959), 54.

3   **Madison, who was siding with France:** See Ralph Louis Ketcham, *James Madison* (New York: Macmillan, 1971), 339.

4   **"met with your father's":** John C. Hamilton, ed., *The Federalist* (Philadelphia: J. B. Lippincott & Co., 1866), xcii.

4   **Hamilton arrived at the law office:** Ibid., xcv.

4   **Coxe immediately wrote back:** Tench Coxe to James Madison, Sept. 26, 1788, *PJM* 11:268–269.

5   **Madison gave printer Jacob Gideon:** In the preface to this edition, Gideon wrote that "the publisher of this volume has been so fortunate as to procure from Mr. Madison the copy of the work which that gentleman had preserved for himself, with corrections of the papers, of which he is the author, in his own hand." George W. Carey and James McClellan, eds., *The Federalist* (1818) (Indianapolis: Liberty Fund, 2001), lxxxv.

5   **"It was furnished to him by me":** Elizabeth Fleet, ed., "Madison's 'Detatched' Memoranda," *Wm. and Mary Q.* 3 (1946): 534–568.

5   **Douglass Adair, an historian:** Adair, 49–57.

6   **"has fairly reached the dignity":** Henry Cabot Lodge, "Introduction," in Lodge, ed., *The Works of Alexander Hamilton* (New York: Putnam, 1904), xv.

6   **Adair reviewed the content:** Adair, 93–102.

6   **Later, Jacob Cooke reviewed:** Jacob E. Cooke, "Introduction," in Cooke, ed., *The Federalist*, 1st ed. (Middletown, Conn.: Wesleyan University Press, 1961).

6   **"a dispute that has not":** Robert Scigliano, "Introduction," in Scigliano, ed., *The Federalist: A Commentary on the Constitution of the United States* (New York: Modern Library, 2000).

6   **Stylometrics is based:** Erica Klarreich, "Bookish Math," *Science News*, Dec. 20, 263: 392–394.

6   **The first statistical study:** Frederick Mosteller and David L. Wallace, *Applied Bayesian and Classical Inference: The Case of the Federalist Papers,* 2d ed. (New York: Springer-Verlag, 1984).

6   **In 2003, a computer scientist:** Glenn Fung, "The Disputed Federalist Papers: SVM Feature Selection via Concave Minimization," *Proceedings of the 2003 Conference on Diversity in Computing*, Atlanta, 2003, 42–44. A thoughtful critic of stylometry noted

that most of the earlier studies of *The Federalist* based their analyses on versions down-loaded from the Internet. While it was easy to perform computer analysis on these versions, they differed from Madison's and Hamilton's original, unedited essays. Joseph Rudman, "The Non-Traditional Case for the Authorship of the Twelve Dis-puted 'Federalist' Papers: A Monument Built on Sand," *Association for Computers and the Humanities and the Association for Literary and LinguisticComputing* (2005). http://mustard.tapor.uvic.ca:8080/cocoon/ach_abstracts/proof/paper_54_rudman.pf. In response, two computer scientists did a study using the 1788 edition of *The Feder-alist* and reached the same conclusion. See Shlomo Levitan and Shlomo Argamon, "Fixing the Federalist: Correcting Results and Evaluating Editions for Automated At-tribution," *Proc. Digital Humanities* (July 2006): 323–328.

CHAPTER 1

11   **They first met:** Despite some uncertainty, historians now assume that Hamilton was born on Jan. 11, 1755. See Ron Chernow, *Alexander Hamilton* (New York: Penguin, 2004), 17.

11   **the "little lion":** John Torrey Morse, *The Life of Alexander Hamilton* (Boston: Little, Brown, 1882), 26.

11   **His private secretary:** Edward Coles to Hugh Blair Grigsby, Dec. 23, 1854, quoted in Stuart Leibiger, *Founding Friendship: George Washington, James Madison, and the Creation of the American Republic* (Charlottesville: University Press of Virginia, 1999), 6. Edward Coles served as President Madison's private secretary from 1809 to 1815.

12   **One woman called him:** Garry Wills, *James Madison* (New York: Times Books, 2002), 19; Margaret Smith to Mrs. Boyd, Aug. 17, 1828, in Gaillard Hunt, ed., *The First Forty Years of Washington Society: Portrayed by the Family Letters of Mrs. Samuel Harrison Smith* (Washington, D.C.: Scribner, 1906), 235.

12   **Thomas Jefferson wrote a congratulatory letter:** Thomas Jefferson to James Madi-son, Apr. 14, 1783, *PJM* 6:459.

12   **"Your inference on that subject":** James Madison to Thomas Jefferson, Apr. 22, 1783, *PJM* 6:481.

12   **John Adams spoke disapprovingly:** John Wood and John Henry Sherburne, *The Suppressed History of the Administration of John Adams* (New York: B. Franklin, 1834), 387 (quoting an 1808 letter from Adams to William Cunningham).

12   **"a superabundance of secretions":** John Adams to Benjamin Rush, Nov. 11, 1806, in Alexander Biddle, *Old Family Letters: Copied from the Originals for Alexander Biddle Series A-B* (Philadelphia: J. B. Lippincott, 1892), 118.

12   **"My heart overflows":** Alexander Hamilton to Elizabeth Schuyler, Aug. 1, 1780, *PAH* 2:397–400. He also wrote a poem, "Answer to the Inquiry Why I Sighed," which ended with the couplet:
"No joy unmixed my bosom warms
But when my angel's in my arms."

According to the editor of Hamilton's papers, the exact date this poem was written is not known. *PAH* 2:352.

12 **"I seldom write":** Alexander Hamilton to Angelica Church, Dec. 7, 1787, *PAH* 4:374–375.

13 **He immersed himself:** Adair, ed., "James Madison's Autobiography," *Wm. and Mary Q.* 2:191, 197.

13 **"During the whole time":** Wills, 35.

13 **"a bastard brat":** John Adams to Benjamin Rush, Jan. 25, 1806, in John A. Schutz and Douglass Adair, eds., *The Spur of Fame: Dialogues of John Adams and Benjamin Rush, 1805–1813* (Indianapolis: Liberty Fund, 2000), 47–48.

13 **He would later pass:** Chernow, 169.

13 **Madison served only briefly:** Jack Rakove, *James Madison and the Creation of the American Republic,* 3rd ed. (New York: Pearson/Longman, 2007), 11.

13 **"the unsettled state":** Adair, 199.

14 **Madison was elected a delegate:** Rakove, *Creation of the American Republic,* 11–12.

14 **Madison convinced the convention:** Ibid., 15.

14 **"recommend themselves to the voters":** Adair, 199.

14 **Madison lost the election:** Rakove, *Creation of the American Republic,* 17.

14 **he became the captain:** Chernow, 72, 85.

14 **"principal and most confidential aide":** Washington Irving, *The Life of George Washington* (New York: G. P. Putnam, 1859), 5:312.

14 **Washington refused:** Chernow, 149.

15 **"I met him":** Alexander Hamilton to Philip Schuyler, Feb. 18, 1781, *PAH* 2:563–568.

15 **"I was always determined":** Ibid.

15 **He was finally given command:** Chernow, 162.

15 **"We have it":** John C. Hamilton, *History of the Republic of the United States of America As Traced in the Writings of Alexander Hamilton and of His Contemporaries,* 3rd ed. (New York: D. Appleton & Co., 1868) 268.

15 **During this decisive battle:** Broadus Mitchell, "Hamilton's Quarrel with Washington, 1781," *Wm. and Mary Q.* 12 (1945): 199–216.

15 **he was elected:** See "Warrant to Alexander Hamilton to Receive Money as Continental Receiver for the State of New York," Apr. 15, 1782, *PAH* 374–375 and 145n3; Nathan Schachner, *Alexander Hamilton* (New York: D. Appleton-Century, 1946), 146–148.

16 **The Articles of Confederation were sent:** Jack Rakove, *The Beginnings of National Politics: An Interpretive History of the Continental Congress* (Baltimore, Md.: Johns Hopkins University Press, 1982), 185. According to Rakove, there is no evidence that "Americans were deeply interested in discussing the nature of the union they were forming. No pamphlets were written about them, and when the Articles were printed in American newspapers they appeared only as another scrap of news."

16 **the currency was trading:** Michael W. Evans, "Foundations of the Tax Legislation Process: The Confederation, Constitutional Convention, and First Revenue Law," *Tax Notes,* Jan. 21, 1991, 283.

17 **"restore the credit"**: George Washington to John Jay, Apr. 1779, in William Jay, ed., *The Life of John Jay: With Selections from His Correspondence and Miscellaneous Papers* (J. & J. Harper, 1833), 45–47.

17 **State tax collection officers**: E. James Ferguson, *The Power of the Purse* (Chapel Hill: University of North Carolina Press, 1961), 141.

17 **"confers on Congress"**: Robert Morris to the President of Congress, Feb. 11, 1782, *RDC* 5:152–159.

17 **"I look forward"**: James Madison to Thomas Jefferson, Mar. 27, 1780, *PJM* 2:6.

17 **Madison argued that Congress**: James Madison to Thomas Jefferson, Apr. 16, 1781, *PJM* 3:71–72; "Proposed Amendment of Articles of Confederation," Mar. 12, 1781, *PJM* 3:17–19.

17 **"to employ the force"**: May 2, 1781, *JCC* 20:470.

18 **"to vest a power"**: Feb. 3, 1781, *JCC* 19:111–112. Congress did not expect to raise enough money under this plan to carry on all the business of the government. The more modest goal was to raise enough money to pay the interest and, eventually, the principal on the national debt, which would then permit Congress to obtain more European loans. See Rakove, *Beginnings of National Politics*, 283.

18 **"He who opposes"**: Robert Morris to the governors of the states, Jan. 3, 1782, *RDC* 5:84–85. Although directed to the governors of the three states that had not passed the impost, the letter was sent to all thirteen state governors.

18 **"repugnant to the liberty"**: "Letter from the lower house of the assembly of the state of Rhode Island and Providence Plantations to the President of Congress," Nov. 30, 1782, *JCC* 23:788.

18 **"Col. Hamilton took his seat"**: James Madison to Edmund Randolph, Nov. 26, 1782, *LDC* 19:420–423.

18 **Unlike Madison**: Charles A. Cerami, *Young Patriots: The Remarkable Story of Two Men, Their Impossible Plan and the Revolution That Created the Constitution* (Naperville, Ill.: Sourcebooks, 2005), 18.

19 **Congress accepted Hamilton's proposal**: Dec. 6, 1782, *JCC* 23:771.

19 **within a few days had written**: Ibid., 798.

19 **If a government is given**: *Federalist 23* (Hamilton). The quotations from the essays of *The Federalist* are taken from the version edited by Jacob E. Cooke in 1961.

19 **Madison's home state of Virginia**: Samuel Osgood to John Lowell, Jan. 6, 1783, *LDC* 19:540. See also Edmund Randolph to James Madison, Dec. 13, 1782, *PJM* 5:399.

19 **"The most intelligent members"**: James Madison's "Notes of Debates," Dec. 24, 1782, *LDC* 19:501–502.

20 **retired soldiers were not receiving**: See Ferguson, 156.

20 **"The uneasiness of the soldiers"**: Apr. 29, 1783, *JCC* 24:291.

20 **"all prospect of obtaining continental funds"**: Alexander McDougall and Mathias Ogden to Henry Knox, Feb. 8, 1783, in Jared Sparks, ed., *The Writings of George Washington* (Boston: Little, Brown, 1855), 3:552–554.

21 **"The army," he wrote, "have swords"**: Gouverneur Morris to John Jay, Jan. 1, 1783, in Jared Sparks, *The Life of Gouverneur Morris* (Boston: Gray & Bowen, 1832), 248–249.

21 **General Alexander McDougall, had been:** *Journals of the Provincial Congress, of the State of New-York* I:321 (Feb. 23, 1776). See generally, *PAH* 1:182.

21 **The second, Colonel Mathias Ogden:** See *PAH* 1:182; Willard Sterne Randall, *Alexander Hamilton: A Life* (New York: HarperCollins, 2003), 276–277.

21 **"intimate friend" of Hamilton's:** Forrest McDonald, *Alexander Hamilton: A Biography* (New York: Norton, 1979), 46; see also Randall, 276–277.

22 **"to unite the influence":** Alexander McDougall to Henry Knox, Jan. 9, 1783, *LMCC* 7:14.

22 **The officers, using the advice:** Richard Kohn, "The Inside History of the Newburgh Conspiracy: America and the Coup d'Etat," *Wm. and Mary Q.* 27 (1970): 187, 188–189.

22 **"at least a mutiny":** James Madison's "Notes of Debates," Jan. 13, 1783, *LDC* 19:580.

22 **"permanent provision for the public debts":** Robert Morris to the President of Congress, Jan. 24, 1783, *RDC* 6:228–229.

22 **"This letter made a deep":** James Madison's "Notes of Debates," Jan. 24, 1783, *LDC* 19:610.

22 **"funds adequate to the object":** Ibid., 611.

22 **"even Rhode Island":** Jan. 25, 1783, *LDS* 19:616.

23 **Congress began its funding:** The debate summarized here can be found at James Madison's "Notes of Debates," Jan. 27–28, 1783, *LDC* 19:616–621, 624–631.

24 **"told him privately":** James Madison's "Notes of Debates," Jan. 29, 1783, *LDC* 19:635–647.

25 **"despondence & timidity":** James Madison to Edmund Randolph, Feb. 4, 1783, *LDC* 19:656–657.

25 **"we seem only to have gone":** James Madison to Edmund Randolph, Feb. 11, 1783, *LDC* 19:675–676.

25 **Colonel Brooks was given two letters:** The letter from Gouverneur Morris states explicitly that it was being given to Brooks. The fact that the Hamilton letter was also given to Brooks was described in George Bancroft, *History of the Formation of the Constitution of the United States of America* (New York: D. Appleton, 1882), 67. There is some disagreement about the exact dates of the letters. The editors of the *Papers of Alexander Hamilton* believe Hamilton's letter was written on February 13, which would have meant it was impossible for Brooks to deliver it, as Brooks arrived at Newburgh on that day. *PAH* 3:255n1.

25 **"The army may now influence":** Gouverneur Morris to Henry Knox, Feb. 7, 1783, *LMCC* 7:34–35.

25 **Hamilton's first direct communication:** James Thomas Flexner, *The Young Hamilton* (Boston: Little, Brown, 1978), 402.

25 **"The great desideratum":** Alexander Hamilton to George Washington, Feb. 13, 1783, *PAH* 3:253–255.

26 **"on a very confidential subject":** Alexander Hamilton to George Washington, Mar. 5, 1783. *PAH* 3:282–283.

26 **"It would at this day":** George Washington to Alexander Hamilton, Mar. 4, 1783, *PAH* 3:277–279.

26   **Gouverneur Morris was similarly:** See, e.g., Gouverneur Morris to General Greene, Feb. 15, 1783, in Sparks, *The Life of Gouverneur Morris*, 250–251.

26   **"When Soldiers advance":** General Greene to Gouverneur Morris, Apr. 3, 1783 (ibid., 251).

27   **Congress learned on February 13:** Elias Boudinot to Nathanael Greene, Feb. 13, 1783, *LDC* 19:688.

27   **In response, several of the delegates:** The meeting is described in James Madison's "Notes of Debates," Feb. 20, 1783, *LDC* 19:717–719.

28   **"a revenue established within each State":** James Madison's "Notes of Debates," Feb. 21, 1783, *LDC* 19:720–723.

28   **Madison wrote the committee's report:** Mar. 6, 1783, *JCC* 24:170–174.

28   **He later attempted:** Mar. 20, 1783, *JCC* 24:198–202.

28   **"a country that tramples":** Irving, *Life of George Washington*, 4:408.

29   **"I will feed them":** Notes on a conversation with Duer, in Rufus King, *The Life and Correspondence of Rufus King* (1894; New York: Da Capo, 1971), 1:621–622. William Duer, who provided the quote of Morris's statement, was later invited by Hamilton to work with him on *The Federalist*. See chap. 4.

29   **The seventy-by-forty-foot wood:** Kohn, 190.

30   **"Gentlemen, you will permit me":** Quoted in William Safire, *Lend Me Your Ears: Great Speeches in History* (New York: W. W. Norton, 1997), 96.

30   **"unshaken confidence":** Apr. 29, 1783, *JCC* 24:310.

30   **"There was something so natural":** Samuel Shaw and Josiah Quincy, *The Journals of Major Samuel Shaw: The First American Consul at Canton: With a Life of the Author* (Boston: Wm. Crosby and H. P. Nichols, 1847), 104.

30   **"There is something very mysterious":** George Washington to Alexander Hamilton, Mar. 12, 1783, *PAH* 3:286–288. That same day, Washington also wrote a letter to Joseph Jones with virtually the same accusatory language. George Washington to Joseph Jones, Mar. 12, 1783, in W. B. Allen, ed., *George Washington: A Collection* (Indianapolis: Liberty Classics, 1988), 241.

30   **"the propriety of uniting":** Alexander Hamilton to George Washington, Mar. 17, 1783, *PAH* 3:290–293.

31   **Washington replied that even:** George Washington to Alexander Hamilton, Apr. 4, 1783, *PAH* 3:315–316.

31   **Hamilton's defense is an interesting:** Alexander Hamilton to George Washington, Apr. 8, 1783, *PAH* 3:317–321.

31   **Congress finally approved:** "Address to the States," Apr. 26, 1783, *JCC* 24:277–285.

32   **"the rigid adherence":** James Madison to Thomas Jefferson, Apr. 22, 1783, *LDC* 20:202–203.

32   **Congress authorized Madison:** "Address to the States," Apr. 26, 1783, *JCC* 24:277–285.

32   **Congress approved a compromise proposal:** *JCC* 24:362–364 (May 26, 1783).

32   **a small contingent from Pennsylvania:** Kenneth Bowling, "New Light on the Philadelphia Mutiny of 1783: Federal-State at the Confrontation at the Close of the War for Independence," *The Pennsylvania Magazine of History and Biography*, 101 (Oct. 1977): 419–450.

33   **"to obtain Justice":** James Madison's "Notes of Debates," June 19, 1783, *LDC* 20:346n3.

33   **"such measures as they should":** Ibid., 345.

33   **Boudinot named Hamilton:** Bowling, *New Lights,* 419–450. The other two members of the committee were Richard Peters of Pennsylvania and Oliver Ellsworth of Connecticut.

33   **"some outrage should":** Hamilton's "Report to Congress," July 1, 1783, *JCC* 24:241. The difficulty Hamilton faced in trying to convince Pennsylvania to stop the mutinous soldiers can readily be appreciated by observing that Pennsylvania's secretary of state was none other than John Armstrong, who had written the mutinous Newburgh Address just three months earlier. Armstrong, in fact, recorded in the minutes of the Executive Council that he had concluded that, in dealing with the approaching soldiers, "the language of invitation, and good humour became more advisable than any immediate exertion of authority." Pennsylvania Council Minutes 13:603, quoted in James Madison's "Notes of Debates," June 19, 1783, *LDC* 20:346n4.

33   **Hamilton responded by ordering:** Committee of Congress to William Jackson, June 19, 1783, *LDC* 20:344.

34   **"we shall instantly let in":** Letter to President Dickinson, June 21, 1783, in Varnum Collins, *The Continental Congress at Princeton* (Princeton, N.J.: The University Library, 1908), 20.

34   **It is unclear whether he had simply heard:** There is great uncertainty over the precise timing of the events of Saturday, June 21. Most interestingly, it is unclear whether the troops had already surrounded the State House when Boudinot called for Congress to meet. In a letter to George Washington, Boudinot said that he had issued the call at one PM, but in a later writing says the meeting was called at twelve thirty. James Madison wrote that the troops arrived after Congress was called into session (James Madison's "Notes of Debates," June 21, 1783, *LDC* 20:352). Kenneth Bowling has concluded that Madison's account was inaccurate. Bowling, 431–434.

34   **called for an emergency meeting:** Elias Boudinot's "Draft Statement on the Mutiny" [est. June 26, 1783], *LDC* 20:367–368.

34   **"without some outrages":** James Madison's "Notes of Debates," June 21, 1783, *LDC* 20:351–353.

34   **"spirituous drink from the tipling houses":** Ibid.

34   **"offering a mock obstruction":** Ibid.

34   **"supporting the dignity":** June 21, 1783, *JCC* 24:410.

35   **"vigorous measures should be taken":** Hamilton's "Report to Congress," July 1, 1783, *JCC* 24:416–417.

35   **The officers whom the soldiers:** Ibid.

35   **"were getting Drunk very fast":** Elias Boudinot's "Draft Statement on the Mutiny," *LDC* 20:368.

35   **Hamilton wrote his formal statement:** Committee of Congress to Elias Boudinot, June 24, 1783, *LDC* 20:362. It is noteworthy that although there were three members of this committee, only Hamilton and Oliver Ellsworth signed this statement, and Ellsworth's signature was subsequently crossed out.

35 **Boudinot quickly issued an order:** Elias Boudinot's "Draft Statement on the Mutiny," *LDC* 20:368.

35 **"This Town is too small":** Eleazer McComb to Nicholas Van Dyke, June 30, 1783, *LDC* 20:379.

35 **"small scattered village":** Charles Thomson to Hannah Thomson, July 4, 1783, *LDC* 20:396–397.

35 **"a single accommodation for writing":** James Madison to Thomas Jefferson, Sept. 20, 1783, *LDC* 20: 694–696.

35 **"we are exceedingly crowded":** James Madison to James Madison Sr., Aug. 30, 1783, *LDC* 20:606. See also James Madison to Edmund Randolph, Aug. 30, 1783, *LDC* 20:607.

36 **"The grand Sanhedrin":** Broadus Mitchell, *Alexander Hamilton: Youth to Maturity* (New York: Macmillan, 1957), 322.

36 **"soured the climate":** Chevalier de la Luzerne to Charles Gravier de Vergennes, Nov. 1, 1783, in Bowling, 419–450n66.

36 **the "ship Congress":** (Philadelphia) *Independent Gazetteer*, Aug. 1783, quoted in Bowling, 419–450.

36 **"I wish Jersey":** Elias Boudinot to Elisha Boudinot, June 23, 1783, *LDC* 20:356.

36 **Hamilton, in contrast:** See, for example, the resolution Hamilton wrote on July 2, 1783, stating that Congress should return to Philadelphia after the mutiny was suppressed. *JCC* 24:424.

36 **"hoped perhaps that a military demonstration":** Bowling, *New Lights,* 419–450.

37 **"vindicate myself from the insinuation":** Alexander Hamilton to James Madison, July 6, 1783, *PAH* 3:412. This was the second version of a letter to Madison that Hamilton wrote. An earlier, longer letter was written on June 29 but apparently was never sent. *PAH* 3:408–409.

37 **"opposed to the removal":** James Madison to Alexander Hamilton, Oct. 16, 1783, *LDC* 21:67.

37 **As historian Jack Rakove has noted:** Rakove, *Beginnings of National Politics,* 324.

38 **"I should write Coll Hamilton":** Robert Livingston to James Madison, July 15, 1783, *PAH* 3:415.

38 **"we have talked over the subject":** Alexander Hamilton to Robert Livingston, July 23, 1783, *PAH* 3:414.

Chapter 2

39 **she sent Madison a letter:** See Ralph Louis Ketcham, *James Madison* (New York: Macmillan, 1971), 110, and "Madison's Unrequited Love: How a Long Island Teen Broke the Future President's Heart," http://www.newsday.com/community/guide/li-history/ny-history-hs427a,0,6961091.story.

39 **"the uncertain state":** James Madison to Thomas Jefferson, Aug. 11, 1783, *PJM* 7:268. See also Irving Brant, *James Madison: The Nationalist* (Indianapolis: Bobbs-Merrill, 1948), 284–287.

40 **"rocking the cradle":** Alexander Hamilton to Marquis de Lafayette, Nov. 3, 1782, *PAH* 3:191–193.

40 **He declined requests:** Alexander Hamilton to Samuel Loudon, Dec. 27, 1783, *PAH* 3:481.

40 **New York's Confiscation Act:** The formal name of the Confiscation Act was "An Act for the Forfeiture and Sale of the Estates of Persons who have adhered to the Enemies of this State, and for declaring the Sovereignty of the People of this State, in respect to all Property within the same," New York assembly, 3rd sess. 1779, chap. XXV, passed Oct. 22, 1779.

40 **The Trespass Act:** "An Act for granting a more effectual relief in cases of certain trespass," New York assembly, 6th sess 1783, chap. XXXI, passed Mar. 17, 1783.

40 **"great number of useful citizens":** Alexander Hamilton to George Clinton, June 1, 1783, *LDC* 20:292–296.

40 **"there shall be no future confiscations":** The Paris Peace Treaty of Sept. 3, 1783.

41 **"the disaffected were secured":** Hamilton, *Second Letter from Phocion,* April 1784, *PAH* 3:530–558.

41 **The most important case:** Hamilton's briefs for this case and the opinion of the court can be found in Julius Goebel Jr., ed., *The Law Practice of Alexander Hamilton* (New York: Columbia University Press, 1964), 1:336–419. For an excellent discussion of this case, see William Michael Treanor, "Judicial Review Before Marbury," *Stan. L. Rev.* 58 (2005): 455.

42 **"the Mayor's court have assumed":** "Open Letter from Melancton Smith and Others," *The New York Packet and the American Advertiser,* Nov. 4, 1784, reprinted in Goebel, 1:313.

42 **"subversive of all law":** New York Assembly resolution, *N.Y. Assembly J.*, Oct. 4–Nov. 29, 1784, reprinted in Goebel, 1:312.

43 **he presented his "Memorial":** James Madison, "Memorial and Remonstrance against Religious Assessments," June 20, 1785, *PJM* 8:298–304.

44 **"met with the approbation of the Baptists":** Elizabeth Fleet, ed., "Madison's 'Detatched Memoranda,' *Wm. and Mary Q.* 3 (1946): 555–557.

44 **"the Channel of conveyance":** George Washington to Thomas Johnson, July 20, 1770, in Dorothy Twohig and Philander Chase, eds., *The Papers of George Washington.* Colonial Series. (Charlottesville: University of Virginia Press, 1992), 8:360.

45 **"opening and extending":** George Washington Ward, *Early Development of Chesapeake and Ohio Canal Project* (Baltimore: Johns Hopkins University Press, 1899), 15. Virginia formally chartered the corporation in October 1784, Maryland in early 1785. For a discussion of the history of the Potomac Company, see Douglas Littlefield, "The Potomac Company: A Misadventure in Financing an Early American Internal Improvement Project," *The Business History Review* 58 (1984): 562–585.

45 **He drafted a resolution":** "Resolutions Authorizing an Interstate Compact on Navigation and Jurisdiction on the Potomac," Dec. 28, 1784, *PJM* 8:206–207. See also Lance Banning, *The Sacred Fire of Liberty: James Madison and the Founding of the Federal Republic* (Ithaca, N.Y.: Cornell University Press, 1995), 51.

45 **neglected to inform:** See Mervin B. Whealy, "'The Revolution Is not Over': The Annapolis Convention of 1786," *Maryland Historical Magazine* 81 (Fall 1986): 228, 229.

45   **They decided to proceed:** George Mason to James Madison, Aug. 9, 1785, *PJM* 8:337–338. See generally, Jeff Broadwater, *George Mason: Forgotten Founder* (Chapel Hill: University of North Carolina Press, 2006), 153–156.

45   **George Washington, eager to ensure:** Gaillard Hunt, *The Life of James Madison* (New York: Doubleday, Page & Co., 1902), 111–112.

45·   **"the most amicable spirit":** James Madison to Thomas Jefferson, Apr. 27, 1785, *PJM*: 8:265–270.

46   **Madison enthusiastically supported:** "Act Ratifying the Chesapeake Compact with Maryland, ca. 24–26 Dec. 1785," *PJM* 8:457–461. The Virginia Senate approved the bill on Dec. 30, 1785. James Madison to James Monroe, Dec. 30, 1785, *PJM* 8:465–466.

46   **"advantage should be taken":** Edward Coles, "Letters of Edward Coles," *Wm. and Mary Q.*, 7 (1927): 158–173.

46   **Madison added a provision:** "Resolution Calling for the Regulation of Commerce by Congress," Nov. 14, 1785, *PJM* 8:413–414.

46   **"I think it better to trust":** James Madison to George Washington, Dec. 9, 1785, *PJM* 8:438–440.

46   **"the requisite augmentation":** Although there has been some dispute over whether Madison was really the person who initially proposed what would become the Annapolis convention, most historians now credit Tyler. See *PTJ* 9:204–208; *PJM* 8:470–471. Joseph Jones had written to Madison earlier, on June 12, 1785, suggesting "a Convention of Deputies from the several States for the purpose of forming Commercial regulations." Joseph Jones to James Madison, June 12, 1785, *PJM* 8:292–293. There is no record of Madison indicating approval of Jones's proposal at that time.

46   **"will have fewer enemies":** James Madison to George Washington, Dec. 9, 1785, *PJM* 8:438–440.

47   **Bill for Establishing:** James Madison to Thomas Jefferson, Jan. 22, 1786, *PJM* 8:472, 473–474.

47   **"general meeting of Commssrs":** Ibid., 472, 476–477.

47   **"examine the relative situations":** Resolution of the General Assembly of Virginia, Jan. 21, 1786, reprinted in *PTJ* 2:545; *PJM* 8:471.

48   **"kept in reserve":** James Madison to Thomas J. Wharton, August 1827, in Philip R. Fendall, ed., *Letters and Other Writings of James Madison* (1865) 3:586–587.

48   **"a highly respected member":** Ibid., and James Madison to Noah Webster, Mar. 10, 1826, in Noah Webster, *Collection of Papers on Political Literary and Moral Subjects* (New York: B. Franklin, 1968), 172.

48   **he also wrote to James Monroe:** James Madison to James Monroe, Jan. 22, 1786, *PJM* 8:483–484.

48   **Edmund Randolph informed Madison:** Edmund Randolph to James Madison, Mar. 1, 1786, *PJM* 8:494–495.

48   **"thought prudent to avoid":** James Madison to Thomas Jefferson, Mar. 18, 1786, *PJM* 8:501–502.

49   **"I almost despair":** Ibid.

49   **"far from entertaining sanguine expectations":** James Madison to James Monroe, Mar. 14, 1786, *PJM* 8:497–498.

49   **"sent to the state legislature":** J. C. Hamilton, *History of the Republic of the United States of America As Traced in the Writings of Alexander Hamilton and of His Contemporaries* (New York: D Appleton & Co., 1857), 374–375.

49   **"They would have revolted":** James Madison to James Monroe, Mar. 19, 1786, *PJM* 8:504–506.

50   **"Many Gentlemen both within":** James Madison to Thomas Jefferson, Aug. 12, 1786, *PJM* 9:93–99.

50   **"It is regretted by many":** George Washington to Marquis de Lafayette, May 10, 1786, *PGW-CS* 4:41, 42.

50   **Hamilton, however, was intent:** Henry Cabot Lodge, *Alexander Hamilton* (Boston: Houghton Mifflin, 1898), 53.

50   **"calling immediately a Convention":** Alexander Hamilton to James Duane, Sept. 3, 1780, *PAH* 2:400–418.

50   **"general Convention of the States":** Resolution of the New York Legislature, July 20, 1783, *PAH* 3:110–113. According to biographer Ron Chernow, it is likely that Hamilton, who was not then even in the legislature, drafted this resolution. Chernow, *Alexander Hamilton* (New York: Penguin, 2004), 171.

50   **According to the minutes:** James Madison's "Notes of Debates," Apr. 1, 1783, *LDC* 20:127.

51   **"constitutional imbecility":** "Hamilton's Defense of Congress," July 1783, *PAH* 3:426–430.

51   **propose "such alterations":** "Hamilton's Draft Resolution," July 1783, *PAH* 3:420–426.

51   **"the present opportunity for obtaining":** Egbert Benson, *Memoir Read Before the Historical Society of the State of New-York, December 31, 1816* (Henry C. Sleight, printer, 2nd ed. 1825), 98.

51   **"partiality in a commercial convention":** J. C. Hamilton, 374–375.

51   **go to "some trouble":** Hugh Williamson to Governor Caswell, Oct. 27, 1786, in Walter Clark, ed., *The State Records of North Carolina* (1900), 18:772–774; see also Samuel A. Ashe, *Biographical History of North Carolina from Colonial Times to the Present* (Greensboro, N.C.: C. L. Van Noppen, 1908).

51   **"with as accurate a state":** Edmund Randolph to James Madison, June 12, 1786, *PJM* 9:75.

52   **"occasional purchase of rare":** James Madison to Thomas Jefferson, Mar. 16, 1784, *PJM* 8:6, 11.

52   **"whatever may throw light":** James Madison to Thomas Jefferson, Mar. 16, 1784, *PJM* 8:6, 9–11.

52   **"such books as may be":** James Madison to Thomas Jefferson, Apr. 27, 1785, *PJM* 8:265–266.

52   **"be deprived of the amusement":** James Madison to Thomas Jefferson, Jan. 22, 1786, *PJM* 8:472–481.

52 **"had the leisure":** James Madison to Thomas Jefferson, Mar. 18, 1786, *PJM* 8:500–501.

52 **"Ancient & Modern Confederacies":** *PJM* 9:4–24.

53 **"When I consider the men":** Stephen Higginson to John Adams (July 1786), in Thomas W. Higginson, *The Life and Times of Stephen Higginson* (Boston: Houghton Mifflin, 1907), 72–73.

53 **"no reasonable expectations of advantage":** Theodore Sedgwick to Caleb Strong, Aug. 6, 1786, *LDC* 23:436. These sentiments were echoed by Rufus King: "It is doubtful what the real sentiments of Virginia are on the question of commercial powers. This is certain, that the proposition for the Annapolis convention, which originated in the Assembly of Virginia, did not come from the persons favorable to a commercial system common to all the States, but from those, who in opposition to such a general system, have advocated the particular regulations of individual States." Rufus King to Jonathan Jackson, June 11, 1786, *LDC* 23:352–354.

54 **"give umbrage to Congress":** 60 Votes and Proceedings of the Senate of the State of Maryland, 1st Sess 84–85 (Mar. 8, 1785). *See also* Whealy, 231.

54 **"But what a dreadful":** Edmund Randolph to James Madison, June 12, 1786, *PJM* 9:75.

54 **"one hundred beds":** See Broadus Mitchell, *Alexander Hamilton: Youth to Maturity* (New York: Macmillan, 1957), 360; Donald Jackson and Dorothy Twohig, eds., *The Diaries of George Washington* (Charlottesville: University Press of Virginia, 1979), 6:102.

55 **Although there had been some limited:** For example, in Apr. 1784, Hamilton wrote Madison, seeking his support for the request of a Joseph Francois Perault, who was asking for reimbursement from Virginia for supplies and money furnished to Virginian troops during the Revolutionary War. Hamilton wrote, "I have assured him that he will find in you a friend to justice and an able advocate for whatever ought and is possible to be done for him." Alexander Hamilton to James Madison, Apr. 18, 1784, *PJM* 8:19. According to the editors of Madison's papers, Perault's claims were apparently denied by "Governor Harrison in Council." *PJM* 8:19.

55 **While some later commentators:** About a month after the Annapolis convention, the French chargé d'affaires, Louis Otto, wrote, "The authors of this proposition had no hope, nor even desire, to see the success of this assembly of commissioners, which was only intended to prepare a question much more important than that of commerce." Louis Otto to Charles Gravier, Count de Vergennes, Oct. 10, 1786, in Albert Bushnell Hart, *American History Told by Contemporaries* (London: Macmillan, 1901), 185, 186–187.

55 **"the prospect of a sufficient":** James Madison to Ambrose Madison, Sept. 8, 1786, *PJM* 9:120.

55 **only twelve commissioners:** They were George Read, John Dickinson, and Richard Bassett from Delaware; Abraham Clarke, William C. Houston, and James Schureman from New Jersey; Alexander Hamilton and Egbert Benson from New York; Tench Coxe from Pennsylvania; and Edmund Randolph, James Madison, and St. George Tucker from Virginia.

55 **Tench Coxe of Pennsylvania attempted:** "Tench Coxe to the Virginia Commissioners at Annapolis," Sept. 13, 1786, *PJM* 9:124–126. After being told that the commissioners would not "enter into any discussion of this business," Coxe wrote a formal letter to Madison, Randolph, and Tucker, asking them to tell the Virginia legislature about Pennsylvania's nondiscriminatory trade policy and the violation of the "great principles and Spirit of Union," created by the trade policies of the other states. See also Jacob E. Cooke, *Tench Coxe and the Early Republic* (Chapel Hill: University of North Carolina Press, 1978), 94–98.

56 **"inexpedient for this Convention":** This quote is from Egbert Benson's handwritten "minutes" of the Annapolis convention. They are incomplete and filled with cross-outs and some illegible writings. They can be found in the Thomas Addis Emmet Collection in the Rare Books and Manuscripts Division, Center for the Humanities, The New York Public Library [hereafter "Benson's minutes"]. This quote is on p. 9399. According to Benson, he was on an earlier committee which recommended a second committee be created to draft the final report.

56 **Edmund Randolph was named:** Brant, *James Madison: The Nationalist*, 385. Randolph's draft can be located in the Library of Congress's collection of Madison's papers, available on-line at http://hdl.loc.gov/loc.mss/mjm.02_0752_0753.

56 **Almost immediately, Hamilton managed:** Madison would later write, "Mr. Hamilton was certainly the member who drafted the address." James Madison to Noah Webster, Oct. 12, 1804, *WJM* 165. Similarly, Benson later wrote that "the draft was by Mr. Hamilton, although not formally one of the committee." Benson, *Memoir.*

56 **In the 1780s:** See Rakove, *Creation of the American Republic,* 61. ("Only the rare assembly in eighteenth-century America managed to muster a quorum on time.")

56 **"to communicate to the Convention":** Letter from Thomas Cushing, Francis Dana, and Samuel Breck to Alexander Hamilton and Egbert Benson, Sept. 10, 1786, *PAH* 3:685.

56 **"papers and other information":** Hugh Williamson to Governor Caswell, Oct. 27, 1786, Walter Clark, ed., *The State Records of North Carolina* (1900) 18:772–774. See also Ashe, *A Biographical History of North Carolina.*

57 **The late-arriving commissioners:** The stories of their journeys are taken from the letters they wrote to their respective state governors. See Letter from Thomas Cushing, Samuel Breck, and Francis Dana to Governor Bowdoin, Sept. 16, 1786; Hugh Williamson to Governor Caswell, Oct. 27, 1786; Ashe, *The State Records of North Carolina,* 18:772–774.

57 **Robert C. Livingston, had virtually:** Ibid.

57 **Suspicions were raised:** Louis Otto to Charles Gravier, Count de Vergennes, Oct. 10, 1786, in Hart, 186–187.

57 **had "hastily" acted:** Federal Farmer I, Oct. 8, 1787, in Storing 2:223, 227. It is unknown who wrote this pamphlet, but many historians believe it was Richard Henry Lee, of Virginia. The complete title of the pamphlet was "Observations Leading to a Fair Examination of the System of Government Proposed by the Late Convention; and to Several Essential and Necessary Alterations to it, In a Number of Letters from the Federal Farmer to the Republican."

57   **The most likely reason:** See, e.g., Norman Risjord, *Chesapeake Politics, 1781–1800* (New York: Columbia University Press, 1978), 266, who concluded, "The Annapolis convention then quickly adjourned lest new delegates arrive who wanted to enter some caveats on the record." Some historians do not see such a result-oriented motive in the decision not to wait for the late-arriving commissioners. See, e.g., Whealy, 235.

57   **"more radical reform":** James Madison to Noah Webster, Oct. 12, 1804. Robert Bruger, ed. Papers of James Madison, Secretary of State Series (Charlottesville: University of Virginia Press, 1986), 8:159–162.

57   **"Since my Journey to Annapolis":** Tench Coxe to James Madison, Sept. 9, 1789. U.S. Department of State, *Documentary History of the Constitution of the United States of America, 1786–1870* (Washington, D.C.: GPO, 1905), 5:204.

57   **"all such Measures as may appear":** The phrase "cement the union" appears in Benson's report, "Benson's minutes," p. 3999; Benson, unlike Hamilton, was on the committee charged with drafting the report.

58   **It appears that many:** Broadus Mitchell, *Alexander Halilton: Youth to Maturity* (New York: Macmillan, 1957), 361–363.

58   **"You had better yield":** John C. Hamilton, *The Life of Alexander Hamilton* (1841), 376.

58   **He permitted his draft:** Proceedings and Report of Commissioners, *DHRC* 1: 181–185.

59   **"an infinity of circumlocutions":** Louis Otto to Charles Gravier, Count de Vergennes, Oct. 10, 1786, in Hart, 186–187.

CHAPTER 3

61   **termed "a gamble":** Jack Rakove, *The Beginnings of National Politics: An Interpretive History of the Continental Congress* (Baltimore: Johns Hopkins University Press, 1982), 375.

61   **"The recommendation from the Meeting":** James Madison to Thomas Johnson, Dec. 4, 1786, *PJM* 9:189–192.

61   **Madison presented a bill:** "Bill Providing for Delegates to the Convention of 1787," *PJM* 9:163–164.

61   **"I smelt a rat":** Hugh Blair Grigsby, *The History of the Virginia Federal Convention of 1788 With Some Account of Eminent Virginians of That Era Who Were Members of the Body.* Vol. I (Richmond: Virginia Historical Society, 1890), 32, n2.

62   **Congress received the report:** Sept. 20, 1786, *JCC* 31:678–680.

62   **it appointed a committee:** Oct. 11, 1786, *JCC* 31:770.

62   **"in the opinion of Congress":** Feb. 21, 1787, *JCC* 32:73–74.

62   **"expressed a strong dislike":** Letters of H.G. XI, Mar. 6, 1789, *PAH* 5:289–290.

62   **"render the next session":** Nathan Schachner, "Alexander Hamilton Viewed by His Friends: The Narratives of Robert Troup and Hercules Mulligan," *Wm. and Mary Q.* 4 (1947): 203, 216.

63   **Congress requested that Clinton:** Ferguson, *Power of the Purse* (Chapel Hill: University of North Carolina Press, 1961), 239–240.

63   **"singularly forced" reasoning:** "First Speech on the Address of the Legislature to Governor George Clinton's Message," Jan. 19, 1787, *PAH* 4:3–12.

63   **Hamilton warned that rejection:** "Remarks on an Act Granting Congress Certain Imposts and Duties," Feb. 15, 1787, *PAH* 4:71–92.

63   **met with "contemptuous silence":** "Rough Carver," *New York Daily Advertiser*, Sept. 3, 1787, reprinted in *DHRC* 19:36.

63   **the impost was defeated:** "Remarks on an Act Granting Congress Certain Imposts and Duties," Feb. 15, 1787, *PAH* 4:71–92 (71n, 92n). Madison referred to the New York vote as the "definitive veto on the Impost." Madison to George Washington, Feb. 21, 1787, *PJM* 9:285.

63   **Hamilton introduced a resolution:** "Resolution on the Appointment of Delegates," Feb. 26, 1787, *PAH* 4:101.

63   **the legislature voted to send:** *DHRC* 19:xlvii.

63   **"tried integrity and abundant experience":** "Remarks on a Motion that Five Delegates be Appointed," Apr. 16, 1787, *PAH* 4:148.

63   **"likely to be a clog":** James Madison to George Washington, Mar. 18, 1787, *PJM* 9:315.

63   **"prevailing mood of uncertainty":** Rakove, *Beginning of National Politics,* 379.

64   **The first of these letters:** James Madison to Thomas Jefferson, Mar. 19, 1787, *PJM* 9:317–322.

64   **expect "leading propositions":** James Madison to Edmund Randolph, Apr. 8, 1787, *PJM* 9:368–371.

65   **Madison's last letter:** James Madison to George Washington, Apr. 16, 1787, *PJM* 9:382–387.

66   **he was also completing:** "Vices of the Political System of the United States," *PJM* 9:348–357. The editors of the *Papers of James Madison* estimate that he wrote this study intermittently between February and April 1787 (*PJM* 9:346).

66   **By now his reading had expanded:** This point is discussed in both Douglass Adair, "That Politics May be Reduced to a Science: David Hume, James Madison, and the Tenth Federalist," in Trevor Colbourn, *Fame and the Founding Fathers* (New York: W. W. Norton, 1974), 138–151, and Garry Wills, *Explaining America: The Federalist* (New York: Penguin, 1982), 21–22.

66   **Madison's extraordinary accomplishment:** For a wonderful analysis of Madison's creativity in his writing of "Vices of the Political System of the United States," see Jack Rakove, "Thinking Like a Constitution," *Journal of the Early Republic* 24 (Spring 2004): 1–26.

67   **Madison was putting together:** As Rakove has noted, "Vices" is "a political actor's own working paper, revealing his recognition or understanding of the necessity of being able to translate conclusions derived from observation into theorized statements that explain why those observations only exemplify deeper structural problems that can be predicted to recur under circumstances not yet experienced." "Thinking Like a Constitution," 10.

67   **They would meet every day:** George Mason to George Mason Jr., May 20, 1787, in Max Farrand, ed., *The Records of the Federal Convention of 1787* (New Haven, Conn.: Yale University Press, 1911) 3:22–23.

67 **More important, his major proposals:** Banning, *The Sacred Fire of Liberty: James Madison and the Founding of the Federal Republic* (Ithaca, N.Y.: Cornell University Press, 1995), 115. The text of the Virginia plan can be found at *PJM* 10:15–17.

68 **Madison obtained for himself:** James Madison, "Preface to Debates in the Convention of 1787," reprinted in Farrand's Records 3:539. It is believed that Madison wrote this preface during the 1830s.

68 **Madison kept the most complete notes:** While many people consider Madison's notes, "the primary source of contemporary understanding of what transpired during the Convention" (Rakove, *Beginnings of National Politics,* 399), some have questioned the accuracy of Madison's account. See, e.g., William Winslow Crosskey, "The Ex-Post-Facto and the Contracts Clauses in the Federal Convention: A Note on the Editorial Ingenuity of James Madison," *U. Chi. L. Rev.* 35 (1968): 248.

68 **"almost killed him":** Farrand's Records 3:550, quoting H. B. Grigsby, *History of Virginia Federal Convention of 1788* (Richmond: Virginia Historical Society, 1890), 1:95n.

68 **They held long conversations:** Alexander Hamilton to Edward Carrington, May 26, 1792, *PAH* 11:426–445.

68 **A particularly intriguing indication:** Worthington Chauncey Ford, "Alexander Hamilton's Notes in the Federal Convention of 1787," *The American Historical Review* 10 (Oct. 1904): 97, 98.

68 **"The way to prevent":** Both Ford and the editors of Hamilton's papers agree that the date of this entry was June 1. Ibid., "Notes Taken in Constitutional Convention," *PAH* 4:161.

69 **including the phrase "enlarge the sphere":** Farrand's Records 1:134.

69 **"of the opinion that the leading":** Robert Yates and John Lansing to Governor Clinton, July 10, 1787, *Elliot's Debates* 1:480.

69 **William Paterson of New Jersey proposed:** Farrand's Records 1:242–245.

69 **"We would sooner submit":** Ibid., 1:242n.

69 **He began by declaring":** It is not surprising that a speech of five hours would be difficult to capture accurately. There are many different versions available, from the notes of Madison, Robert Yates, John Lansing Jr., and Rufus King. In addition, Hamilton wrote an outline of notes in preparation for his speech. See *PAH* 4:178–211. Madison later said that Hamilton "happened to call on me when putting the last hand to it, and who acknowledged its fidelity, without suggesting more than a very few verbal alterations which were made." James Madison, "Preface to Debates in the Convention of 1787," reprinted in Farrand's Records 3:539. The quotes from Hamilton's speech are from Madison's notes.

70 **According to Robert Yates:** Farrand's Records 1:301.

70 **"has been praised by everybody":** Robert Yates, *Secret Proceedings and Debates of the Convention Assembled at Philadelphia, in the Year 1787, for the Purpose of Forming the Constitution of the United States of America* (Richmond, Va.: W. Curtiss, 1839), 158.

70 **Madison delivered his longest speech:** Farrand's Records 1:314.

71 **"persuasion, rational argument":** Jack Rakove, "The Great Compromise: Ideas, Interests, and the Politics of Constitution Making," *Wm. and Mary Q.* 44 (1987): 424–457.

71   **On June 29 he left Philadelphia:** *PAH* 4:223n3. See also Alexander Hamilton to Thomas Mullett, July 23, 1787, *PAH* 4:232 (describing preparations for trial).

71   **"I am seriously":** Alexander Hamilton to George Washington, July 3, 1787, *PAH* 4:223–225.

71   **"no opposition . . . should discourage":** George Washington to Alexander Hamilton, July 10, 1787, *PAH* 4:225.

71   **Hamilton did not return:** *PAH* 4:235n1.

71   **"ground of compromise":** Farrand's Records 2:9.

72   **"the negative on the laws":** Ibid., 2:27.

72   **"Overall, of seventy-one":** Forrest McDonald, *Novus Ordo Seclorum: The Intellectual Origins of the Constitution* (Lawrence: University Press of Kansas, 1985), 208–209.

72   **Despite his setbacks:** One commentator decided that a better moniker for Madison was "the Godfather of the Constitution." See Bruce G. Kauffmann, "James Madison: Godfther of the Constitution," http://www.earlyamerica.com/review/summer97/madison.html. .

72   **"I hazard an opinion":** James Madison to Thomas Jefferson, Sept. 6, 1787, *PJM* 10:163–164.

72   **"to let me know":** Alexander Hamilton to Rufus King, Aug. 20, 1787, *PAH* 4:235.

72   **"his dislike of the Scheme":** Farrand's Records 2:524 (Sept. 6, 1787).

73   **Mason's opposition came primarily:** Ibid., 2:587–588 (Sept. 12, 1787).

73   **"I confess that there":** Ibid., 2:641–642 (Sept. 17, 1787). The elderly Franklin actually wrote out these words and had them read aloud by fellow Pennsylvania delegate James Wilson.

73   **"might do infinite mischief":** Farrand's Records 2:645–646 (Sept. 17, 1787).

74   **He managed to seize the quill:** Constitution of the United States, *PAH* 4:274.

CHAPTER 4

75   **In a letter published:** "To the Daily Advertiser," July 21, 1787, in *PAH* 4:229–232. The letter was originally published anonymously, but Hamilton's identity was discovered quickly, and he later wrote that he had left his name with the newspaper from the beginning in case anyone wanted to discover the letter's author.

75   **"certain Aristocratic junto":** "Rusticus," *New-York Journal*, Sept. 13, 1787, *DHRC* 14:24–26. "A Republican," *New Youk Journal*, Sept. 6, 1787, *DHRC* 19:16–20.

76   **The most vituperative:** Inspector wrote three essays that appeared in the *New-York Journal* on Sept. 20, Oct. 4, and Oct. 18, 1787. The first is reprinted in *DHRC* 19:31–33.

76   **"This I confess":** Alexander Hamilton to George Washington, Oct. [8–10] 1787, *DHRC* 19:34–35.

76   **"when the situation":** George Washington to Alexander Hamilton, Oct. 18, 1787, PAH 4:284–285.

76   **"Least, however, you may":** Edward Carrington to James Madison, Sept. 23, 1787, *LDC* 24:435–436.

77   **"mere act of Congress":** James Madison to George Washington, Sept. 30, 1787, *PJM* 10:179–181.

77 **"to the several legislatures":** *JCC* 33:549 (Sept. 28, 1787).

77 **"unsuspecting goodness and zeal":** Oct. 5, 1787, Herbert J. Storing, *The Complete Anti-Federalist* (Chicago: University of Chicago Press, 1981), 2:136, 137–138.

78 **Two who appeared:** Historians are not certain about the identities of either writer. It is suspected that Federal Farmer was Richard Henry Lee and that Brutus was Hamilton's fellow New York delegate to the convention, Robert Yates. See Storing, 2:214–216, 358.

78 **"The president is connected":** Federal Farmer III, Oct. 10, 1787, Storing, 2:234, 237.

78 **"A free republic":** Oct. 18, 1787, Storing, 2:363, 368.

78 **"the new Constitution":** Alexander Hamilton to George Washington, Oct. [8–10], 1787, *DHRC* 19:34–35.

78 **"in general been pretty":** James Madison to Ambrose Madison, Oct. 11, 1787, *PJM* 10:191–192.

78 **"the Newspapers here begin":** James Madison to George Washington, Oct. 18, 1787, *PJM* 10:197.

78 **"a new Combatant":** James Madison to Edmund Randolph, Oct. 21, 1787, *PJM* 10:199–200.

78 **"the artillery of its opponents":** Alexander Hamilton to George Washington, Oct. 30, 1787, *PAH* 4: 306–307.

79 **needed to be in Albany:** Jacob E. Cooke, "Alexander Hamilton's Authorship of the 'Caesar' Letters," *Wm. and Mary Q.* 17 (1960): 78–85. We know that Hamilton had left New York City before October 1 since Madison had written to Tench Coxe on that date that "Col. Hamilton happens not to be in the City at present." James Madison to Tench Coxe, Oct. 1, 1787, *PJM* 10:183.

79 **the seventy-foot vessel:** For a good description of the type of boat Hamilton sailed on, see William E. Verplanck and Moses W. Collyer, *Sloops of the Hudson River* (New York: G. P. Putnam's Sons, 1908).

79 **It was there that Hamilton:** According to Hamilton's son, the outline for *The Federalist* was written while Hamilton was returning to New York City. J. C. Hamilton, *History of the Republic of the United States As Traced in the Writings of Alexander Hamilton and of His Contemporaries* (New York: D. Appleton, 1857), 369. According to Hamilton's widow, the outline was written while Hamilton was traveling north. Katherine Schuyler Baxter, *A Godchild of Washington: A Picture of the Past* (London: F. T. Neely, 1897), 219.

79 **Hamilton selected Publius:** See, generally, Martin Diamond, *The Federalist,* in William A. Schambra, ed., *As Far as Republican Principles Will Admit* (Lanham, Md.: National Book Network, 1992), 38; Douglass Adair, "A Note on Certain of Hamilton's Pseudonyms," *Wm. and Mary Q.* 12 (1955): 282–297. Hamilton had actually used the pseudonym Publius several years earlier. In 1778, he had written three essays as Publius, castigating future Supreme Court Justice Samuel Chase for allegedly working with merchants to raise the price of flour being purchased for French troops who had arrived to fight the British. Ron Chernow, *Alexander Hamilton* (New York: Penguin, 2004), 118.

79   **"It was rumoured that he"**: Livy, *The History of Rome* (Whitefish, Mont.: Kessinger, 2004), 1:64. Livy, whose full name was Titus Livius, lived from 59 BCE to 17 CE.

80   **The terms "Federalist" and "Anti-Federalist"**: Thus, in 1786, Madison wrote, "I am somewhat apprehensive . . . that Col. Mason may not be fully cured of his Antifederal prejudices." James Madison to James Monroe, May 13, 1786, *PJM* 9:54–55. Bernard Bailyn traces the distinction between "fæderal" and "anti-fæderal" to a 1786 writing by Noah Webster, *The Debate Over the Constitution* (New York: Viking Press, 1993), 1:1049.

80   **First, they claimed, with some validity**: See, e.g., W. B. Allen and Gordon Lloyd, eds., "Preface" to *The Essential Antifederalist* (Lanham, Md.: University Press of America, 1985), describing the "democratic nationalism" of the Federalists. Allen and Lloyd do not believe that the Federalists' use of the term was illegitimate, a view shared by Storing. See Herbert Storing, *What the Anti-Federalists Were For*, in Storing 1:9–10.

80   **"the odious term anti-Federalists"**: "Aristocrotis," *The Government of Nature Delineated*, in Storing 3:196, 209.

80   **"if any names are applicable"**: Federal Farmer VI, Dec. 25, 1787, Storing 2:256, 259.

80   **"Their names then ought"**: Statement of Elbridge Gerry, *Annals of Congress* (Aug. 15, 1789), 1:759.

80   **one of "candor"**: *See* Albert Furtwangler, "Strategies of Candor in the Federalist," *Early American Literature* 14 (1979): 91, 107, describing Hamilton's pledge of candor as one to "present genuine, forthright insights about the nature and promise of the Constitution."

81   **"I do not mean"**: Federal Farmer I, Oct. 8, 1787, Storing 2:223, 224. See also Cato I, Sept. 27, 1787, Storing 2:104, 105. He began his argument: "Without directly engaging as an advocate for this new form of national government, or as an opponent. . . .'"

82   **"consist of twenty Numbers"**: Archibald McLean to Robert Troup, Oct. 11, 1788, in Allan McLane Hamilton, *The Intimate Life of Alexander Hamilton* (New York: Scribner's, 1910), 82. Some historians spell the printer's name M'Lean." *DHRC* 13:491.

82   **he was "warmly pressed"**: Gouverneur Morris to William Hill Wells, Feb. 24, 1815, in Jared Sparks, *The Life of Gouverneur Morris* (Boston: Little, Brown, 1855), 3:338–339.

82   **William Duer, an old friend**: For an excellent biography of Duer, see Robert F. Jones, *The King of the Alley: William Duer, Politician, Entrepreneur, and Speculator, 1768–1799* (Philadelphia: American Philosophical Society, 1992). See also Stanley Elkins and Eric McKitrick, *The Age of Federalism* (New York: Oxford University Press, 1993), 272–276.

82   **Not only was she wealthy**: Charles R. Geisst, *Wall Street: A History* (New York: Oxford University Press, 1997), 12.

82   **"tho' intelligent & sprightly"**: Elizabeth Fleet, ed., "Madison's 'Detatched Memoranda,'" *Wm. and Mary Q.* 3:534–568.

83   **"diminution of State authority"**: "Philo-Publius I" in *DHRC* 19:148–150.

83   **It was published**: Ibid. It was published in the *New York Daily Advertiser* on Oct. 30, 1787.

83   **"first inside trader":** Geisst, 12.

83   **At the same time:** Richard Brookhiser, *Alexander Hamilton, American* (New York: Free Press, 1999), 86.

84   **"the outdoor talk of Col. Duer":** Noah Webster to James Greenleaf, Sept. 20, 1789, in Emily Ellsworth Ford, ed., *Notes on the Life of Noah Webster* (New York: B. Franklin, 1912), 207.

84   **"in the style of a nobleman":** William Parker Cutler and Julia Perkins Cutler, eds., *Life, Journals and Correspondence of Rev. Manasseh Cutler, LL. D* (Cincinnati: R. Clarke & Co., 1888), 241.

84   **"a coat of arms":** John C. Miller, *Alexander Hamilton: Portrait in Paradox* (New York: Harper, 1959), 244.

84   **"not less than fifteen":** Cutler, 241.

84   **"gambling scoundrels":** Thomas Jefferson to Thomas Mann Randolph, Mar. 16, 1792, in Ford, 6:408.

84   **"had serious fears":** Alexander Hamilton to William Duer, Aug. 17, 1791, *PAH* 9:74–75.

84   **"shopkeepers, Widows, orphans":** Seth Johnson to Andrew Cragie, Mar. 25, 1792, quoted in Stuart Banner, *Anglo-American Securities Regulation: Cultural and Political Roots, 1690–1860* (New York: Cambridge University Press, 1998), 144.

84   **"We will have Mr. Duer":** Chernow, 383.

84   **He died destitute:** Jones, 202–203.

85   **"Let Congress legislate":** John Jay to George Wahinngton, Jan. 7, 1787, *PGW-CS,* 4:502–504.

85   **These pieces were concerned:** Robert A. Ferguson, "The Forgotten Publius: John Jay and the Aesthetics of Ratification," *Early American Literature* 34 (1999): 223.

85   **"This country and this people":** *Federalist 2* (Jay).

85   **"Different commercial concerns":** *Federalist 5* (Jay).

86   **Jay was incapacitated:** "John Jay and the Constitution" (based on the notes of Professor Richard B. Morris and his staff) in the "Papers of John Jay," an on-line dat abase: http://www.columbia.edu/cu/lweb/digital/exhibitions/constitution/essay.htm.

86   **"as deep and wicked":** *The Baltimore Md. Journal,* Nov. 30, 1787, *PJM* 10:299n3.

86   **"I am anxious":** George Washington to James Madison, Dec. 7, 1787, *PJM* 10:296–298.

86   **an "arrant forgery":** James Madison to George Washington, Dec. 20, 1787, *PJM* 10:333–334.

86   **Doctors' Riot of 1788:** There are many competing versions as to what transpired during the Doctors' Riot. This account is drawn from the following, not entirely consistent, accounts: Joel Tyler Headley, *The Great Riots of New York, 1712 to 1873* (Indianapolis: Bobbs-Merrill), 1970; Robert Swan, "Prelude and Aftermath of the Doctors' Riot of 1788," *New York History* 81 (2000): 417, 447–452; Whitfield J. Bell, "Doctors' Riot, New York, 1788," *Bulletin of the New York Academy of Medicine,* 47 (1971): 1501–1503; Monaghan Lowenthal, *This Was New York: The Nation's Capital in 1789* (1943), 199–200; George Pellew, *John Jay* (Boston: Houghton Mifflin, 1890); Linda

Grant De Pauw, *The Eleventh Pillar: New York State and the Federal Constitution* (Ithaca, N.Y.: Cornell University Press, 1966), 151.

87   **"sundry doctors and others"**: Swan, 447–452.

87   **"Bring out your doctors"**: Headley, 36.

87   **"My God, Jay"**: Lowenthal, 200.

87   **"two large holes"**: De Pauw, 151.

87   **For several days**: Landa M. Freeman et al., eds., *Selected Letters of John Jay and Sarah Livingston Jay* (2004), 181.

87   **"the undertaking was proposed"**: Fleet, 534–568.

88   **"I beg the favor"**: Tench Coxe to James Madison, Sept. 27, 1787, *PJM* 10:175–176.

88   **"as soon as he returns"**: James Madison to Tench Coxe, Oct. 1, 1787, *PJM* 10:183.

88   **"wish that you and Col. H."**: Tench Coxe to James Madison, Oct. 21, 1787, *PJM* 10:201–202.

88   **"Col. Hamilton had returned"**: James Madison to Tench Coxe, Oct. 26, 1787, *PJM* 10:222–223.

88   **"I returned hither"**: James Madison to Edmund Randolph, Nov. 18, 1787, *PJM* 10:252–253.

88   **"I will not conceal"**: James Madison to George Washington, Nov. 18, 1787, *PJM* 10:253–254.

89   **"it is proposed"**: *Federalist 7* (Hamilton). In the Cooke edition of *The Federalist,* this note is given at page 610.

89   **"Madison's definite promise of aid"**: Douglass Adair, *Authorship of the Disputed Federalist Papers,* 85, n86.

89   **In the six months**: Ibid., 75.

89   **"It frequently happened"**: Fleet, 534–568.

89   **"in the General's study"**: Nathan Schachner, "Alexander Hamilton Viewed by His Friends," *Wm. and Mary Q.* 4:220. In the 1790s, Hamilton was promoted to the rank of general and his friends would refer to him with that title.

89   **"cramming us with the voluminous"**: De Pauw, 110.

89   **"the performance must have borne"**: Fleet, 534–568.

90   **The arguments and historical examples**: See Adair, *Authorship of the Disputed Federalist Papers,* 83–84.

90   **virtually all of the opening essays**: William Lee Miller, *The Business of May Next: James Madison and the Founding* (Charlottesville: University Press of Virginia, 1994), 158–163.

90   **Madison would leave**: Chernow, 251; Miller, *Alexander Hamilton: Portrait in Paradox,* 191.

90   **"In the beginning"**: Fleet, 565.

90   **"rendered so inconvenient"**: Ibid. Madison would occasionally claim that he and Hamilton had decided not to stop reviewing one another's essays due to political disagreements: "It was found most agreeable to each, not to give a positive sanction to all the doctrines and sentiments of the other; there being a known difference in the general complexion of their political theories." See also James Madison to

Thomas Jefferson, Aug. 10, 1788, *PJM* 11:227 (stating that "the writers are not mutually answerable for all the ideas of each other there being seldom time for even a perusal of the pieces by any but the writer before they are wanted at the press and sometimes hardly by the writer himself."). The fact that Hamilton and Madison continued to discuss *Federalist* essays even after Madison left New York belies this notion.

91 **"What had been prepared":** See Madison's footnote to *Federalist 18* which is added to the 1818 Gideon edition of *The Federalist.*

91 **"the Printer means":** James Madison to Edmund Randolph, Dec. 2, 1787, *PJM* 10:289–290.

91 **"By a Citizen of New-York":** "Advertisement for the Book Edition of *The Federalist*," *New York Independent Journal,* Jan. 2, 1788, *DHRC* 20:564.

91 **"to be clothed":** *Federalist 23* & *30* (Hamilton).

92 **while Hamilton attended:** The winter term of the New York Supreme Court had begun on Jan. 8, 1788. John Chester Miller, *Alexander Hamilton and the Growth of the New Nation* (New Brunswick, N.J.: Transaction, 2003), 192.

92 **"It is impossible":** *Federalist 37* (Madison).

92 **become "very ominous":** James Madison to George Washington, Jan. 20, 1788, *PJM* 10:399.

92 **"the discord and ferment":** *Federalist 38* (Madison). Madison also addressed the difficulties of multiple constitutional conventions in *Federalist 49* and *50*. See generally Jack Rakove, "The Super-Legality of the Constitution, or, a Federalist Critique of Bruce Ackerman's Neo-Federalism," *Yale L.J.* 108 (1999): 1931, 1956.

93 **They convinced Governor John Hancock:** Edward C. Bannfield, "Was the Founding an Accident?" in Charles R. Kesler, ed., *Saving the Revolution: The Federalist Papers and the American Founding* (London: Collier Macmillan, 1987), 271.

93 **He devoted several essays:** For a discussion on *The Federalist*'s analysis of federalism, see chap. 9.

93 **"neither a national":** *Federalist 39* (Madison).

93 **a mere "parchment barrier":** *Federalist 48* (Madison).

93 **The only way:** For a discussion on *The Federalist*'s analysis of separation of powers, see chap. 8.

93 **Madison then turned:** Adair, *Authorship of the Disputed Federalist Papers,* 88.

94 **"according to their respective Numbers":** U.S. Constitution, art. 1, sec. 2, cl. 2.

94 **for purposes of representation:** The idea of counting slaves as three-fifths of a free person was not invented at the convention; the Continental Congress had previously utilized the fraction in its apportionment of federal expenses. John Kaminski, *A Necessary Evil? Slavery and the Debate Over the Constitution,* 1st ed. (Madison, Wis.: Madison House, 1995), 20–23. It should also be noted that the southern delegates wanted slaves counted as full persons, as that would have given the southern states more representation in the House.

94 **Both he and Jay:** Brookhiser, 175–176. It is generally presumed that Hamilton did not own any slaves himself.

94 **"he never would concur":** Farrand's Records 1:221.

94   **"informed that it was probable"**: "Minutes of the Manumission Society of New-York," Aug. 17, 1787, 36. The minutes are located in the New York Historical Society and can be seen online at Columbia University's Website: http://wwwapp.cc.columbia.edu/ldpd/app/jay/image?key=columbia.jay.00630&p=36. John Jay was on the committee which drafted the antislavery petition.

94   **"the great evil"**: James Madison to Robert J. Evans, June 15, 1819, *WJM* 8:439–447.

94   **"idle and depraved"**: Rakove, *Creation of the American Republic*, 213.

95   **"wrong to admit"**: Farrand's Records 2:417.

95   **"importation of such Persons"**: U.S. Constitution, art. 1, sec. 9, cl. 1.

95   **"scruples against admitting"**: James Madison to Robert Walsh, Nov. 27, 1819, *WJM* 9:1–13.

95   **"the Federal Government was never"**: "Address for the Promotion of Colored Enlistments," July 6, 1863, in Philip S. Foner, *The Life and Writings of Frederick Douglass* (New York: International, 1950), 3:365.

95   **"Abolish slavery tomorrow"**: Ibid. The fact that the Constitution omitted the word "slavery" also permitted Abraham Lincoln to argue that the Founding Fathers never accepted or approved of the institution. See Miller, *The Business of May Next,* 121.

95   **"one of our Southern brethren"**: *Federalist 54* (Madison).

96   **"time, places and, manner"**: U.S. Constitution, art. 1, sec. 4, cl. 1. The only provision Congress could not control was that state legislators would choose senators.

96   **"I am sorry to inform"**: George Washington to James Madison, Dec. 7, 1787, *PGW-CS,* 5:477–480; William Moore to James Madison, Feb. 5, 1788, reprinted in William Cabell Rives, *History of the Life and Times of James Madison* (Boston: Little, Brown, 1859), 549.

96   **"I think you had better"**: James Madison Sr. to James Madison Jr., Jan. 30, 1788, *PJM,* 10:446.

97   **"Many have asked me"**: George Washington to James Madison, Feb. 5, 1788, *PGW-CS,* 6:89.

97   **Before he left New York:** The fact that they held such a discussion is evidenced by Hamilton's letter to Madison of Apr. 3. In referencing Madison's comments, Hamilton stated, "I think, however, the principles we have talked of are not only just, but will apply to the other departments." Alexander Hamilton to James Madison, Apr. 3, 1788, *PAH* 4:644.

97   **En route from New York:** Hamilton began his letter by stating, "I have been very delinquent, my dear sir, in not thanking you for your letter from Philadelphia." Alexander Hamilton to James Madison, Apr. 3, 1788, *PAH* 4:644. Thus, we know that Madison had written his comments while in transit to Virginia.

97   **"The remarks you made"**: The reason for such obscure language was the fear that the letter would be read by the postal carrier, and clearer language might reveal the identity of Publius (see Introduction). Apparently, Madison's comments had involved the way Hamilton would be describing the difficult question of the overlapping jurisdiction of state and federal courts. That this is the subject of Madison's comments can be seen in Hamilton's response. Hamilton wrote, "The States retain all the authorities they were before possessed of, not alienated in the three modes pointed out." In *Federalist 31,*

Hamilton had pointed out that the complete assumption by the federal government of state sovereignty "would only exist in three cases"—where 1) the Constitution did so in express terms; 2) it expressly prohibited the states from exercising the authority; and 3) granting such authority to the states would be "totally CONTRADICTORY and RE-PUGNANT" to the exercise of federal power. When writing *Federalist 82* a month after his letter to Madison, Hamilton addresses the question of whether federal crimes can be tried in state courts by explaining that the determination of whether the federal government has exclusive power would be made according to "one of three cases" which had been "established in a former paper."

97 **He stopped for a few days:** Robert Scigliano, ed., "Introduction," *The Federalist.*

97 **"very strong wind":** Charles Fenton James, *Documentary History of the Struggle for Religious Liberty in Virginia* (New York: Da Capo Press, 1971), 157; Ralph Louis Ketcham, *James Madison* (New York: Macmillan, 1971), 251.

97 **before Madison had left for Virginia:** Adair, *Authorship of the Disputed Federalist Papers,* 108.

98 **Hamilton would be solely responsible:** Hamilton's analysis of the roles of the different branches is discussed in chap. 8.

98 **"THIS DAY IS PUBLISHED":** "Advertisement," *New York Independent Journal,* Mar. 22, 1788, in *DHRC* 20:880–881.

98 **"superfine Royal Writing Paper":** The type of paper used is described in "Advertisement for the Book Edition of *The Federalist*," *New York Independent Journal,* Jan. 2, 1788, *DHRC* 20:564. The binding is described in William Loring Andrews, "Early American Bookbinding and Kindred Subjects," in *The Bookman: A Magazine of Literature and Life* 15 (1903): 164, 165–166.

98 **"neatly enough bound":** See Alexander Hamilton to James Madison, May 19, 1788, *PAH* 4:649; Alexander Hamilton to George Washington, Aug. 13, 1788, *PAH* 5:201–202.

98 **"assisting the public judgment":** "Preface" to *The Federalist* (McLean edition, 1788), in *DHRC* 20:881.

99 **"If our suspicions":** Alexander Hamilton to James Madison, Apr. 3, 1788, *PAH* 4:644.

99 **"the bulwarks of a limited constitution":** *Federalist 78* (Hamilton). For a discussion of *The Federalist*'s view of the courts, see chap. 8 on separation of powers.

99 **the issue had been raised:** Statement of George Mason, Sept. 12, 1787, Farrand's Records 2:587–588.

100 **Wilson delivered a speech:** The full text of Wilson's speech can be found in Paul Leicester Ford, *Pamphlets on the Constitution of the United States, Published During Its Discussion by the People 1787–1788* (New York: 1888; reprinted by Da Capo Press, 2000), 157.

100 **"the single most influential":** *The Debate over the Constitution,* 1:1142.

100 **"If every thing":** Brutus II, in Storing, 2:372, 376.

101 **"not only unnecessary":** *Federalist 84.* Hamilton returned briefly to the problem of the lack of a bill of rights in *Federalist 85* and argued that it would be easier to obtain amendments after the Constitution was ratified. He contended that any change in the document prior to ratification would "require the concurrence of thirteen States,"

while the amendment process would only require approval of three-fourths of the states. This is hardly a perfect argument. Since ratification required only nine states, the "amended" Constitution would be ratified and effective with less than two-thirds of the states approving. Also, he begged the question that there was no guarantee of future amendments.

101 **Most significant, Hamilton:** Rakove, "Thinking Like a Constitution," *Journal of the Early Republic* 24 (2004): 19.

101 **"Once the concept":** Ibid., 18.

102 **One of the clues:** The first person to note that the relationship between Hamilton and Madison could be observed through the closings of their letters was Robert Scigliano. See his "Introduction," *The Federalist*, xiii. Stuart Leibiger also used a study of letter closings to demonstrate the growing friendship of George Washington and James Madison. See *Founding Friendship: George Washington, James Madison, and the Creation of the American Republic* (Charlottesville: University Press of Virginia, 1999), 2–3.

103 **Madison ended his letter:** James Madison to Alexander Hamilton, June 9, 1788, *PJM* 11:101.

103 **"Yet I own I fear":** Alexander Hamilton to James Madison, June 21, 1788, *PJM* 11:165.

103 **"The business is in":** James Madison to George Washington, June 13, 1788, *DHRC* 10:1619.

103 **"the greatest orator":** Charles F. Horne, *Statesmen and Sages: Great Men and Famous Women* (2003), 4:238.

103 **"he spoke so low":** See *PJM* 11:78.

104 **"Conditional amendments":** James Madison to George Nicholas, Apr. 8, 1788; *PJM,* 11:11–14.

104 **"a bill of rights":** Thomas Jefferson to James Madison, Dec. 20, 1787; *PTJ,* 12:440.

104 **"I wish with all my soul":** Thomas Jefferson to Alexander Donald, Feb. 7, 1788; *PTJ,* 12:570.

104 **If Virginia were to follow:** Speech of Patrick Henry, June 12, 1788, *DHRC,* 10:1210.

104 **"Constitution shall have been discussed":** Resolution, June 3, 1788, *DHRC,* 9:914. For a discussion of Mason's strategy, see Lance Banning, *The Sacred Fire of Liberty: James Madison and the Founding of the Federal Republic* (Ithaca, N.Y.: Cornell University Press, 1995), 237, stating that Mason called for the clause-by-clause review because he did not want a final vote "before the opposition could develop its appeal for previous amendments."

104 **At Madison's request:** Alexander Hamilton to James Madison, May 19, 1788, *PAH* 649–650.

105 **"to coach specific speakers":** Adair, *Authorship of the Disputed Federalist Papers,* 70n60.

105 **it was Hamilton who used:** Hamilton had had sixty copies rushed to a supporter in Albany for distribution prior to the election of delegates to New York's ratifying convention. Archibald McLean to Steven Van Renssalear, Apr. 10, 1788, *DHRC* 20:906–907.

105 **When the convention opened:** De Pauw, 184.

105 **"the friends to the rights"**: George Clinton to John Lamb, June 21, 1788, in Isaac Q. Leake, ed., *Memoir of the Life and Times of General John Lamb* (Albany, N.Y.: J. Munsell, 1850), 315.

105 **"I request you to dispatch"**: Alexander Hamilton to James Madison, May 19, 1788, *PAH* 4:650.

105 **Hamilton had made a similar**: Alexander Hamilton to John Sullivan, June 6, 1788, *PAH* 5:2.

105 **an express rider arrived**: See "News of New Hampshire and Virginia Ratification Arrives in New York," *DHRC* 21:1210–1211.

106 **Madison had been able**: See Lance Banning, "Sectionalism and the General Good," in Michael Gillespie and Michael Lienesch, eds., *Ratifying the Constitution* (Lawrence: University Press of Kansas, 1989), 285.

106 **The delegates voted to recommend**: See "Debates in the Virginia Convention," June 27, 1788, *DHRC* 10:1554.

106 **"This day put an end"**: James Madison to Alexander Hamilton, June 27, 1788, *PJM* 11:181.

106 **"returned, with the same zealous"**: "Convention of Virginia," in the *New-York Journal*, July 3, 1788, *DHRC* 21:1215.

106 **"TEN guns were fired"**: Ibid.

106 **To Hamilton's surprise**: De Pauw, 215.

107 **"If this can"**: Alexander Hamilton to James Madison, July 19, 1788, *PJM* 11:188.

107 **"this idea of reserving"**: James Madison to Alexander Hamilton, July 20, 1788, *PJM* 11:189.

107 **"It is not a little strange"**: James Madison to George Washington, July 21, 1788, *PJM* 11:190–191.

107 **Hamilton read Madison's warning**: George Bancroft, *History of the Formation of the Constitution of the United States of America* (New York: D. Appleton, 1882), 459.

107 **"Upon the whole"**: Alexander Hamilton to James Madison, July 22, 1788, *PJM* 11:192.

108 **The convention would ratify**: "Circular Letter," July 28, 1788, *DHRC*, 13:306–307.

108 **Among the amendments**: The proposed amendments are printed in, *DHRC*, 13:301–305.

108 **"the circumstances involved"**: James Madison to George Washington, Aug. 24, 1788, *LDC* 25:319–321.

108 **when news of New York's official ratification**: "The Federal Ship Hamilton," *DHRC* 21:1592–1593.

CHAPTER 5

109 **"our mutual Friend Hamilton"**: William Duer to James Madison, Nov. 25, 1788, *PJM* 11:367–368.

110 **If every elector voted:** After the fiasco of the election of 1800, which was decided by the House after thirty-six ballots, the Twelfth Amendment was proposed and ratified, requiring that electors vote for one presidential and one vice-presidential candidate.

110 **"it would be disagreeable":** Alexander Hamilton to James Madison, Nov. 23, 1788, *PAH* 5:235–237.

110 **Together they devised a plan:** As Stuart Leibiger has noted, "Madison made sure that Alexander Hamilton had arranged for some electors to throw away votes." *Founding Friendship: George Washington, James Madison, and the Creation of the American Republic* (Charlottesville: University Press of Virginia, 1999), 103.

110 **"scurvy manner in which":** John Adams to Benjamin Rush, May 17, 1789, in Alexander Biddle, *Old Family Letters Copied from the Originals for Alexander Biddle; Series A-B* (Philadelphia: J. B. Lippincott, 1892), 36.

110 **"the government may sincerely":** Alexander Hamilton to James Madison, Nov. 23, 1788, *PAH* 5:235–237.

110 **"unworthy of the confidence":** Henry Lee to James Madison, Nov. 19, 1788, in Ralph Louis Ketcham, *James Madison* (New York: Macmillan, 1971), 275.

111 **"face of a keen":** Willliam C. Rives, *History of the Life and Times of James Madison* (Boston: Little, Brown), 2:656.

111 **"scar of a wound":** Paul F. Boller Jr., *Presidential Anecdotes,* 2nd ed. (New York: Oxford University Press, 1996), 47.

111 **"the most satisfactory provisions":** James Madison to George Eve, Jan. 2, 1789, *PJM* 11:402.

111 **"There is no part":** *Federalist 35* (Hamilton).

112 **"perhaps best qualified":** James Madison to Thomas Jefferson, May 27, 1789.

112 **Washington agreed with Madison's assessment:** Chernow, 287.

112 **"how Hamilton and Madison":** J. C. Hamilton, *History of the Republic of the United States of America As Traced in the Writings of Alexander Hamilton and of His Contemporaries* (New York: D. Appleton, 1857), 29.

112 **"Congress had authorized":** "Resolution," *House Journal,* Sept. 21, 1789, 1:117; Alexander Hamilton to James Madison, Oct. 12, 1789, *PAH* 5:439.

112 **"a clever man":** Conversation with George Beckwith, Oct. 1789, *PAH* 5:482, 488.

112 **On November 19, he wrote:** James Madison to Alexander Hamilton, Nov. 19, 1789, *PAH* 5:526.

113 **"like individuals, who observe":** "Report on Public Credit" Jan. 9, 1790, *PAH* 6:65–168.

113 **"of eighty pounds":** Edgar S. Maclay, ed., *Journal of William Maclay* (New York: Appleton and Co., 1890), 327

113 **Madison rose to speak:** Speech, Feb. 11, 1790, *PJM* 13:34–39.

114 **joined together in 1783:** Feb. 18, 1783, James Madison's "Notes of Debates," *LDC* 19:703–704.

114 **"would be a task":** "Address to the States," Apr. 26, 1783, *PJM* 6:493.

114 **When Hamilton heard rumors:** Alexander Hamilton to Edward Carrington, May 26, 1792, *PAH.*

114 **"was less in view"**: Douglass Adair, "James Madison's Autobiography," *Wm. and Mary Q.* 2:204–205. Some historians contend that Madison's change of heart "is better explained as the opening move in a resumption of state-oriented politics" (James Ferguson, *Power of the Purse* [Chapel Hill: University of North Carolina Press, 1961], 298), while others see it as representing an error in judgment in which "his intellect was on the same side as his feelings." Banning, *The Sacred Fire of Liberty: James Madison and the Founding of the Federal Republic* (Ithaca, N.Y.: Cornell University Press, 1995), 316.

114 **"breach of faith"**: "Report on Public Credit," Jan. 9, 1790, *PAH* 6.

114 **"in general well digested"**: James Madison to Edmund Pendleton, Mar. 4, 1790, *PJM* 13:85.

114 **"be the last"**: Speech of Mar. 12, 1790, *PJM* 13:80.

114 **"laid the foundation"**: "Defence of the Funding System," July 1795, *PAH* 18:1, 73.

115 **Without assumption**: See Stanley Elkins and Eric McKitrick, *The Age of Federalism* (New York: Oxford University Press, 1993), 118–119.

115 **"these defects [ought]"**: "Speech on Assumption," Apr. 22, 1790, *PJM* 13:167.

115 **"we were perfectly agreed"**: Alexander Hamilton to Edward Carrington, May 26, 1792, *PAH* 11:426–445.

116 **According to Jefferson**: "Jefferson's Account of the Bargain on the Assumption and Residence Bills," *PTJ* 17:205–207.

116 **most famous dinners**: Among the many works concerning this dinner, see Kenneth R. Bowling, *The Creation of Washington D.C.: The Idea and Location of the American Capital* (Fairfax, Va.: George Mason University Press, 1991); Norman K. Risjord, "The Compromise of 1790: New Evidence on the Dinner Table Bargain," *Wm. and Mary Q.* 33 (1976): 309–314; Kenneth R. Bowling, "Dinner at Jefferson's: A Note on Jacob E. Cooke's 'The Compromise of 1790,'" *Wm. and Mary Q.* 28 (1971): 629–648; Cooke, "The Compromise of 1790," *Wm. and Mary Q.* 27 (1970): 523–545.

116 **a deal was brokered**: Some historians doubt that a deal actually occurred, contending that there were separate deals on assumption and capital and that Jefferson's dinner had no effect on either. See, e.g., Cooke, ibid.; Joshua D. Clinton, "Testing Explanations of Strategic Voting in Legislatures: A Reexamination of the Compromise of 1790," *American Journal of Political Science* 48 (2004): 675. Others, however, remain convinced that in describing the deal, Jefferson was "right about the essentials" (Banning, 321). See also Elkins and McKitrick, 156 ("All things considered, there is really no better shorthand for what happened than the story told by Thomas Jefferson").

116 **"this despicable grog-shop contest"**: Fisher Ames to Thomas Dwight, June 11, 1790, in Charlene Bickford, ed., *Documentary History of the First Federal Congress of the United States of America*: http://adh.sc.edu [accessed Feb. 26, 2007].

117 **"the project of Philadelphia"**: "Memorandum," June 30, 1790, in *The Life and Correspondence of Rufus King* (New York: Putnam, 1894), 384.

117 **Several other negotiations**: Joseph Ellis argues that the dinner was part of a larger realm of negotiations and that the most important benefit for Madison was the recalculation of the debt. *Founding Brothers: The Revolutionary Generation* (New York: Knopf, 2000), 48–80.

117 **"after Hamilton assured"**: Leibiger, 132.

117 **Virginia also received:** Ferguson, 321.

117 **"Even the powers":** Article in *New-York Journal,* July 27, 1790, quoted in *PTJ* 17:182.

118 **"added to the number":** Franklin B. Sawvel, ed., *The Complete Anas of Thomas Jefferson* (1903), 34.

118 **"of all the errors":** Thomas Jefferson to George Washington, Sep. 9, 1792, *PTJ* 24:352.

118 **The Bank of the United States:** See, e.g., Leibiger, 134; Banning, 325.

118 **Hamilton had long believed:** See Alexander Hamilton to James Duane, Sept. 3, 1780, *PAH* 2:418; Alexander Hamilton to Robert Morris, Apr. 30, 1781, *PAH* 2:604–635.

118 **Now he was attempting:** "Second Report on the Further Provision Necessary for Establishing Public Credit (Report on a National Bank)," Dec. 13, 1790, *PAH* 236, 258.

118 **Many feared that the bank:** See, e.g., Marie B. Hecht, *Odd Destiny: The Life of Alexander Hamilton* (New York: Macmillan, 1982), 504.

118 **Madison led the opposition:** There is also evidence that he was motivated, at least in part, by a fear that a national bank, located in Philadelphia, would lead to pressure to keep the nation's capital in that city as well. Kenneth Bowling, "The Bank Bill, the Capital City, and President Washington," *Capital Studies* I (1972): 59–71.

118 **Madison laid out his argument:** "Speech on the National Bank," Feb. 2, 1791, *PJM* 15:94ff.

118 **"necessary and proper":** U.S. Constitution, art. I, sec 8, cl. 18.

119 **"You must answer them":** The story of Hamilton's writing his opinion on the bank comes from notes which a law student, and a future president, Rutherford B. Hayes, took from a lecture which Supreme Court Justice Joseph Story gave at Harvard. See Charles Richard Williams, *Life of Rutherford Birchard Hayes* (Boston: Houghton Mifflin, 1914), 1:42. See also George Washington to Alexander Hamilton, Feb. 16, 1791, *PAH.*

119 **"told his wife":** See Williams, 1:42. Hamilton's cover letter to Washington stated that the writing of the opinion had "occupied him the greatest part of last night." Alexander Hamilton to George Washington, Feb. 23, 1791, *PAH* 8:61.

119 **Hamilton presented Washington:** "Opinion on the Constitutionality of an Act to Establish a Bank," Feb. 23, 1791, *PAH* 8:63–134.

120 **the end of the ten-day period:** U.S. Constitution, art. I, sec. 7, cl. 2.

120 **George Washington decided:** Twenty-eight years later, in 1819, Chief Justice John Marshall and a unanimous Supreme Court would agree that the establishment of the bank was indeed constitutional, relying heavily on Hamilton's analysis; *McCulloch v. Maryland* 17 U.S. 316 (1819). The bank which was upheld in *McCulloch* was actually the second bank of the United States. The charter for the first bank was not renewed when it expired in 1811, and the second bank was created in 1816, at the request of then-President James Madison.

120 **espouse "republican principles":** Quoted in Lewis Leary, *That Rascal Freneau: A Study in Literary Failure* (New Brunswick, N.J.: Rutgers University Press, 1941), 188.

See also Philip Marsh, "Philip Freneau and James Madison," *Proceedings of the N.J. Historical Society* 65 (1947):189–194.

120 **To help support this venture:** Banning, 340.

121 **"gives so little":** Thomas Jefferson to Philip Freneau, Feb. 28, 1791, *PTJ* 19:35.

121 **"intermeddle with the Treasury Department":** James Madison to Thomas Jefferson, July 24, 1791, *PJM* 14:52–53.

121 **"an obvious intrusion":** Michael P. Riccards, *A Republic, If You Can Keep It* (1987), 134.

121 **The comptroller position became open:** The story of the communications surrounding Coxe's attempt to be appointed comptroller is found in Julian Boyd, "Editorial Note," *PTJ* 20:219–232. At the time of his attempt, Coxe was working as an assistant to Hamilton in the Treasury Department.

121 **Jefferson passed along:** In fact, in his letter to Washington, Jefferson mentioned another possible candidate, Thomas Heyward of South Carolina, in case Washington was interested in geographic diversity (what Jefferson termed "distributive justice.") Ibid.

121 **"encamp hostile officers":** J. C. Hamilton, 513.

121 **Madison encountered Hamilton:** Madison's version of this discussion is contained in a letter he wrote to Jefferson. James Madison to Thomas Jefferson, July 24, 1791, *PJM* 14:52–53.

122 **Madison tried to increase:** Leary, 196.

122 **"it is downright despotism":** Ibid., 202–203.

122 **Madison contributed nineteen anonymous:** See generally, Douglas W. Jaenicke, "Madison v. Madison: The Party Essays v. The Federalist Papers," in R. A. Maedment and John Zvesper, eds., *Reflections on the Constitution: The American Constitution After Two Hundred Years* (Manchester: Manchester University Press, 1989), 116–135.

122 **"those who study":** James Madison, "The Union. Who Are Its Real Friends?" March 31, 1792, *PJM* 274–275.

122 **"a personal and political friend":** Hamilton's discussion of his feelings is described in a letter written by New York City financier Isaac Bronson to Hamilton's son, John C. Hamilton, on Mar. 2, 1834. The letter is reprinted in Abraham H. Venit, "An Unwritten Federalist History," *The New England Quarterly* 21, no. 2. (June 1948): 241, 243–244.

122 **Hamilton wrote one:** Alexander Hamilton to Edward Carrington, May 26, 1792, *PAH* 11:433.

122 **The emotional letter was detailed:** The letter runs 6,081 words, while *Federalist* essays *77*, *78*, and *79* total 6,092 words.

124 **"perfidious desertion of the principles":** Isaac Bronson to John C. Hamilton, Mar. 2, 1834, in Venit, 243–244.

124 **"Madison was always":** Hamilton, 686.

124 **he "was weak":** Richard Brookhiser, *Alexander Hamilton, American* (New York: Free Press, 1999), 53.

124 **"speculators and Tories":** Elkins and McKitrick, 234, quoting James Madison to Thomas Jefferson, May 1, 1791, *PJM* 14:16.

124 **"the nation's liberty":** Thomas A. Mason, Robert A. Rutland, and Jeanne K. Sisson, *PJM* 15:332.

124 **"as a neutral disinterested umpire":** Gordon S. Wood, *Revolutionary Characters* (2006), 164–165.

124 **"emerging realities of national politics":** Jack Rakove, *James Madison and the Creation of the American Republic,* 3rd ed. (New York: Pearson/Longman, 2007), 119.

125 **"I deserted Colonel Hamilton":** "N. P. Trist Memoranda," Sept. 17, 1834, Max Farrand, trans., *The Records of the Federal Convention of 1787* (New Haven, Conn.: Yale University Press, 1911), 3:534.

125 **"his personal and political enemy":** John Beckley to James Madison, Sept. 2, 1792, *PJM* 14:355–356.

125 **"finally baffle all her enemies":** James Madison to George Nicholas, Mar. 15, 1793, in Ralph Louis Ketcham, *James Madison* (New York: Macmillan, 1971), 339–340.

125 **"a womanish attachment":** Alexander Hamilton to Edward Carrington, May 26, 1792, *PAH* 11:433.

126 **"Proclamation of Neutrality":** See "Proclamation," in James D. Richardson, ed., *A Compilation of the Messages and Papers of the Presidents: 1789–1897* (Washington, D.C.: GPO, 1896), *PAH*, 15:330–343.

126 **Hamilton penned seven essays:** The first essay appeared in the *Gazette of the United States* on June 29, 1793.

127 **"For God's Sake":** Thomas Jefferson to James Madison, July 7, 1793, *PTJ* 26:444.

127 **Madison reluctantly took up:** The first Helvidius essay was published in the *Gazette of the United States* on Aug. 24. Madison's reluctance can be seen from a letter he wrote to Jefferson about the writing of the Helvidius essays: "I have forced myself into the task of a reply. I can truly say I find it the most grating one I ever experienced." James Madison to Thomas Jefferson, July 30, 1793, *PJM* 15:48.

127 **the eponymous Jay treaty:** For a detailed analysis of the treaty, see Samuel Flagg Bemis, *Jay's Treaty: A Study in Commerce and Diplomacy* (Westport, Conn.: Greenwood Press, 1962), and Jerald Combs, *The Jay Treaty: Political Battleground of the Founding Fathers* (Berkeley: University of California Press, 1970).

127 **"likely that no other":** Elkins and McKitrick, 410.

128 **he attended an outdoor debate:** Chernow, 490.

128 **Over the next five months:** There were a total of thirty-eight Camillus essays; Rufus King wrote ten others under the same pseudonym. *PAH* 18:475.

128 **"Hamilton is really a colossus":** Thomas Jefferson to James Madison, Sept. 21, 1795, *PJM* 16:88–89.

129 **Hamilton challenged anyone:** In addition to Madison, Hamilton also mentioned Rep. Abraham Baldwin of Georgia.

129 **Madison demanded:** See, e.g., James Madison, Jay's Treaty Speech, Mar. 10, 1796, *PJM* 16: 255–263.

129 **both his constitutional:** Elkins and McKitrick, 449.

130 **"valedictory address from me":** George Washington to James Madison, May 20, 1792, *PJM* 14:310–312.

130 **"the many ties":** James Madison to George Washington, June 20, 1792, *PJM* 14:319–324.

131 **"diminution of zeal":** Madison had written in 1792 that Washington's stepping down as president of the United States should not be interpreted as coming from the "smallest deficiency of zeal for its future interests, or of grateful respect for its past kindness." "Madison's Form for an Address as Drafted by Him for Washington," in Victor Hugo Paltsits, *Washington's Farewell Address: In Facsimile, with Transliterations of all the Drafts of Washington, Madison, & Hamilton, Together with their Correspondence and Other Supporting Documents* (New York: New York Public Library, 1935), 160.

131 **"compleatly in the snares":** James Madison to James Monroe, Sept. 29, 1796, *PJM* 16:403.

132 **"We proceeded deliberately":** John Jay to Judge Peters, Mar. 29, 1811, in William Jay, *The Life of John Jay with Selections from His Correspondence and Miscellaneous Papers* (New York: J&J Harper, 1833), 2:336–346.

CHAPTER 6

135 **The essays have been cited:** Buckner F. Melton Jr. and Jennifer J. Miller, "The Supreme Court and *The Federalist:* A Supplement, 1996–2001," *Ky. L.J.* 90 (2002): 415.

135 ***Calder v. Bull:*** 3 U.S. 386 (1798).

135 **more than half of the decisions:** Ira C. Lupu, "Time, the Supreme Court, and *The Federalist,*" *Geo. Wash. L. Rev.* 66 (1998): 1324, 1329.

135 **"It would not be stretching":** Clinton Rossiter, ed., *The Federalist Papers* (1961), vii.

135 **"an almost total failure":** William Jeffrey Jr., "The Letters of 'Brutus'—A Neglected Element in the Ratification Campaign of 1787–88," *U. Cinn. L.Rev.* 40 (1971): 643, 663.

136 **"cannot be relied on":** J. Michael Martinez and William D. Richardson, "The Federalist Papers and Legal Interpretation," *S.D.L. Rev.* 45 (2000): 307, 332.

136 **the two were intimately involved:** This observation also applies to the third author of *The Federalist,* John Jay, who was the president of the Continental Congress in 1778, a member of the delegation that negotiated the Treaty of Paris ending the Revolutionary War, and the secretary for foreign affairs from 1784 to 1789.

136 **Madison undertook a mammoth study:** "Ancient & Modern Confederacies," *PJM* 9:4–24, and "Vices of the Political System of the United States," *PJM* 9:348–357.

136 **"the specie & current cash":** Alexander Hamilton to Timothy Pickering, Apr. 20, 1781, *PAH* 2:595–596.

136 **"powerful cement of our union":** Alexander Hamilton to Robert Morris, Apr. 30, 1781, *PAH* 2:604, 635. See also Ron Chernow, *Alexander Hamilton* (New York: Penguin, 2004), 156.

137 **"it is now settled":** Dan T. Coenen, "A Rhetoric for Ratification: The Argument of *The Federalist* and Its Impact on Constitutional Interpretation," *Duke L. J.* 56 (2006): 469. See also William N. Eskridge Jr., "Should the Supreme Court Read *The Federalist* but Not Statutory Legislative History?" *Geo. Wash. L. Rev.* 66 (1998): 1301, 1309,

which states that "the authors of *The Federalist* wrote the essays for just one state's ratifying convention, New York's."

137 **only twelve newspapers:** Elaine F. Crane, "Publius in the Provinces: Where was '*The Federalist*' Reprinted Outside New York City?" *Wm. and Mary Q.* 21 (1964): 589, 590.

137 **"*The Federalist* was not widely":** Vasan Kesavan and Michael Stokes Paulsen, "The Interpretive Force of the Constitution's Secret Drafting History," *Geo. L.J.* 91 (2003): 1154.

137 **"Publius did not reach":** Crane, 591.

137 **Hamilton sent several essays:** *PAH* 4:332–333.

137 **Madison sent essays:** *PJM* 10:445.

137 **"appears to have sprung":** Philadelphia *Independent Gazetteer,* Jan. 16, 1788, reprinted in *DHRC* 13:493.

138 **"if any thing new":** *DHRC* 13:491.

138 **"as we are in greater want":** William R. Davie to James Iredell, Jan. 22, 1788, *The Papers of James Iredell,* 2:218. In early January, Iredell also sent several *Federalist* essays to another North Carolinian, Charles Johnson (*DHRC* 13:491; *The Papers of James Iredell* 2:598–599). In March a North Carolina lawyer, Archibald Maclaine, would complain that he did not think that *The Federalist* was "well calculated for the common people." Archibald Maclaine to James Iredell, Mar. 4, 1788, *DHRC* 13:494.

138 **"we have christened":** Samuel Tenney to Nathaniel Gilman, Mar. 12, 1788, *DHRC* 13:488; see chap. 1.

138 **Connecticut's Jeremiah Wadsworth wrote:** Jeremiah Wadsworth to Rufus King, Dec. 16, 1787, *DHRC* 3:497; Jeremiah Wadsworth to Henry Knox, Dec. 23, 1787, *DHRC* 3:501.

138 **Advertisements for the book:** Advertisements ran in New York's *Independent Journal* six times in January, and in New York's *Packet* ten times. The *Norfolk and Portsmouth Journal* ran an advertisement Jan. 30 and Virginia's *Independent Chronicle* ran advertisements on Feb. 6 and Mar. 12 *DHRC* 15:23.

138 **"[A]mongst the numerous publications":** Advertisement, reprinted in *DHRC* 15:224.

138 **Hamilton made sure:** *DHRC* 13:491.

138 **there is solid evidence:** *DHRC* 16:468, 18:85.

139 **Connecticut's Jeremiah Wadsworth was not:** Another leader of the fight for ratification in Connecticut, Samuel William Johnson, also received copies of *The Federalist.* Roger Alden to Samuel William Johnson, *LDC* 24:603.

139 **"Enclosed I send you":** Charles Thomson to James McHenry, Apr. 19, 1788, *LMCC* 8:720–722.

139 **"The greater part":** George Nicholas to James Madison, Apr. 5, 1788, *PJM* 11:9–10.

139 **Madison responded three days later:** James Madison to George Nicholas, Apr. 8, 1788, *PJM* 11:13–14.

139 **Hamilton subsequently arranged:** Alexander Hamilton to James Madison, May 19, 1788, *PAH,* 4:649–650: June 8, 1788, *PAH,* 5:2–4.

139 **"there is no good evidence that anyone":** David McGowan, "Ethos in Law and History: Alexander Hamilton, *The Federalist,* and the Supreme Court," *Minn. L. Rev.* 85 (2000): 755, 756. See also Coenen, who says that "historians have concluded that the papers had little impact on the ratification decision even in New

York" (532); Albert Furtwangler, *The Authority of Publius: A Reading of the Federalist Papers* (Ithaca, N.Y.: Cornell University Press, 1984), 23, says, "In terms of affecting votes or justifying the outcome in any state convention, *The Federalist* was in fact very marginal."

139 **"despite *The Federalist*"**: Forrest McDonald, *Alexander Hamilton: A Biography* (New York: W. W. Norton, 1979), 114. The actual popular vote was probably closer than this, but it is undeniable that close to two-thirds of the elected delegates were Anti-Federalists.

140 **"there is no evidence that Publius"**: De Pauw, 114.

140 **"worked only a small influence"**: Rossiter, ed., "Introduction," in *The Federalist Papers* (1961), xi.

140 **"expression not only of the popular will"**: Charles R. Kesler, "Introduction," in *Saving the Revolution: The Federalist Papers and the American Founding* (London: Collier Macmillan, 1987), 1, 4.

141 **"I have read every"**: George Washington to Alexander Hamilton, Aug. 28, 1788, *PGW-CS* 6:480, 481.

141 **"have thrown new light"**: George Washington to John Armstrong, Apr. 25, 1788, *PGW-CS* 6:224, 226.

141 **Others in the midst:** Of course, not every reader valued *The Federalist*. One writer complained of "the dry trash of Publius in 150 numbers," *New-York Journal*, May 16, 1788, quoted in Furtwangler, 21. Louis Otto, the French chargé d'affaires, was notably unimpressed as well, writing that "the work is of no use to the well-informed, and it is too learned and too long for the ignorant." Farrand, *The Records of the Federal Convention of 1787*, 3:234.

141 **"most valuable disquisitions"**: Tench Coxe to James Madison, Jan. 16, 1788, *DHRC* 13:492.

141 **"candor, ingenuity, depth of thought"**: Samuel Tenney to Nathaniel Gilman, Mar. 12, 1788, *DHRC* 13:492.

141 **"the best thing I have seen"**: James Kent to Nathanial Lawrence, Dec. 8, 1787, *DHRC* 14:390.

142 **"a work which I hope"**: James Iredell, "Answers to Mr. Mason's objections to the new Constitution, recommended by the late Convention," in Paul Leicester Ford, *Pamphlets on the Constitution of the United States Published During Its Discussion by the People 1787–1788* (1888; New York: Da Capo Press, 1968).

142 **"expose the real circumstances"**: John Marshall, *The Life of George Washington* (Fredericksburg, Va.: The Citizens' Guild, 1926), 4:241.

142 **"well calculated . . . to impress"**: *American Magazine,* June 1788, in *DHRC* 18:86. Although it is not 100 percent certain that Webster wrote the review, he is considered the most likely author. Webster was the publisher of *American Magazine* and wrote many of its pieces. The author of the review criticized Publius for his grammar, specifically for using the word "was" when the proper tense would be the "future or conditional 'should be' or 'might be.'" Such criticisms would not be unexpected from the future author of *An American Dictionary of the English Language*.

142 **"its authors wrote it":** Coenen, 469, 536.

142 **"a piece of political advocacy":** John F. Manning, "Textualism and Original Understanding: Textualism and the Role of *The Federalist* in Constitutional Adjudication," *Geo. Wash. L. Rev.* 66 (1998): 1337, 1339.

143 **"*The Federalist* was at bottom":** Douglass Adair, "Authorship of the Disputed *Federalist Papers*," in Trevor Colbourn, ed., *Fame and the Founding Fathers* (New York: W. W. Norton, 1974), 82.

143 **"designed to place the Constitution":** James W. Ducayet, "Publius and Federalism: On the Use and Abuse of *The Federalist* in Constitutional Interpretation," *N.Y.U. L. Rev.* 68 (1993): 821, 845–846. See also Jacobus tenBroek, "Use by the United States Supreme Court of Extrinsic Aids in Constitutional Construction," *Cal. L. Rev.* 27 (1939): 157, 163.

143 **Hamilton's earlier attempt:** See chap. 4.

143 **"These papers," Madison wrote:** *Federalist 37* (Madison).

143 **"I have not failed":** *Federalist 85* (Hamilton).

144 **"A Writer under the signature":** Roger Alden to Samuel William Johnson, Dec. 31, 1787, *LDC* 24:603.

144 **"Precisely because Publius's purpose":** Coenen, 539.

144 **the fact that thousands:** See, e.g., Eskridge, 1308.

145 **a split developed:** See chap. 5.

145 **Politicians debate the conflicting values:** See, e.g., Robert S. Erikson, Norman R. Luttberg, and Kent L. Tedin, *American Public Opinion: Its Origins, Content, and Impact,* 2nd ed. (New York: Wiley, 1980), 183.

145 **the moment before the national big bang:** The fact that Hamilton and Madison diverged so sharply so soon after writing *The Federalist* has sometimes led commentators to find a split personality in the essays. Most of these differences have been exaggerated with the benefit of our knowledge of the animosity which followed; see chap. 9.

145 **Is there a role:** In his excellent historical study of *The Federalist,* Gary Wills concluded that the main reason a modern reader should be interested in Publius is that "Madison explains himself in *The Federalist* . . . [and] . . . in explaining himself he tells us what Washington meant to his peers and friends and followers, what Jefferson meant," and thus "he does explain America." *Explaining America: The Federalist* (New York: Penguin, 1982), 270. In the revised edition of his book, Wills says that he overemphasized the "difference between Madison's time and ours" (p. x), but does not say if that realization altered his view on the contemporary utility of *The Federalist.*

145 **"Whatever may have been":** Alexander Hamilton, "Opinion on the Constitutionality of an Act to Establish a Bank," Feb. 23, 1791, *PAH* 8:111.

145 **"the manner in which":** Alexander Hamilton, "The Defence No. XXXVI," Jan. 2, 1796, *PAH* 20:3, 5.

146 **During the 1791 debate:** Jack N. Rakove, "The Original Intention of Original Understanding," *Constitutional Commentary* 13 (1996): 159, 173.

146 **"[his] argument rested on text":** Ibid., 179, citing Madison's speech in the House of Representatives on Mar. 10, 1796.

146 **"was nothing more than the draft":** *Annals of Congress* 5:776 (Apr. 6, 1796). In this speech, Madison also stated: "Whatever veneration might be entertained for the body of men who formed our constitution, the sense of that body could never be regarded as the oracular guide in the expounding the constitution. . . . If we were to look therefore, for the meaning of the instrument, beyond the face of the instrument, we must look for it not in the general convention, which proposed, but in the state conventions, which accepted and ratified the constitution."

146 **"the legitimate meaning":** James Madison to Thomas Ritchie, Sept. 15, 1821, in Farrand's Records (New Haven, Conn.: Yale University Press, 1923), 3:447.

146 **They used temporary:** See Rakove, *Origional Intention,* 186.

147 **"Such is the character":** *McCulloch v. Maryland,* 17 U.S. (4 Wheat.) 316, 413–414 (1819).

147 **"No language is so copious":** *Federalist* 37 (Madison).

147 **"When the Almighty":** Ibid.

147 **many questions about the meaning:** See Frederick Schauer, "Easy Cases," *S. Cal. L. Rev.* 58 (1985): 399.

147 **This is an "easy" case:** Those with an argumentative bent could point out that "natural born" could be read to exclude those born via caesarean section. See Paul Brest, "The Misconceived Quest for the Original Understanding," *B.U.L. Rev.* 60 (1980): 204, 207.

147 **A significant number:** Schauer added that for a question to be "easy" the answer should be "consistent both with the purpose behind the rule and with the social, political, and moral climate in which the question is answered" ("Easy Cases," 416). While knowing and agreeing with the purpose of a specific term may be useful, if the language is clear enough, the purpose behind it may be irrelevant. For example, the requirement that senators be at least thirty years old and presidents at least thirty-five, was based on the view that it "confines the electors to men of whom the people have had time to form a judgment, and with respect to whom they will not be liable to be deceived by those brilliant appearances of genius and patriotism which, like transient meteors sometimes mislead as well as dazzle" *Federalist 64* (Jay). Even if it were determined that in the modern age of communication and information retrieval, the populace would have time to "form a judgment" of a particularly astute thirty-four-year-old, that youngster would still be ineligible for the White House.

147 **"commerce . . . among the several states":** U.S. Const., art I, sec. 8.

147 **a bill to regulate nuclear wastes:** See May 2, 2000, vote in Senate on S.1287, regulating nuclear waste storage.

148 **preclude judicial review:** *Marbury v. Madison,* 5 U.S. (1 Cranch) 137 (1803).

148 **does not discuss a legislative veto:** See, e.g., *I.N.S. v. Chadha,* 462 U.S. 919, 977 (1983) (White dissenting): "That disagreement stems from the silence of the Constitution on the precise question: The Constitution does not directly authorize or prohibit the legislative veto."

148 **has "nothing to say":** See, e.g., *Cruzan v. Director, Mo. Dep't of Health,* 497 U.S. 261, 300 (1990) (Scalia concurring), in which Justice Scalia concluded that there

was no constitutional right to die because "the Constitution has nothing to say about the subject."

148 **the Court must determine:** Cf. Rakove, *Origional Intention*, 163, who says that future Supreme Court Justice James Iredell argued against a bill of rights on the theory that future generations would reason that "if some rights were enumerated and others not, they would need no other evidence to conclude that the omissions were deliberate."

148 **the "originalists" and the "non-originalists":** See Antonin Scalia, "Originalism: The Lesser Evil," *U. Cin. L. Rev.* 57 (1989): 849; Stephen Breyer, *Active Liberty: Interpreting Our Democratic Constitution* (New York: Knopf, 2005) and "Our Democratic Constitution," *N.Y.U.L. Rev.* 77 (2002): 245.

149 **"people in little boxes":** Nick Madigan, "Who's Shouting Now?" *Baltimore Sun,* Dec. 24, 2006.

149 **"Originalism," when first used:** Edwin Meese, "Speech Before the American Bar Association" (July 9, 1985), *The Great Debate: Interpreting Our Written Constitution* (The Federalist Society, 1986), 9.

149 **After withering attacks:** See, e.g., Jack N. Rakove, "Mr. Meese, Meet Mr. Madison," in *Interpreting the Constitution: The Debate Over Original Intent* (Boston: Northeastern University Press, 1990); Leonard W. Levy, *Original Intent and the Framers' Constitution* (London: Collier Macmillan, 1988); Paul Finkelman, "The Constitution and the Intentions of the Framers: The Limits of Historical Analysis," *U. Pitt. L. Rev.* 50 (1989): 349.

149 **search for "original meaning":** In the mid-1980s Justice Scalia urged originalists to "change the label from the Doctrine of Original Intent to the Doctrine of Original Meaning." Kesavan and Paulsen, 1140, citing Antonin Scalia, "Speech Before the Attorney General's Conference on Economic Liberties" (June 14, 1986), in *Office of Legal Policy, Original Meaning Jurisprudence: A Sourcebook* (U.S. Dept. of Justice, 1987), 106.

149 **"What I look for":** Scalia, *A Matter of Interpretation* (Princeton, N.J.: Princeton University Press, 1997), 38.

150 **"would have been understood":** Kesavan and Paulsen, 1132. To some, this approach is called either textualism or "textualism-originalism."

150 **Justice Clarence Thomas's concurring opinion:** *McIntyre v. Ohio Elections Commission,* 514 U.S. 334 (1995).

150 **"give meaning to all constitutional provisions":** Erwin Chemerinsky, *Interpreting the Constitution* (New York: Praeger, 1987), 109.

151 **One of the most striking examples:** *Bolling v. Sharpe,* 347 U.S. 497, 500 (1954).

151 **"the most fundamental original intention":** Breyer, *Active Liberty,* 131–132.

151 **"the right of individuals":** Ibid., 21. Historian Morton J. Horwitz contends that it is a misreading of history to assume that democracy was a "foundational concept of American constitutional law before the twentieth century. Democracy was consistently a negative term for most of the Framers' generation." "The Constitution of Change: Legal Fundamentality Without Fundamentalism," *Harv. L. Rev.* 107 (1993): 32.

151 **an "historical baseline":** Kesavan and Paulsen, 1126.

152 **"relatively high level of generality":** See Brest, 223.

152　**They look to the more general purpose:** Ronald Dworkin, "Comment," in Scalia, *A Matter of Interpretation,* 119. Dworkin has referred to this as "semantic originalism," in contrast to the more traditional approach of defining purpose very narrowly, which he terms "expectation originalism."

152　**The strongest rationale for an originalist approach:** Kesavan and Paulsen, 1128. Supporters also claim that originalism serves democratic principles by permitting elected officials to make "value choices." That argument, however, begs the question of which value choices the Constitution removes from majoritarian determination. For example, as Justice Brandeis said, freedom of speech was guaranteed by the First Amendment against infringement by "the occasional tyrannies of governing majorities, *Whitney v. California,* 274 U.S. 357, 376 (1927) (Brandeis concurring).

152　**"The Constitution is supreme law":** Rakove, *The Original Intention of Original Understanding,* 161. This quote represents Rakove's depictions of those who call themselves originalists. It was not meant to describe his personal views.

152　**"mistake their own predilections":** Scalia, "Originalism: The Lesser Evil," 863.

152　**"History is inevitably ambiguous":** *Interpreting the Constitution,* 18. See also Eskridge, 1310: "The originalist evidence does not provide any greater interpretive closure—and hence does not constrain willful judges." See Matthew J. Festa, "Dueling Federalists: Supreme Court Decisions with Multiple Opinions Citing 'The Federalist,' 1986–2007," *Seattle U. L. Rev.* 31 (2007): 75.

153　**adoption of an eighteenth-century mind-set:** See Steven Carter, "The Right Questions in the Creation of Constitutional Meaning," *B.U.L. Rev.* 61 (1986): 71, 76: "The word 'originalism' nowadays has understandably become a red flag to many theorists, carrying as it does lurid images of reaction and retrenchment run rampant."

153　**"those who would restrict claims":** Justice William J. Brennan, "Speech to the Text and Teaching Symposium," Georgetown University (Oct. 12, 1985), in *The Great Debate: Interpreting Our Written Constitution,* 24.

153　**"A position that upholds":** Ibid.

153　***Brown v. Board of Education* was incorrectly decided:** See, e.g., Alexander M. Bickel, "The Original Understanding and the Segregation Decision," *Harv. L. Rev.* 69 (1955): 1, 58; Michael J. Klarman, "Brown, Originalism, and Constitutional Theory: A Response To Professor McConnell," *Va. L. Rev.* 81 (1995): 1881. Some scholars disagree, and believe that *Brown* is consistent with originalism. See Michael W. McConnell, "Originalism and the Desegregation Decisions," *Va. L. Rev.* 81 (1995): 947.

153　**Justice Scalia has written:** Scalia, *A Matter of Interpretation,* 132, 139.

154　**"Because it was written 200 years ago":** Eskridge, 1310.

154　**"the nature of government has changed":** Ibid.

154　**"We may also suspect":** *Youngstown Sheet & Tube Co. v. Sawyer,* 343 U.S. 579, 650 (1952) (Jackson concurring).

154　**"The Federalist papers remain relevant":** Bernard Bailyn, *To Begin the World Anew: The Genius and Ambiguities of the American Founders* (New York: Knopf, 2003), 124.

155　**"machine that would go of itself":** See, Michael Kammen, *A Machine That Would Go of Itself: The Constitution in American Culture* (New York: Knopf, 1986).

155   **"Bill of Rights—useful—not essential":** Notes for Speech in Congress [ca. June 8, 1789], *PJM* 12:193, 16:724. See, generally, Richard Labunski, *James Madison and the Struggle for the Bill of Rights* (New York: Oxford University Press, 2006).

155   **complaining that the time:** See, e.g., Robert A. Rutland, "The Trivialization of the Bill of Rights: One Historian's View of How the Purposes of the First Ten Amendments Have Been Defiled," *Wm. and Mary L. Rev.* 31 (1990): 287, 292.

155   **"merely a tub to the whale":** *Gazette of the United States* (N.Y.), Aug. 15, 1789, in Helen E. Veit et al., eds., *Creating the Bill of Rights: The Documentary Record from the First Federal Congress* (Baltimore: Johns Hopkins University Press, 1991), 157, 175.

156   **"milk & water propositions":** George Mason to John Mason (July 31, 1789), in Robert Rutland, ed., *The Papers of George Mason, 1725–1792* (Chapel Hill: University of North Carolina Press, 1970), 3:1164. As an example of the general apathy which greeted the Bill of Rights, one New York newspaper, *The Daily Advertiser,* which "had been filled with essays during the ratification campaign, published only four articles dealing with the Constitution between June 1789, when Madison introduced his amendments, and January 1790, when New York acted on them." De Pauw, 272.

156   **When a controversy over ratification:** See, e.g., John P. Kaminski, "The Making of the Bill of Rights: 1787–1792," in Stephen L. Schechter and Richard B. Bernstein, eds., *Contexts of the Bill of Rights* (Albany: New York State Commission on the Bicentennial of the United States Constitution, 1990), 18, 46.

156   **"the conformity of the proposed constitution":** *Federalist 1* (Hamilton).

157   **"muddled thinker, given":** Raoul Berger, *Government by Judiciary: The Transformation of the Fourteenth Amendment,* 2nd ed. (Cambridge, Mass.: Harvard University Press, 1977), 164.

157   **"every word" of the Fourteenth Amendment:** *Cong. Globe,* 39th cong., 1st sess., 1034 (1866).

157   **"at best . . . inconclusive":** *Loving v. Virginia,* 388 U.S. 1, 9–10 (1967). See also *Brown v. Board of Education,* 347 U.S. 483, 489 (1954).

157   **Because ratification was required:** Joseph B. James, *The Ratification of the Fourteenth Amendment* (Macon, Ga.: Mercer University Press, 1984), 216.

158   **"holy writ":** See Seth Barrett Tillman, "The Federalist Papers as Reliable Historical Source Material for Constitutional Interpretation," *W. Va. L. Rev.* 105 (2003): 601, 617.

158   **the appointment will be effective:** While it was not until the Twelfth Amendment that it was ensured that the president and vice president would be of the same party, the structure of the original Constitution still permitted a unity of interest between the two, and thus did not mandate that no appointment could be approved in a split Senate. For other technical errors in *The Federalist,* see Tillman, 603–615.

158   **slaves were to be regarded as three-fifths:** U.S. Constitution, art. 1, sec. 2.

158   **While he did not express support:** Madison did permit himself to condemn in emphatic language the "barbarism" of the international slave trade, which under article I, section 9 of the Constitution, could be prohibited in 1808. *Federalist 42* (Madison).

159 **"Publius had informed him":** William Smith to E. Rutledge, June 21, 1789, in *South Carolina Historical Magazine* 69: 6, 8 (South Carolina Historical Society, 1968), as quoted in Rakove, "The Original Intention of Original Understanding," *Const. Commentary* 13, 170–171.

159 ***The Federalist* may fairly enough":** James Madison to Thomas Jefferson, Feb. 8, 1825, *WJM* 9:218–220.

159 **"considered as of great authority":** *Cohens v. Virginia,* 19 U.S. 264, 418 (1821).

160 ***McCulloch v. Maryland:*** 17 U.S. 316 (1819).

160 **"in applying their opinions":** *McCulloch v. Maryland,* 17 U.S. 316, 433–435 (1819).

160 **"common sense" indicates:** *Federalist 83* (Hamilton).

161 **"wished to erect a political system":** Robert Alan Dahl, *A Preface to Democratic Theory* (Chicago: University of Chicago Press, 1956), 31.

161 **A careful reading of history:** See, e.g., Gordon Wood, *Revolutionary Characters: What Made the Founders Different* (New York: Penguin, 2006), 143–172.

CHAPTER 7

163 **the most famous writing:** David F. Epstein, *The Political Theory of the Federalist* (Chicago: University of Chicago Press, 1984), 59.

163 **"most often anthologized":** Albert Furtwangler, *The Authority of Publius: A Reading of the Federalist Papers* (Ithaca, N.Y.: Cornell University Press, 1984), 112.

163 **"turn first to No. 10":** Garry Wills, *Explaining America: The Federalist* (New York: Doubleday, 1981), xi.

164 **"failed to comprehend the argument":** Larry D. Kramer, "Madison's Audience," *Harv. L. Rev.* 112 (1999): 611, 670.

164 **Several of Hamilton's later:** See, e.g., *Federalist 60, 61 & 68* (Hamilton).

164 **"an economic document":** Charles A. Beard, *An Economic Interpretation of the Constitution of the United States* (New York: Macmillan, 1913), 188.

164 **"in no uncertain language":** Ibid., 156.

164 **Later historians have discredited:** See Richard A. Posner, "The Constitution as an Economic Document," *Geo. Wash. L. Rev.* 56 (1987): 4. See, generally, Forrest McDonald, *"We The People: The Economic Origins of the Constitution"* (Chicago: University of Chicago Press, 1958). As always, there are some who still believe that there is validity in Beard's thesis. See, e.g., James Grey Pope, "An Approach to State Constitutional Interpretation," *Rutgers L.J.* 24 (1993): 985, 994n54: "The facile tendency to assert that Beard has been conclusively 'refuted' is groundless."

164 **"The history of modern scholarly analysis":** Banning, 205.

164 **"short of despotism":** Centinel 1, Oct. 5, 1787, in Storing 2:136, 141.

165 **"with considerable address":** James Madison to Edmund Randolph, Oct. 21, 1787, *PJM* 10:199–200.

165 **"A free republic cannot succeed":** Brutus I, Oct. 18, 1787, in Storing 2:363, 368.

165 **"Vices of the Political System":** *PJM* 9:348–357. "Vices" was probably written from February through April 1787.

165 **Madison had further refined:** James Madison to Thomas Jefferson, Oct. 24, 1787, *PJM* 10:206–215. Before the convention, Madison had also written to George Washington revealing the beginning of his theory. James Madison to George Washington, Apr. 16, 1787, *PJM* 9:382–387.

166 **"an elaborate tree-like system":** Mary Louise Gill, "Method and Metaphysics in Plato's 'Sophist and Statesman,'" in Edward N. Zalta, ed., *The Stanford Encyclopedia of Philosophy* (Winter 2005): http://plato.stanford.edu/archives/win2005/entries/plato-sophstate/.

167 **Madison's explication:** Madison drew on the work of David Hume in creating his concept of faction and of the various ways factions could be dealt with. See Douglass Adair, "That Politics May Be Reduced to a Science"; David Hume, James Madison, and the Tenth Federalist," in Trevor Colborn, ed., *Fame and the Founding Fathers* (New York: W. W. Norton, 1974), 138–151; and Wills, 216–237. Madison, however, was not simply parroting Hume, and the final product reflects Madison's own experiences and political creativity. See Edmund Morgan, "Safety in Numbers: Madison, Hume and the Tenth Federalist," *Huntington Library Quarterly* 49 (1986): 95–112; Theodore Draper, "Hume and Madison: The Secrets of Federalist Paper No. 10," *Encounter* 58 (1982); Banning, 204.

167 **It was this section:** The other part of *Federalist 10* with strong economic class implications is Madison's list of "improper or wicked" projects: "A rage for paper money, for an abolition of debts, for an equal division of property."

167 **"great mass of the little propertied":** Martin Diamond, "The Federalist," in William A. Schambra, ed., *As Far as Republican Principles Will Admit* (Lanham, Md.: National Book Network, 1992), 54.

169 **"We have seen the mere distinction":** "Statement of James Madison," June 6, 1787, in Farrand, *The Records of the Federal Convention of 1787,* 1:135.

170 **"wherever the real power":** James Madison to Thomas Jefferson, Oct. 17, 1788, *PJM* 9:297–298.

170 **"the occasional tyrannies":** *Whitney v. California,* 274 U.S. 357, 375 (1927) (Brandeis concurring).

170 **This definition would today:** Diamond, 44.

171 **based on the Roman ideal:** Mortimer Sellers, *American Republicanism: Roman Ideology in the United States Constitution* (New York: New York University Press, 1994), 6.

171 **Brutus had distinguished:** Brutus I, Oct. 18, 1787, in Storing 2:363, 369. That Brutus is the source of Madison's definition was first recognized in Emery G. Lee, "Representation, Virtue, and Political Jealousy in the Brutus-Publius Dialogue," *The Journal of Politics* 59 (1997): 1073–1095.

173 **The United States, according to Madison:** The western expansion of the United States coincided with improvements in transportation, such as the railroad, so that Madison's ideal size for a republic was not exceeded. It is interesting to ponder the "natural" limits of a republic in a time of supersonic air transport.

CHAPTER 8

175 **"power to advance":** *Federalist 41* (Madison).

175 **"all men having power":** "Statement of James Madison," July 11, 1787, Farrand, *The Records of the Federal Convention of 1787*, 1:584.

175 **"the people are the only":** *Federalist 49* (Madison).

176 **"the capacity of mankind":** *Federalist 39* (Madison).

176 **"the total exclusion":** *Federalist 63* (Madison).

176 **"a remote choice":** *Federalist 39* (Madison).

176 **"The eighteenth-century mind":** Gordon Wood, *Creation of the American Republic, 1776–1787* (Chapel Hill: University of North Carolina Press, 1969), 68.

176 **"to obtain for rulers":** *Federalist 57* (Madison).

176 **"If men were angels":** *Federalist 51* (Madison).

177 **"Men of factious tempers":** *Federalist 10* (Madison).

177 **"may forget their obligations":** *Federalist 62* (Madison).

177 **"The natural cure":** *Federalist 21* (Hamilton). See also *Federalist 52* (Madison) ("Frequent elections are unquestionably the only policy by which [a] dependence and sympathy can be effectually secured") and *Federalist 57* (Madison) ("The elective mode of obtaining rulers is the characteristic policy of republican government.").

177 **"A dependence on the people":** *Federalist 51* (Madison).

177 **The British system:** See Wood, 20. According to Wood, "Monarchy and democracy would each prevent the other from sliding off toward an extremity on the power spectrum; and to keep the government from oscillating like a pendulum the aristocracy would act as a centering stabilizer" (198).

178 **"there would be an end":** Baron de Montesquieu, trans., Thomas Nugent, *The Spirit of Laws* (Littleton, Colo.: F. B. Rothman, 1991), 1:174.

178 **"compleat separation of the great":** Centinel II, Oct. 24, 1787, in Storing 2:143, 151.

178 **"power is of an encroaching nature":** *Federalist 48* (Madison).

178 **"Ambition must be made":** *Federalist 51* (Madison).

179 **"The legislative department is every where":** *Federalist 48* (Madison).

179 **"concurrence of two distinct bodies":** *Federalist 62* (Madison).

180 **"The injury which may possibly":** *Federalist 73* (Hamilton).

180 **"own temporary errors and delusions":** *Federalist 63* (Madison).

180 **"an additional security":** *Federalist 73* (Hamilton).

180 **"far less probable":** Ibid.

180 **permit the president to act with "energy":** *Federalist 70* (Hamilton).

181 **"Decision, activity, secrecy":** Ibid.

181 **"The FIRST relates":** *Federalist 41* (Madison).

181 **"causes of hostility":** *Federalist 6* (Hamilton).

181 **"nations in general":** *Federalist 4* (Jay).

181 **"Security against foreign danger":** *Federalist 41* (Madison).

181 **government "ought to be cloathed":** *Federalist 23* (Hamilton).

181 **"to raise armies":** Ibid.

181   **The Constitution specifies:** U.S. Constitution, art. I, sec. 8, cl. 1, 12, 13, 14.

182   **"commander-in-chief":** Ibid., art. II, sec. 2.

182   **"would amount to nothing":** *Federalist 69* (Hamilton).

182   **Since the time of President Washington:** See, e.g., John H. Ely, "The American War in Indochina, Part I: The (Troubled) Constitutionality of the War They Told Us About, *Stan. L. Rev.* 42 (1990): 877, 913; Steven G. Calabresi and Christopher S. Yoo, "The Unitary Executive During the First Half-Century," *Case W. Res. L. Rev.* 47 (1997): 1451; Calabresi and Yoo, "The Unitary Executive During the Second Half-Century," *Harv. J.L. & Pub. Pol'y* 26 (2003): 667; Charles Tiefer, "Can Appropriation Riders Speed Our Exit from Iraq?" *Stan. J. Int'l L.* 42 (2006): 291.

183   **the Supreme Court should not "second guess":** *Hamdi v. Rumsfeld*, 542 U.S. 507 (2004).

183   **"direction of war":** *Hamdi v. Rumsfeld*, 542 U.S. 507, 579 (2004) (Thomas dissenting, quoting *Federalist 74*). See also Jide Nzelibe and John Yoo, "Rational War and Constitutional Design," *Yale L.J.* 115 (2006): 2512, 2523, which quotes from the same essay to establish the conclusion that, "From the standpoint of institutional design, it seems that the executive branch has critical advantages over a multi-member legislature in reaching foreign policy and national security decisions that are more accurate."

183   **"a state of war is not":** *Hamdi v. Rumsfeld*, 542 U.S. 507, 536 (2004) (O'Connor plurality opinion). Even though this statement is contained in a plurality opinion, it represents a statement of principle accepted by all of the justices except Justice Thomas.

183   **"the constant aim":** *Federalist 51* (Madison).

183   **The opinion of Justice Scalia:** Not all of Justice Scalia's opinions in which he relied on *The Federalist* are this successful. For example, see the discussion of *Printz* in chap. 10.

184   **"the practice of arbitrary imprisonments":** *Federalist 84* (Hamilton).

184   **Scalia concluded that:** *Hamdi v. Rumsfeld*, 542 U.S. 562 (Scalia dissenting), quoting U.S. Constitution, art. I, sec. 9, cl. 2. The conclusion that, absent suspension of the writ of habeas corpus by Congress, the only way to try a citizen accused of being an enemy combatant was in a criminal court was not accepted by the rest of the Court.

184   *American Insurance Ass'n v. Garamendi:* 539 U.S. 396 (2003).

184   **an agreement signed by President Clinton:** Similar agreements were made by the president and the leaders of France and Austria.

185   **"If we are to be one nation":** *Federalist 42* (Madison). Souter also quoted *Federalist 80* ("The peace of the WHOLE ought not to be left at the disposal of a PART" and *Federalist 44* (Madison) discussing "the advantage of uniformity in all points which relate to foreign powers."

185   **"two thirds of the Senators present concur":** U.S. Constitution, art. II, sec. 2.

185   **There are two types of executive agreements:** See, generally, Louis Henkin, *Foreign Affairs and the U.S. Constitution,* 2nd ed. (New York: Oxford, 1996), 215–229.

185   **fewer than 5 percent:** See *Treaties and Other International Agreements: The Role of the United States Senate,* 98th Cong., 2nd sess., 1984, S. Rep. 205.

186 **"The multitudinous composition"**: *Federalist 75* (Hamilton).

186 **"a nice and uniform"**: Ibid.

186 **"the advantage of numbers"**: Ibid.

186 **"He must either have"**: *Federalist 64* (Jay).

186 **"The security essentially intended"**: *Federalist 66* (Hamilton).

187 **"The President is to have power"**: *Federalist 69* (Hamilton).

187 **"The history of human conduct"**: *Federalist 75* (Hamilton).

187 the **"historical practice"**: *Am. Ins. Ass'n v. Garamendi*, 539 U.S. 396, 416 (2003).

187 **One possible concern:** Indeed, one federal court of appeals declined to rule on the question of whether the fact that NAFTA was not approved as a treaty made it unconstitutional on the grounds that the issue presented "a nonjusticiable political question." *Made in the USA Found. v. United States*, 242 F.3d 1300, 1320 (11th Cir. 2001), *cert. denied, USW v. United States*, 534 U.S. 1039 (2001).

187 **"excellent barrier to the encroachments"**: *Federalist 78* (Hamilton).

188 **"whenever a particular statute"**: *Federalist 78* (Hamilton).

188 **federal judges must be appointed for life:** U.S. Constitution, art. III, sec. 1. The other major guarantee of judicial independence is that their salaries cannot be reduced while in office: "Next to permanency in office, nothing can contribute more to the independence of the judges than a fixed provision for their support," *Federalist 79* (Hamilton).

188 **"the permanent tenure"**: *Federalist 51* (Madison).

188 **all of whom voted to reaffirm:** *Planned Parenthood of Southeastern Pennsylvania v. Casey*, 505 U.S. 833, 846 (1992).

188 **The most articulate Anti-Federalist proponent:** *See* Jack N. Rakove, *Original Meanings: Politics and Ideas in the Making of the Constitution* (New York: Knopf, 1996), 187.

188 **"There is no power above them"**: Brutus XV, Mar. 20, 1788, in Storing 2:437, 439. Brutus's five essays dealing with the judiciary, numbered 11'–15, ran from Jan. 31 to Mar. 20, 1788.

189 **"In their decisions"**: Brutus XI, Jan. 31, 1788, in Storing 2:417, 419.

189 **"a point-by-point rejoinder"**: Shlomo Slonim, "Federalist No. 78 and Brutus' Neglected Thesis on Judicial Supremacy," *Const. Commentary* 23 (2006): 7, 19.

189 **"an intermediate body"**: *Federalist 78* (Hamilton).

189 **"the rights of individuals"**: Ibid.

189 **"a momentary inclination"**: Ibid.

189 **"serious oppressions of the minor party"**: Ibid.

189 **"substitute their own pleasure:"** Ibid.

190 **"to exercise WILL"**: Ibid.

190 **"there is not a syllable"**: *Federalist 81* (Hamilton).

190 **"There never can be danger"**: Ibid.

190 **"wicked and corrupt motives"**: Brutus XV, Mar. 20, 1788, in Storing 2:437, 440.

191 **Under the English common law system:** William Blackstone, *Commentaries on the Laws of England* (Chicago: University of Chicago Press, 1979) 1:*69; see, generally,

Thomas R. Lee, "Stare Decisis in Historical Perspective: From the Founding Era to the Rehnquist Court," *Vand. L. Rev.* 52 (1999): 647.

191 **"may happen that the judge":** Blackstone, 1:*71.

191 **"To avoid an arbitrary discretion":** *Federalist 78* (Hamilton).

191 **"They will be able to extend":** Brutus XV, Mar. 20, 1788, in Storing 2:437, 441. Brutus argued that such a line of cases would lead to the eventual elimination of all state governments.

192 **"to condemn every constitution":** *Federalist 81* (Hamilton).

192 **the "least dangerous" branch:** *Federalist 78* (Hamilton).

192 **"deciding issues no more broadly":** Douglas W. Kmiec, "An 'Honest Broker,'" *Washington Post*, Oct. 4, 2005: A23.

192 **"least responsive to opinion":** See, e.g., Sean Moynihan, "The Case for Constitutional Evolution," *Denv. U.L. Rev.* 81 (2003): 191, 197.

192 **"commands the purse":** *Federalist 78* (Hamilton).

192 **"holds the sword of the community":** The president, Hamilton said, can also curry favor through his power to make appointments to important governmental positions. *Federalist 78* (Hamilton).

192 **"the strength or of the wealth":** *Federalist 78* (Hamilton).

193 **"Particular misconstructions and contraventions":** *Federalist 81* (Hamilton).

193 **"individual oppression may now":** *Federalist 78* (Hamilton).

CHAPTER 9

195 **"I want to tell you":** Jack Bass and Marilyn Thompson, *Strom: The Complicated Personal and Political Life of Strom Thurmond* (New York: Public Affairs, 2005), 117.

195 **"I believe in states' rights":** Douglas Kneeland, "Reagan Campaigns at Mississippi Fair,"*New York Times*, Aug. 4, 1980: A11.

195 **"rooted in the knowledge":** Presidential Executive Order 12612, Oct. 26, 1987.

196 **"many liberals as a smoke screen":** John Kincaid, "The State of American Federalism—1986," *Publius: The Journal of Federalism* 17 (1987): 1–32.

196 **"in delineating the boundary":** *Federalist 37* (Madison).

197 **quote only those statements:** Peter Smith, "Sources of Federalism: An Empirical Analysis of the Court's Quest for Original Meaning," *U.C.L.A. Rev.* 52 (2004): 217.

197 ***Printz v. United States*:** 521 U.S. 898 (1997).

197 **"the Legislatures Courts and Magistrates":** *Printz v. United States*, 521 U.S. 971–972 (Souter dissenting; emphasis in *Federalist 27*).

197 **who so frequently quotes *The Federalist*:** Among the opinions for which Justice Scalia cited *The Federalist* are: *Nev. v. Hicks*, 533 U.S. 353, 367 (2001); *College Sav. Bank v. Fla. Prepaidpostsecondary Ed. Expense Bd.*, 527 U.S. 666, 690 (1999); *Edmond v. United States*, 520 U.S. 651, 659 (1997); *Plaut v. Spendthrift Farm*, 514 U.S. 211, 222 (1995).

198 **"a remarkably 'whole personality'":** Clinton Rossiter, *Alexander Hamilton and the Constitution* (New York: Harcourt, 1964), 58; Garry Wills, *Explaining America: The*

Federalist (New York: Penguin Books, 1982), 78. It is generally though not universally conceded that the earlier contrary conclusion of Alpheus Mason was significantly overstated; see Alpheus Thomas Mason, "The Federalist—A Split Personality," *The American Historical Review* 57, no. 3 (April 1952): 625–643. See, e.g., Martin Diamond, "The Federalist," in William A. Schambra, *As Far as Republican Principles Will Admit* (Lanham, Md.: National Book Network, 1992), 38 (stating that *The Federalist* is "the work of one Publius" who supplies "a consistent, comprehensive, and true account of the Constitution and of the regime it was calculated to engender").

199 **"ambition must be made to counteract ambition":** *Federalist 51* (Madison).

199 **"Power being almost always":** *Federalist 28* (Hamilton).

199 **"a double security arises":** *Federalist 51* (Madison).

199 **"the States in all unenumerated cases":** *Federalist 40* (Madison).

199 **"certain exclusive and very important":** *Federalist 9* (Hamilton).

199 ***United States v. E. C. Knight Co.:*** 156 U.S. 1 (1895).

200 **"trafficked across state lines":** *United States v. Lopez,* 514 U.S. 549, 586–589 (1995) (Thomas concurring). In one sense his definition of commerce is correct. In *The Federalist,* commerce is generally treated as distinct from agriculture and manufacturing. For example, Hamilton at one point refers to a legislator's knowledge of a region's "agriculture, commerce, manufactures" *Federalist 36* (Hamilton). This was the general understanding of Anti-Federalists as well as other Federalist writers. See Randy Barnett, "The Original Meaning of the Commerce Clause," *U. Chi. L. Rev.* 68 (2001): 101; Barnett "New Evidence of the Original Meaning of the Commerce Clause," *Ark. L. Rev.* 55 (2003): 55. Some scholars disagree, believing that commerce had a broader meaning which could include manufacturing and agriculture. Grant S. Nelson and Robert J. Pushaw Jr., "Rethinking the Commerce Clause: Applying First Principles to Uphold Federal Commercial Regulations but Preserve State Control over Social Issues," *Iowa L. Rev.* 85 (1999): 1; Nelson and Pushaw, "A Critique of the Narrow Interpretation of the Commerce Clause," *Nw. U. L. Rev.* 96 (2002): 695.

200 **"productive activities like manufacturing":** *Gonzales v. Raich,* 545 U.S. 1, 58 (2005) (Thomas dissenting); *United States v. Lopez,* 514 U.S. 549, 586–589 (1995) (Thomas concurring).

200 **federal minimum wage and child labor laws:** Similar laws had been held unconstitutional when the Supreme Court formerly utilized the same definition of commerce as that supported by Justice Thomas. See *A. L. A. Schechter Poultry Corp. v. United States,* 295 U.S. 495 (1935); *Hammer v. Dagenhart,* 247 U.S. 251 (1918).

200 **"The powers delegated":** *Federalist 45* (Madison).

200 **"the ordinary administration":** *Federalist 17* (Hamilton).

200 **"must be empowered to pass":** *Federalist 23* (Hamilton).

200 **"maintenance of harmony":** *Federalist 41* (Madison).

200 **One reason that Congress:** Justice Thomas acknowledges that the "necessary and proper" clause increased Congress's power, but he would limit that enhancement to laws which have an "obvious, simple, and direct relation" to the regulation of interstate commerce. *Gonzales v. Raich,* 545 U.S. 1, 61 (2005) (Thomas dissenting).

201   **"the government of the Union":** *Federalist 23* (Hamilton).

201   **"wherever the end is required":** *Federalist 44* (Madison).

201   **"in the commercial sphere":** *United States v. Lopez*, 514 U.S. 549, 574 (1995) (Kennedy concurring).

202   **"which concern all the members":** *Federalist 14* (Madison).

202   **Thomas Jefferson had a grand total:** Jefferson's hog ownership peaked at forty-three in 1781 and had declined to thirty by the end of 1794. See Thomas Jefferson, *Farm Book*, ed. Edwin Morris Betts (Princeton, N.J.: Princeton University Press, 1953), 33 (http://www.thomasjeffersonpapers.org/farm/). Smithfield Foods' 2006 hog totals are available online at http://www.smithfieldfoods.com/Investor/Snapshot/. The size of Smithfield's hog production is also discussed in *Smithfield Foods, Inc. v. Miller*, 241 F. Supp. 2d 978 (D. Iowa 2003).

202   **"able to enlarge its sphere of jurisdiction":** *Federalist 46* (Madison).

202   **"the constitutional equilibrium":** *Federalist 31* (Hamilton).

202   **"by throwing themselves into either scale":** *Federalist 28* (Hamilton).

202   **"the people should in [the] future":** *Federalist 46* (Madison). Hamilton made a similar observation when he remarked: "The people of each State would be apt to feel a stronger bias towards their local governments than towards the government of the Union; unless the force of that principle should be destroyed by a much better administration of the latter" *Federalist 17* (Hamilton).

203   **"the people ought not surely":** *Federalist 46* (Madison).

203   **"The structures, finances, and policies":** John Dinan and Dale Krane, "The State of American Federalism, 2005: Federalism Resurfaces in the Political Debate," *Publius: The Journal of Federalism* 36 (May 17, 2006): 327–374.

203   **"betray their constituents":** *Federalist 28* (Hamilton).

203   **"formidable to the liberties":** *Federalist 29* (Hamilton).

203   **"the advantage of being armed":** *Federalist 46* (Madison).

203   **"a militia amounting to near":** Ibid.

204   **"by the election of more faithful":** *Federalist 44* (Madison).

204   **"auxiliary precautions":** *Federalist 51* (Madison).

204   **"each of the principal branches":** *Federalist 45* (Madison).

204   **presidential electors were chosen:** U.S. Constitution, art. II, sec. 1.

204   **"time, place and manner":** U.S. Constitution, art. I, sec. 4. Congress does have the ability to amend state regulations of federal elections, other than the time for voting for senators.

204   **"feel a dependence":** *Federalist 45* (Madison).

204   ***Garcia v. San Antonio Metropolitan Transit Authority:*** 469 U.S. 528 (1985).

204   **"will partake sufficiently of the spirit":** *Garcia v. San Antonio Metro. Transit Auth.*, 469 U.S. 528, 551 (1985).

205   **"residuary authorities":** *Federalist 33* (Hamilton).

205   **"merely acts of usurpation":** Ibid.

205   **"success of the usurpation":** *Federalist 44* (Madison).

205   **"in controversies relating to the boundary":** *Federalist 39* (Madison).

205   ***United States v. Lopez:*** 514 U.S. 549 (1995).

205   *United States v. Morrison*: 529 U.S. 598 (2000).

205   "**a distinction between**": *United States v. Morrison*, 529 U.S. 598, 618 (2000).

205   "**an unconfined authority**": *Federalist 23* (Hamilton).

205   "**the general government**": *Federalist 14* (Madison).

206   **the Court expressed doubts:** *Solid Waste Agency v. United States Army Corps of Engineers*, 531 U.S. 159 (2001). See also *Rapanos v. U.S.*, 126 S. Ct. 2208, 2225 (2006), in which Justice Scalia, writing for a four-justice plurality, questioned whether the Congress could constitutionally regulate wetlands located near "channels through which water flows intermittently or ephemerally, or channels that periodically provide drainage for rainfall."

206   **the Court permitted Congress:** *Gonzales v. Raich*, 545 U.S. 1 (2005).

207   "**a usurpation of power**": *Federalist 33* (Hamilton).

207   **In 2005 the Supreme Court struck down:** *Granholm v. Heald*, 544 U.S. 460 (2005).

207   "**is a charter for Congress**": *Tyler Pipe v. Washington State Dep't of Revenue*, 483 U.S. 232, 260 (1987) (Scalia dissenting).

207   "**has no basis**": *Am. Trucking Ass'ns v. Mich. PSC*, 545 U.S. 429, 439 (2005) (Thomas concurring).

207   "**unrestrained intercourse between the States**": *Federalist 11* (Hamilton).

207   "**at liberty to regulate**": *Federalist 42* (Madison).

208   "**Whatever practices may have a tendency**": *Federalist 80* (Hamilton). There is some language in *The Federalist* which indicates that Congress was the entity designed to serve as "a superintending authority over the reciprocal trade" of the states. *Federalist 42* (Madison). There is also language that cautions against implying limits on state authority. As Hamilton asserted, normally when the Constitution empowers Congress and restricts a state, as with the ban on coining money, it does so directly: "There has been the most pointed care in those cases where it was deemed improper that the like authorities should reside in the States, to insert negative clauses prohibiting the exercise of them by the States" *Federalist 32* (Hamilton). Hamilton added that the sovereignty of the states would also be eliminated in those cases where giving that particular authority to state governments "would be absolutely and totally CONTRADICTORY and REPUGNANT" to the exercise of the authority given to the federal government (ibid.). It appears that the dormant commerce clause reflects a determination that it would be "absolutely and totally CONTRADICTORY and REPUGNANT" to the constitutional scheme if states were permitted to interfere with interstate commerce or discriminate against out-of-state businesses.

208   **consider the case of Patricia Garrett:** *Board of Trustees of the University of Alabama v. Garrett*, 531 U.S. 356 (2001).

208   **A similar fate befell state probation officers:** *Alden v. Maine*, 527 U.S. 706 (1999).

209   "**It is inherent**": *Federalist 81* (Hamilton), quoted in *Alden v. Maine*, 527 U.S. 706, 717 (1999).

209   "**federal jurisdiction over suits**": *Seminole Tribe v. Fla.*, 517 U.S. 44, 54 (1996), quoting *Hans v. Louisiana*, 134 U.S. 1, 15 (1890) (internal quotation marks omitted).

209 **"assured the people":** *Alden v. Maine*, 527 U.S. 706, 716 (1999).

209 **Thus, the Court has concluded:** Although much of the Supreme Court's doctrine in this area began with cases dealing with the Eleventh Amendment (which was ratified in 1795, see *Seminole Tribe v. Florida*, 517 US 44 [1996]), the Court subsequently declared that "sovereign immunity derives not from the Eleventh Amendment but from the structure of the original Constitution itself," *Alden v. Maine*, 527 U.S. 706, 728 (1999).

210 **"humiliating and degrading":** Brutus XIII, Feb. 21, 1788, in Storing 2:428, 430.

210 **"not to be amenable":** *Federalist 80* (Hamilton).

210 **"rather clearly assumes":** Martha A. Field, "The Eleventh Amendment and Other Sovereign Immunity Doctrines: Part One," *Pa. L.Rev.* 126 (1978): 515, 535n75.

211 **"suits against sovereigns":** Maeva Marcus and James R. Perry, *The Documentary History of the Supreme Court of the United States 1789–1800* (New York: Columbia University Press, 2004), 5:2.

CHAPTER 10

213 **"what is government":** *Federalist 51* (Madison).

213 **based on a conception of the universality:** According to political scientist David Howe, the arguments in *The Federalist* are "based on ideas on universal human nature." "The Political Psychology of the Federalist," *Wm. and Mary Q.* 44 (1987): 485, 486.

213 **the motivations for people's differing beliefs:** For a discussion of Publius's views of these motivations, see James P. Scanlan, "'The Federalist' and Human Nature," *The Review of Politics* 21 (1959): 657.

213 **"timid and cautious":** *Federalist 49* (Madison).

214 **"momentary passions and immediate interest":** *Federalist 6* (Hamilton).

214 **"Because the passions of men":** *Federalist 15* (Hamilton).

214 **"men are ambitious":** *Federalist 6* (Hamilton).

214 **"the impulse and the opportunity":** *Federalist 10* (Madison).

214 **"a nation of philosophers":** *Federalist 49* (Madison).

214 **"best antidote" to extremism:** See, e.g., "President Bush Participates in Joint Press Availability with President Ilves of Estonia," http://www.whitehouse.gov/news/releases/2006/11/20061128–4.html. Vice President Dick Cheney similarly declared that "the best antidote to terror is freedom and democracy" in "Where They Stand," *Detroit Free Press*, Oct. 30, 2004: 8A.

214 **"ideologies of hatred":** Secretary of State Condoleezza Rice, "Opening Remarks before the House Appropriations Subcommittee," Mar. 9, 2006, http://www.state.gov/secretary/rm/2006/62911.htm.

214 **"to sacrifice to its ruling passion":** *Federalist 10* (Madison).

214 **"If a majority be united":** *Federalist 51* (Madison).

215 **"mortal feuds":** *Federalist 16* (Hamilton).

215 **"without the compass of human remedies":** *Federalist 43* (Madison).

215 **"one united people"**: *Federalist 2* (Jay). Jay added that Americans also shared "the same religion." Madison, however, noted that America's religious freedoms were secured by its "multiplicity of sects." *Federalist 51* (Madison).

215 **"that peace or war"**: *Federalist 34* (Hamilton).

215 **"When the sword"**: *Federalist 16* (Hamilton).

216 **"the continual effort and alarm"**: *Federalist 8* (Hamilton).

216 **"sudden breese of passion"**: *Federalist 71* (Hamilton).

216 **"It is the reason, alone"**: *Federalist 49* (Madison).

216 **"suspend the blow"**: *Federalist 63* (Madison).

216 **"it is the duty of the persons"**: *Federalist 71* (Hamilton).

217 **"wisdom . . . patriotism and love of justice"**: *Federalist 10* (Madison).

217 **"misled by the artful"**: *Federalist 63* (Madison).

217 **"commencing Demagogues and ending tyrants"**: *Federalist 1* (Hamilton). Political scientist Tom Krannawitter noted that the actual word "demagogue" appears only in the first and last essays of *The Federalist*. Symbolically, therefore, "self-government, as presented in *The Federalist*, is literally surrounded by the problem of demagoguery." "Constitutional Government and Judicial Power: The Political Science of The Federalist," *Interpretation: A Journal of Political Philosophy* 27 (1999): 43–69.

217 **"The representatives of the people"**: *Federalist 71* (Hamilton).

217 **"may forget their obligations"**: *Federalist 62* (Madison).

217 **"the defect of better motives"**: *Federalist 51* (Madison).

217 **"act with more rectitude"**: *Federalist 15* (Hamilton).

217 **"factious leaders"**: *Federalist 62* (Madison).

217 **"regard to reputation"**: *Federalist 15* (Hamilton).

218 **"improprieties and excesses"**: Ibid.

218 **"the confusion and intemperance of a multitude"**: *Federalist 55* (Madison).

218 **"the mild voice of reason"**: *Federalist 42* (Madison).

218 **"Had every Athenian citizen"**: *Federalist 55* (Madison).

218 ensure **"personal responsibility"**: *Federalist 63* (Madison).

218 the first time in the history: *Oxford English Dictionary*, John Simpson and Edmund Weiner, eds., 2d ed. (1989), 13:742. The O.E.D. cites *Federalist 63* as the initial appearance of the word "responsibility," even though it was used almost three months earlier, on Dec. 18, 1787, in *Federalist 23* (Hamilton). Researchers have also discovered that both Madison and Hamilton used the word as far back as 1780. See Douglass Adair, "The Federalist Papers," in Trevor Colbourn, ed., *Fame and the Founding Fathers* (New York: W. W. Norton, 1974), 366n8 (describing James Madison's use of the word "responsibility" in a report to the Continental Congress on July 22, 1780); Ralph Lerner, "The American Founders' Responsibility," *Wash. & Lee L. Rev.* 56 (1999): 891, 891n1 (describing a letter of Alexander Hamilton to James Duane on Sept. 3, 1780, discussing the responsibility of Congress).

218 **"independent and public spirited men"**: *Federalist 76* (Hamilton).

218 **"discern the true interest"**: *Federalist 10* & *57* (Madison).

218 **"There are men"**: *Federalist 73* (Hamilton).

218 **"This supposition of universal venality"**: *Federalist 76* (Hamilton).

219 **"As there is a degree of depravity"**: *Federalist 55* (Madison).

219 **"virtue and honor among mankind"**: *Federalist 76* (Hamilton).

219 **"nothing less than the chains"**: *Federalist 55* (Madison).

219 **"Man's sense of justice"**: Willliam Vander Hevuel, "Postpone the Visit to Manila," *New York Times*, Sept. 8, 1983: A23.

219 **"the GREATER, not the PERFECT, good"**: *Federalist 41* (Madison).

219 **"a faultless plan"**: *Federalist 37* (Madison).

219 **some "real force"**: *Federalist 85* (Hamilton).

219 **"the necessity of moderating"**: *Federalist 37* (Madison).

220 **"When men exercise their reason"**: *Federalist 50* (Madison).

220 **"the reason of man continues fallible"**: *Federalist 10* (Madison).

220 **"ambition, avarice, personal animosity"**: *Federalist 1* (Hamilton).

220 **"as long as the connection"**: *Federalist 10* (Madison).

220 **"wise and good men"**: *Federalist 1* (Hamilton).

220 **"furnish a lesson of moderation"**: Ibid.

220 **"they themselves also are but men"**: *Federalist 37* (Madison).

221 **"accomplished a revolution"**: *Federalist 14* (Madison).

221 **"Is it not the glory"**: Ibid.

221 **"Let experience the least fallible"**: *Federalist 6* (Hamilton).

221 **"Where annual elections end, tyranny begins"**: *Federalist 53* (Madison). This quote is a paraphrase from a statement John Adams wrote in 1776: "Where annual elections end, there slavery begins." "Thoughts on Government," reprinted in *The Political Writings of John Adams* (2001), 493.

221 **"Let us consult experience"**: *Federalist 52* (Madison).

221 **"proof, and I conceive it"**: Ibid.

222 **"mutual jealousies, fears"**: *Federalist 18* (Madison).

222 **"make no apology"**: *Federalist 20* (Madison).

222 **"Experience is the oracle of truth"**: Ibid.

222 **"furnish no other light"**: *Federalist 37* (Madison).

222 **"render extreme circumspection"**: *Federalist 63* (Madison). For example, Madison notes that the Swiss cantons, "so far as the peculiarity of their case will admit of comparison with that of the United States," confirm the dangers of a loose confederacy. *Federalist 19* (Madison).

223 **"deprive the government"**: *Federalist 49* (Madison).

BIBLIOGRAPHY

Ackerman, Bruce A. *We the People.* Cambridge, Mass.: Belknap Press of Harvard University Press, 1991.

Adair, Douglass, ed. "James Madison's Autobiography." *Wm. and Mary Q.* 2 (1945): 191–209.

———. "A Note on Certain of Hamilton's Pseudonyms." *Wm. and Mary Q.* 12 (1955): 282–297.

———. "That Politics May be Reduced to a Science: David Hume, James Madison, and the Tenth Federalist" and "Authorship of the Disputed Federalist Papers," in Trevor Colbourn, ed., *Fame and the Founding Fathers.* New York: W. W. Norton, 1974.

Adams, John, and Benjamin Rush. *The Spur of Fame: Dialogues of John Adams and Benjamin Rush, 1805–1813.* Ed. John A. Schutz and Douglass Adair. Indianapolis: Liberty Fund, 2000.

Adams, William Howard. *Gouverneur Morris: An Independent Life.* New Haven, Conn.: Yale University Press, 2003.

Allen, W. B., and Kevin A. Cloonan. *The Federalist Papers: A Commentary: "The Baton Rouge Lectures."* New York: P. Lang, 2000.

Allen, W. B., and John C. Fitzpatrick, eds. *George Washington: A Collection.* Indianapolis: Liberty Classics, 1988.

Allen, W. B., Gordon Lloyd, and Margie Lloyd, eds. *The Essential Antifederalist.* Lanham, Md.: University Press of America, 1985.

Ambrose, Douglas, and Robert W. T. Martin. *The Many Faces of Alexander Hamilton: The Life and Legacy of America's Most Elusive Founding Father.* New York: New York University Press, 2006.

Andrews, William L. "Early American Bookbinding and Kindred Subjects." *The Bookman: A Magazine of Literature and Life* 15 (1903): 164–175.

Ashe, Samuel A. *Biographical History of North Carolina from Colonial Times to the Present.* Greensboro, N.C.: C. L. Van Noppen, 1905.

Bailyn, Bernard. *The Debate on the Constitution.* New York: Viking Press, 1993.

———. *To Begin the World Anew: The Genius and Ambiguities of the American Founders.* New York: Knopf, 2003.

Baltz, Shirley Vlasak. *A Closer Look at the Annapolis Convention, September 1786.* Annapolis: Maryland Office for the Bicentennial of the U.S. Constitution, 1986.

Bancroft, George. *History of the Formation of the Constitution of the United States of America.* New York: D. Appleton and Co., 1882.

Banner, Stuart. *Anglo-American Securities Regulation Cultural and Political Roots, 1690–1860.* New York: Cambridge University Press, 1998.

Banning, Lance. *The Sacred Fire of Liberty: James Madison and the Founding of the Federal Republic.* Ithaca, N.Y.: Cornell University Press, 1995.

Barbash, Fred. *The Founding a Dramatic Account of the Writing of the Constitution.* New York: Linden Press/Simon & Schuster, 1987.

Barnett, Randy E. "New Evidence of the Original Meaning of the Commerce Clause." *Ark. L. Rev.* 55 (2003): 847–899.

———. "The Original Meaning of the Commerce Clause." *U. Chi. L. Rev.* 68 (2001): 101–147.

Bass, Jack, and Marilyn Thompson. *Strom: The Complicated Personal and Political Life of Strom Thurmond.* New York: Public Affairs, 2005.

Baxter, Katharine Schuyler. *A Godchild of Washington: A Picture of the Past.* London: F. T. Neely, 1897.

Beard, Charles A. *An Economic Interpretation of the Constitution of the United States.* New York: Macmillan, 1935.

———. *The Enduring Federalist.* New York: F. Ungar Publishing Co., 1959.

Beeman, Richard R., Stephen Botein, and Edward C. Carter, eds. *Beyond Confederation: Origins of the Constitution and American National Identity.* Chapel Hill: University of North Carolina Press, 1987.

Bell, Whitfield J. "Doctors' Riot, New York, 1788." *Bull. N. Y. Acad. Med.* 47 (1971): 1501–1503.

Bemis, Samuel Flagg. *Jay's Treaty: A Study in Commerce and Diplomacy.* Westport, Conn.: Greenwood Press, 1962.

Benson, Egbert. *Memoir, Read Before the Historical Society of the State of New York, December 31, 1816.* Jamaica, N.Y.: Henry C. Sleight, 1848.

Berger, Raoul. *Government by Judiciary: The Transformation of the Fourteenth Amendment.* Cambridge, Mass.: Harvard University Press, 1977.

Bernstein, Richard B., and Kym S. Rice. *Are We to Be a Nation? The Making of the Constitution.* Cambridge, Mass.: Harvard University Press, 1987.

Bickel, Alexander M. "The Original Understanding and the Segregation Decision." *Harv. L. Rev.* 69 (1955): 1–58.

Biddle, Alexander. *Old Family Letters Copied from the Originals for Alexander Biddle; Series A-B.* Philadelphia: J. B. Lippincott, 1892.

Binney, Horace. *An Inquiry into the Formation of Washington's Farewell Address.* New York: Da Capo, 1969.

Blackstone, William. *Commentaries on the Laws of England.* Chicago: University of Chicago Press, 1979.

Boller, Paul F. *Presidential Anecdotes.* New York: Oxford University Press, 1981.

Bowen, Catherine Drinker. *Miracle at Philadelphia: The Story of the Constitutional Convention, May to September, 1787.* Boston: Little, Brown, 1986.

Bowling, Kenneth R. "The Bank Bill, the Capital City and President Washington." *Capitol Studies* 1 (1972): 59–71.

———. *The Creation of Washington, D.C.: The Idea and Location of the American Capital.* Fairfax, Va.: George Mason University Press, 1991.

———. "Dinner at Jefferson's: A Note on Jacob E. Cooke's 'The Compromise of 1790.'" *Wm. and Mary Q.* 28 (1971): 629–648.

———. "New Light on the Philadelphia Mutiny of 1783: Federal-State at the Confrontation at the Close of the War for Independence." *Pennsylvania Magazine of History and Biography* 101 (1977): 419–450.

Boyd, Steven R. *The Politics of Opposition: Antifederalists and the Acceptance of the Constitution.* Millwood, N.Y.: KTO Press, 1979.

Brant, Irving. *The Bill of Rights: Its Origin and Meaning.* Indianapolis: Bobbs-Merrill, 1965.

———. *James Madison and American Nationalism.* Princeton, N.J.: Van Nostrand Reinhold, 1968.

———. *James Madison: Father of the Constitution, 1787–1800.* Indianapolis: Bobbs-Merrill, 1950.

———. *James Madison: The Nationalist, 1780–1787.* Indianapolis: Bobbs-Merrill, 1948.

———. "Settling the Authorship of the Federalist." *Am. Hist. Rev.* 67 (1961): 71–75.

Brennan, William J., Jr. "Speech to the Text and Teaching Symposium," Georgetown University, Oct. 12, 1985. In *The Great Debate: Interpreting Our Written Constitution.* Federalist Society for Law and Public Policy Studies (1986), 11–25.

Brest, Paul. "The Misconceived Quest for the Original Understanding." *B.U.L. Rev.* 60 (1980): 204–223.

Breyer, Stephen G. *Active Liberty: Interpreting Our Democratic Constitution.* New York: Knopf, 2005.

———. "Our Democratic Constitution." *N.Y.U. L. Rev.* 77 (2002): 245–272.

Broadwater, Jeff. *George Mason: Forgotten Founder.* Chapel Hill: University of North Carolina Press, 2006.

Brookhiser, Richard. *Alexander Hamilton, American.* New York: Free Press, 1999.

———. *Gentleman Revolutionary: Gouverneur Morris, the Rake Who Wrote the Constitution.* New York: Free Press, 2003.

Burns, Edward McNall. *James Madison: Philosopher of the Constitution.* New York: Octagon Books, 1968.

Calabresi, Steven G., and Christopher S. Yoo. "The Unitary Executive During the Second Half-Century." *Case W. L. Rev.* 47 (1997): 1451–1561.

Carey, George W. "Publius: A Split Personality?" *Rev. of Pol.* 46 (1984): 5–22.

———, ed. *The Political Writings of John Adams.* Washington, D.C.: Regnery, 2000.

Carter, Steven. "The Right Questions in the Creation of Constitutional Meaning." *B.U.L. Rev.* 66 (1986): 71–91.

Cerami, Charles A. *Young Patriots: The Remarkable Story of Two Men, Their Impossible Plan, and the Revolution That Created the Constitution.* Naperville, Ill.: Sourcebooks, 2005.

Chemerinsky, Erwin. *Interpreting the Constitution*. New York: Praeger, 1987.

Chernow, Ron. *Alexander Hamilton*. New York: Penguin, 2004.

Clark, Bradford R. "Textualism and Federalism: Translating Federalism: A Structural Approach." *Geo. Wash. L. Rev.* 66 (1998): 1161–1197.

Clinton, Joshua D., and Adam Meirowitz. "Testing Explanations of Strategic Voting in Legislatures: A Reexamination of the Compromise of 1790." *American Journal of Political Science* 48 (2004): 675–689.

Coenen, Dan T. "A Rhetoric for Ratification: The Argument of 'The Federalist' and Its Impact on Constitutional Interpretation." *Duke L. J.* 56 (2006): 469–543.

——. *The Story of the Federalist: How Hamilton and Madison Reconceived America*. New York: Twelve Tables Press, 2007.

Cogan, Neil H., ed. *The Complete Bill of Rights: The Drafts, Debates, Sources, and Origins*. New York: Oxford University Press, 1997.

Coles, Edward. "Letters of Edward Coles." *Wm. and Mary Q.* 7 (1927): 158–173.

Collins, Varnum L. *The Continental Congress at Princeton*. Princeton, N.J.: The University Library, 1908.

Combs, Jerald A. *The Jay Treaty: Political Battleground of the Founding Fathers*. Berkeley: University of California Press, 1970.

Cooke, Jacob E. "Alexander Hamilton's Authorship of the 'Caesar Letters.'" *Wm. and Mary Q.* 17 (1960): 78–85.

——. "The Compromise of 1790." *Wm. and Mary Q.* 27 (1970): 523–545.

——. *Tench Coxe and the Early Republic*. Chapel Hill: University of North Carolina Press, 1978.

Cornell, Saul. *The Other Founders: Anti-Federalism and the Dissenting Tradition in America, 1788–1828*. Chapel Hill: University of North Carolina Press, 1999.

Crane, Elaine F. "Publius in the Provinces: Where Was 'The Federalist' Reprinted Outside New York City?" *Wm. and Mary Q.* 21 (1964): 589–592.

Currie, David P. *The Constitution in Congress: The Federalist Period 1789–1801*. Chicago: University of Chicago Press, 1997.

Cutler, William Parker, and Julia Perkins Cutler, eds. *Life, Journals and Correspondence of Rev. Manasseh Cutler, LL.D.* Cincinnati: R. Clarke & Co., 1888.

Dahl, Robert Alan. *A Preface to Democratic Theory*. Chicago: University of Chicago Press, 1956.

De Pauw, Linda Grant. *The Eleventh Pillar: New York State and the Federal Constitution*. Ithaca, N.Y.: Cornell University Press, 1966.

Diamond, Martin. *As Far as Republican Principles Will Admit*. Ed. William A. Schambra. Lanham, Md.: National Book Network, 1992.

Dietze, Gottfried. *The Federalist: A Classic on Federalism and Free Government*. Baltimore, Md.: Johns Hopkins University Press, 1999.

Dinan, John, and Dale Krane. "The State of American Federalism, 2005: Federalism Resurfaces in the Political Debate." *Publius: The Journal of Federalism* 36 (2006): 327–374.

Draper, Theodore. "Hume and Madison: The Secrets of Federalist Paper No. 10." *Encounter* 58 (1982): 34–47.

Ducayet, James W. "Publius and Federalism: On the Use and Abuse of the Federalist in Constitutional Interpretation." *N.Y.U. L. Rev.* 68 (1993): 821–869.

Durchslag, Melvyn R. "The Supreme Court and the Federalist Papers: Is There Less Here Than Meets the Eye?" *Wm. and Mary Bill Rts. J.* 14 (2005): 243–316.

Elkins, Stanley M., and Eric L. McKitrick. *The Age of Federalism.* New York: Oxford University Press, 1993.

Ellis, Joseph J. *Founding Brothers: The Revolutionary Generation.* New York: Knopf, 2000.

Ely, John H. "The American War in Indochina, Part I: The (Troubled) Constitutionality of the War They Told Us About." *Stan. L. Rev.* 42 (1990): 877–926.

Engeman, Thomas S., Edward J. Erler, and Thomas B. Hofeller. *The Federalist Concordance.* Chicago: University of Chicago Press, 1988.

Epstein, David F. *The Political Theory of the Federalist.* Chicago: University of Chicago Press, 1984.

Erikson, Robert S., Norman R. Luttbeg, and Kent L. Tedin. *American Public Opinion: Its Origins, Content, and Impact.* 2d ed. New York: Wiley, 1980.

Eskridge, William N., Jr. "Should the Supreme Court Read the Federalist But Not Statutory Legislative History?" *Geo. Wash. L. Rev.* 66 (1998): 1301–1323.

Evans, Michael W. "Foundations of the Tax Legislation Process: The Confederation, Constitutional Convention, and First Revenue Law." *Tax Notes Magazine,* Jan. 21, 1991: 283.

Farrand, Max, trans. *The Records of the Federal Convention of 1787.* New Haven, Conn.: Yale University Press, 1923. (Originally published 1911)

Ferguson, E. James. *The Power of the Purse.* Chapel Hill: University of North Carolina Press, 1961.

Ferguson, Robert A. "The Forgotten Publius: John Jay and the Aesthetics of Ratification." *Early American Literature* 34 (1999): 223–240.

Festa, Matthew J. "Dueling Federalists: Supreme Court Decisions with Multiple Opinions Citing 'The Federalist,' 1986–2007." *Seattle U. L. Rev.* 31 (2007): 75.

Field, Martha. "The Eleventh Amendment and Other Sovereign Immunity Doctrines: Part One." *U. Pa. L. Rev.* 126 (1977): 515.

Finkelman, Paul. "The Constitution and the Intentions of the Framers: The Limits of Historical Analysis." *U. Pitt. L. Rev.* 50 (1989): 349–398.

Fiske, John. *The Critical Period of American History, 1783–1789.* Boston: Houghton Mifflin, 1888.

Flack, Horace Edgar. *The Adoption of the Fourteenth Amendment.* Birmingham, Ala.: Palladium Press, 2003.

Fleet, Elizabeth, ed. "Madison's 'Detatched Memoranda.'" *Wm. and Mary Q.* 3 (1946): 534–568.

Flexner, James Thomas. *The Young Hamilton.* Boston: Little, Brown, 1978.

Foner, Philip Sheldon, ed. *The Life and Writings of Frederick Douglass.* New York: International, 1950.

Ford, Emily Ellsworth Fowler, and Emily Ellsworth Ford Skeel. *Notes on the Life of Noah Webster.* New York: Priv. Print, 1912.

Ford, Paul Leicester, ed. *Pamphlets on the Constitution of the United States Published During Its Discussion by the People 1787–1788 .* New York: Da Capo, 1968.

———. *The Works of Thomas Jefferson.* London: Putnam, 1904.

Ford, Worthington Chauncey. "Alexander Hamilton's Notes in the Federal Convention of 1787." *American Historical Review* 10 (1904): 97–109.

Fraser, Steve. *Every Man a Speculator: A History of Wall Street in American Life.* New York: HarperCollins, 2005.

Freeman, Landa M., Louise V. North, and Janet M. Wedge. *Selected Letters of John Jay and Sarah Livingston Jay: Correspondence by or to the First Chief Justice of the United States and His Wife.* Jefferson, N.C.: McFarland & Co, 2004.

Fung, Glenn. "The Disputed Federalist Papers: SVM Feature Selection Via Concave Minimization." *Proceedings of the 2003 Conference on Diversity in Computing* (Atlanta, 2003), 42–46.

Furtwangler, Albert. *The Authority of Publius: A Reading of the Federalist Papers.* Ithaca, N.Y.: Cornell University Press, 1984.

———. "Strategies of Candor in the Federalist." *Early American Literature* 14 (1979): 91–109.

Geisst, Charles R. *Wall Street: A History.* New York: Oxford University Press, 1997.

Gibson, Alan Ray. *Interpreting the Founding Guide to the Enduring Debates over the Origins and Foundations of the American Republic.* Lawrence: University Press of Kansas, 2006.

Gill, Mary Louise. "Method and Metaphysics in Plato's 'Sophist and Statesman.'" *Stanford Encyclopedia of Philosophy.* Ed. Edward N. Zalta: http://plato.stanford.edu/archives/win2005/entries/plato-sophstate/.

Gillespie, Michael Allen, and Michael Lienesch. *Ratifying the Constitution.* Lawrence: University Press of Kansas, 1989.

Goebel, Julius, ed. *The Law Practice of Alexander Hamilton.* New York: Columbia University Press, 1964.

Grigsby, Hugh Blair. *The History of Virginia Federal Convention of 1788.* Richmond: Virginia Historical Society, 1890.

Grofman, Bernard, and Donald A. Wittman, eds. *The Federalist Papers and the New Institutionalism.* New York: Agathon Press, 1989.

Hamilton, Allan McLane. *The Intimate Life of Alexander Hamilton.* New York: Scribner's, 1910.

Hamilton, John C. *History of the Republic of the United States of America, As Traced in the Writings of Alexander Hamilton and of His Contemporaries.* New York: D. Appleton & Co., 1857.

Hart, Albert Bushnell. *American History Told by Contemporaries.* London: Macmillan, 1898.

Headley, Joel Tyler. *The Great Riots of New York, 1712–1873.* Indianapolis: Bobbs-Merrill, 1970.

Hecht, Marie B. *Odd Destiny: The Life of Alexander Hamilton.* New York: Macmillan, 1982.

Henderson, H. James. *Party Politics in the Continental Congress.* New York: McGraw-Hill, 1974.

Hendrickson, Robert A. *The Rise and Fall of Alexander Hamilton.* New York: Van Nostrand Reinhold, 1981.

Henkin, Louis. *Foreign Affairs and the Constitution.* 2nd ed. New York: Oxford, 1996.

Higginson, Thomas W. *Life and Times of Stephen Higginson.* Boston: Houghton Mifflin, 1907.

Horwitz, Morton J. "The Constitution of Change: Legal Fundamentality Without Fundamentalism." *Harv. L. Rev.* 107 (1993): 32–117.

Howe, David W. "The Political Psychology of the Federalist." *Wm. and Mary Q.* 44 (1987): 485–486.

Hunt, Gaillard. *The Life of James Madison.* New York: Doubleday, Page & Co., 1902.

Iredell, James. *The Papers of James Iredell.* Raleigh, N.C.: Division of Archives and History, Department of Cultural Resources, 1976.

Jackson, Donald D., and Dorothy Twohig, eds. *The Diaries of George Washington.* Charlottesville: University Press of Virginia, 1976.

Jaenicke, Douglas W. "Madison v. Madison: The Party Essays v. The Federalist Papers." In R. A. Maidment and John Zvesper, eds. *Reflections on the Constitution: The American Constitution After Two Hundred Years.* Manchester, UK: Manchester University Press, 1989.

James, Charles F. *Documentary History of the Struggle for Religious Liberty in Virginia.* New York: Da Capo, 1971. (Originally published 1899)

James, Joseph B. *The Ratification of the Fourteenth Amendment.* Macon, Ga.: Mercer University Press, 1984.

Jay, William. *The Life of John Jay: With Selections from His Correspondence and Miscellaneous Papers.* New York: J&J Harper, 1833.

Jefferson, Thomas. *The Complete Anas of Thomas Jefferson.* Ed. Franklin B. Sawvel. New York: Round Table Press, 1903.

———. *Farm Book.* Ed. Edwin Morris Betts. Princeton, N.J.: Princeton University Press, 1953.

Jefferson, Thomas, and James Madison. *The Republic of Letters: The Correspondence Between Thomas Jefferson and James Madison, 1776–1826.* Ed. James Morton Smith. New York: W. W. Norton, 1995.

Jeffrey, William, Jr. "The Letters of 'Brutus'—A Neglected Element in the Ratification Campaign of 1787–88." *U. Cin. L. Rev.* 40 (1971): 643–777.

Johnson, Calvin H. *Righteous Anger at the Wicked States: The Meaning of the Founders' Constitution.* Cambridge, U.K.: Cambridge University Press, 2005.

Jones, Robert Francis. *The King of the Alley: William Duer, Politician, Entrepreneur, and Speculator, 1768–1799.* Philadelphia: American Philosophical Society, 1992.

Kaminski, John P. "The Making of the Bill of Rights: 1787–1792." In Stephen L. Schechter and Richard B. Bernstein, eds. *Contexts of the Bill of Rights.* Albany: New York State Commission on the Bicentennial of the United States Constitution, 1990.

Kaminski, John P., and Richard Leffler. *A Necessary Evil: Slavery and the Debate Over the Constitution.* Madison, Wisc.: Madison House, 1992.

Kammen, Michael G. *A Machine That Would Go of Itself: The Constitution in American Culture.* New York: Knopf, 1986.

Kauffmann, Bruce G. "James Madison: Godfather of the Constitution." *Early America Review* (1997): http://www.earlyamerica.com/review/summer97/madison.html.

Kaufman, Burton I. *Washington's Farewell Address: The View from the 20th Century.* Chicago: Quadrangle Books, 1969.

Kesavan, Vasan, and Michael S. Paulsen. "The Interpretive Force of the Constitution's Secret Drafting History." *Geo. L. J.* 91 (2003): 1113–1214.

Kesler, Charles R., ed. *Saving the Revolution: The Federalist Papers and the American Founding.* London: Collier Macmillan, 1987.

Ketcham, Ralph Louis. *James Madison.* New York: Macmillan, 1971.

Kincaid, John. "The State of American Federalism—1986." *Publius: The Journal of Federalism* 17 (1987): 1–32.

King, Rufus. *The Life and Correspondence of Rufus King.* New York: Putnam, 1894.

Klarman, Michael J. "Brown, Originalism, and Constitutional Theory: A Response to Professor McConnell." *Va. L. Rev.* 81 (1995): 1881–1936.

Klarreich, Erica. "Bookish Math." *Science News,* Dec. 20, 2003: 392–394.

Koch, Adrienne. *Jefferson and Madison: The Great Collaboration.* New York: Knopf, 1950.

Kohn, Richard H. *Eagle and Sword: The Federalists and the Creation of the Military Establishment in America, 1783–1802.* New York: Free Press, 1975.

———. "The Inside History of the Newburgh Conspiracy: America and the Coup d'Etat." *Wm. and Mary Q.* 27 (1970): 187–220.

Kramer, Larry D. "Madison's Audience." *Harv. L. Rev.* 112 (1999): 611–679.

Krannawitter, Tom L. "Constitutional Government and Judicial Power: The Political Science of *The Federalist.*" *Interpretation: A Journal of Political Philosophy* 27 (1999): 43–69.

Kurland, Philip B., and Ralph Lerner, eds. *The Founders' Constitution.* Chicago: University of Chicago Press, 1987.

Labunski, Richard E. *James Madison and the Struggle for the Bill of Rights.* New York: Oxford University Press, 2006.

Leake, Isaac Q., ed. *Memoir of the Life and Times of General John Lamb.* Albany, N.Y.: J. Munsell, 1857.

Leary, Lewis Gaston. *That Rascal Freneau: A Study in Literary Failure.* New Brunswick, N.J.: Rutgers University Press, 1941.

Lee, Emery G. "Representation, Virtue, and Political Jealousy in the Brutus-Publius Dialogue." *Journal of Politics* 59 (1997): 1073–1095.

Lee, Thomas R. "*Stare Decisis* in Historical Perspective: From the Founding Era to the Rehnquist Court." *Vand. L. Rev.* 52 (1999): 647–735.

Leibiger, Stuart Eric. *Founding Friendship: George Washington, James Madison, and the Creation of the American Republic.* Charlottesville: University Press of Virginia, 1999.

Lerner, Ralph. "The American Founders' Responsibility." *Wash. and Lee L. Rev.* 56 (1999): 891, 891n1.

Levitan, Shlomo, and Shlomo Argamon. "Fixing the Federalist: Correcting Results and Evaluating Editions for Automated Attribution." *Proc. Digital Humanities* (July 2006): 323–328.

Levy, Leonard W. *Original Intent and the Framers' Constitution.* London: Collier Macmillan, 1988.

Littlefield, Douglas. "The Potomac Company: A Misadventure in Financing an Early American Internal Improvement Project." *Business History Review* 58 (1984): 562–585.

Livy. *The History of Rome.* Whitefish, Mont.: Kessinger, 2004.

Lodge, Henry Cabot. *Alexander Hamilton.* Boston: Houghton Mifflin, 1882.

Lupu, Ira C. "Time, the Supreme Court, and the Federalist." *Geo. Wash. L. Rev.* 66 (1998): 1324–1336.

Lynch, Joseph M. *Negotiating the Constitution: The Earliest Debates Over Original Intent.* Ithaca, N.Y.: Cornell University Press, 1999.

Maclay, William. *Journal of William Maclay.* Ed. Edgar Stanton Maclay. New York: Appleton & Co., 1890.

Madison, James. *Letters and Other Writings of James Madison: Fourth President of the United States.* Philadelphia: J. B. Lippincott & Co, 1865.

Main, Jackson Turner. *The Antifederalists: Critics of the Constitution, 1781–1788.* Chapel Hill: University of North Carolina Press, 2004.

Manning, John F. "Textualism and Original Understanding: Textualism and the Role of 'The Federalist' in Constitutional Adjudication." *Geo. Wash. L. Rev.* 66 (1998): 1337–1365.

Marcus, Maeva, and James R. Perry, eds. *The Documentary History of the Supreme Court of the United States, 1789–1800.* New York: Columbia University Press, 2004.

Marshall, John. *The Life of George Washington.* Fredericksburg, Va.: The Citizens' Guild, 1926.

Martinez, J. Michael, and William D. Richardson. "The Federalist Papers and Legal Interpretation." *S.D.L. Rev.* 45 (2000): 307–333.

Mason, Alpheus T. "*The Federalist*—A Split Personality." *Am. Hist. Rev.* 57 (1952): 625–643.

Mason, George. *The Papers of George Mason, 1725–1792.* Ed. Robert A. Rutland. Chapel Hill: University of North Carolina Press, 1970.

Matthews, Richard K. *If Men Were Angels: James Madison and the Heartless Empire of Reason.* Lawrence: University Press of Kansas, 1995.

McCoy, Drew R. *The Last of the Fathers: James Madison and the Republican Legacy.* New York: Cambridge University Press, 1989.

McDonald, Forrest. *Alexander Hamilton: A Biography.* New York: W. W. Norton, 1979.

———. *Novus Ordo Seclorum: The Intellectual Origins of the Constitution.* Lawrence: University Press of Kansas, 1985.

———. *We the People: The Economic Origins of the Constitution.* New Brunswick, N.J.: Transaction, 1992.

McGowan, David. "Ethos in Law and History: Alexander Hamilton, the Federalist, and the Supreme Court." *Minn. L. Rev.* 85 (2000): 755–898.

Meese, Edwin, III. "Speech Before the American Bar Association." *The Great Debate: Interpreting Our Written Constitution.* The Federalist Society, 1986, 1–10.

Melton, Buckner F., Jr. "The Supreme Court and the Federalist: A Citation List and Analysis, 1789–1996." *Ky. L. J.* 855 (1996): 243–256.

Melton, Buckner F., Jr., and Carol W. Melton. "The Supreme Court and the Federalist: A Supplement, 2001–2006." *Ky. L. J.* 95 (2006): 749–764.

Melton, Buckner F., Jr., and Jennifer J. Miller. "The Supreme Court and the Federalist: A Supplement, 1996–2001." *Ky. L. J.* 90 (2001): 415–440.

Miller, John C. *Alexander Hamilton and the Growth of the New Nation.* New Brunswick, N.J.: Transaction, 2004.

———. *Alexander Hamilton: Portrait in Paradox.* New York: Harper, 1959.

Miller, William Lee. *The Business of May Next: James Madison and the Founding.* Charlottesville: University Press of Virginia, 1992.

Millican, Edward. *One United People: The Federalist Papers and the National Idea*. Lexington: University Press of Kentucky, 1990.

Mitchell, Broadus. *Alexander Hamilton: Youth to Maturity*. New York: Macmillan, 1957.

———. "Hamilton's Quarrel with Washington, 1781." *Wm. and Mary Q.* 12 (1945): 199–216.

Molot, Jonathan. "The Rise and Fall of Textualism." *Columb. L. Rev.* 106 (2006): 1–69.

Monaghan, Frank, and Marvin Lowenthal. *This Was New York: The Nation's Capital in 1789*. Garden City, N.Y.: Doubleday, Doran & Co., 1943.

Montesquieu, Baron de. *The Spirit of Laws*. Trans. Thomas Nugent Alembert and J. V. Prichard. Littleton, Colo.: F. B. Rothman, 1991.

Morgan, Edmund. "Safety in Numbers: Madison, Hume, and the Tenth Federalist." *Huntington Library Quarterly* 49 (1986): 95–112.

Morris, Richard Brandon. *Witnesses at the Creation: Hamilton, Madison, Jay, and the Constitution*. New York: Holt, Rinehart & Winston, 1985.

Morse, John Torrey. *The Life of Alexander Hamilton*. Boston: Little, Brown, 1876.

Mosteller, Frederick, and David L. Wallace. *Applied Bayesian and Classical Inference: The Case of The Federalist Papers*. 2nd ed. New York: Springer-Verlag, 1984.

———. *Inference and Disputed Authorship: The Federalist*. Stanford, Calif.: Center for the Study of Language and Information, 2007.

Moynihan, Sean. "The Case for Constitutional Evolution." *Denv. U. L. Rev.* 81 (2003): 191–211.

Nelson, Grant S., and Robert J. Pushaw. "A Critique of the Narrow Interpretation of the Commerce Clause." *NW. U. L. Rev.* 96 (2002): 695–719.

———. "Rethinking the Commerce Clause: Applying First Principles to Uphold Federal Commercial Regulations But Preserve State Control Over Social Issues." *Iowa L. Rev.* 85 (1999): 1–170.

Nzelibe, Jide, and John Yoo. "Rational War and Constitutional Design." *Yale L. J.* 115 (2006): 2512–2541.

O'Neill, Johnathan. *Originalism in American Law and Politics: A Constitutional History*. Baltimore, Md.: Johns Hopkins University Press, 2005.

Packard, Francis R., and Robert P. Parsons. *History of Medicine in the United States*. New York: P. B. Hoeber, 1931.

Palmer, Robert. *The Age of the Democratic Revolution: A Political History of Europe and America 1760–1800*. Princeton, N.J.: Princeton University Press, 1959.

Paltsits, Victor Hugo. *Washington's Farewell Address: In Facsimile, with Transliterations of all the Drafts of Washington, Madison, & Hamilton, Together with their Correspondence and Other Supporting Documents*. New York: New York Public Library, 1935.

Pellew, George. *John Jay*. Boston: Houghton Mifflin, 1890.

Pole, J. R., ed. *The American Constitution—For and Against: The Federalist and Anti-Federalist Papers*. New York: Hill and Wang, 1987.

Pomerantz, Sidney. *New York: An American City, 1783–1803*. New York: Columbia University Press, 1938.

Posner, Richard A. "The Constitution as an Economic Document." *Geo. Wash. L. Rev.* 56 (1987): 4–25.

Potter, Kathleen O. *The Federalist's Vision of Popular Sovereignty in the New American Republic.* New York: LFB Scholarly Publications, 2002.

Rakove, Jack N. *The Beginnings of National Politics an Interpretive History of the Continental Congress.* Baltimore: Johns Hopkins University Press, 1982.

———. *Declaring Rights: A Brief History with Documents.* Boston: Bedford, 1998.

———. "The Great Compromise: Ideas, Interests, and the Politics of Constitution Making." *Wm. and Mary Q.* 44 (1987): 424–457.

———. *Interpreting the Constitution: The Debate Over Original Intent.* Boston: Northeastern University Press, 1990.

———. *James Madison and the Creation of the American Republic.* 3rd ed. New York: Pearson/Longman, 2007.

———. "The Original Intention of Original Understanding." *Const. Comm.* 13 (1996): 159–186.

———. *Original Meanings: Politics and Ideas in the Making of the Constitution.* 1st ed. New York: Knopf, 1996.

———. "The Super-Legality of the Constitution, or, a Federalist Critique of Bruce Ackerman's Neo-Federalism." *Yale L. J.* 108 (1999): 1931–1958.

———. "Thinking Like a Constitution." *Journal of the Early Republic* 24 (2004): 1–26.

Rakove, Jack N., and Oscar Handlin. *James Madison and the Creation of the American Republic.* Glenview, Ill.: Scott, Foresman/Little, Brown Higher Education, 1990.

Randall, Willard Sterne. *Alexander Hamilton: A Life.* New York: HarperCollins, 2003.

Rhodehamel, John H. *The Great Experiment: George Washington and the American Republic.* San Marino, Calif.: Huntington Library, 1998.

Riccards, Michael P. *A Republic, If You Can Keep It: The Foundation of the American Presidency, 1700–1800.* Contributions in Political Science, no. 167. New York: Greenwood Press, 1987.

Richardson, James D., ed. *A Compilation of the Messages and Papers of the Presidents, 1789–1897.* Washington: Government Printing Office, 1897.

Risjord, Norman K. *Chesapeake Politics, 1781–1800.* New York: Columbia University Press, 1978.

———. "The Compromise of 1790: New Evidence on the Dinner Table Bargain." *Wm. and Mary Q.* 33 (1976): 309–314.

Rives, William C. *History of the Life and Times of James Madison.* Boston: Little, Brown, 1859.

Rosen, Gary. *American Compact: James Madison and the Problem of Founding.* Lawrence: University Press of Kansas, 1999.

Rossiter, Clinton Lawrence. *Alexander Hamilton and the Constitution.* New York: Harcourt, Brace & World, 1964.

Rudman, Joseph. "The Non-Traditional Case for the Authorship of the Twelve Disputed 'Federalist' Papers: A Monument Built on Sand." *Association for Computers and the Humanities and the Association for Literary and Linguistic Computing,* 2005. http://mustard.tapor.uvic.ca:8080/cocoon/ach_abstracts/proof/paper_54_rudman.pdf.

Rutland, Robert Allen. *James Madison: The Founding Father.* Columbia: University of Missouri Press, 1997.

———. *The Ordeal of the Constitution*. Norman: University of Oklahoma Press, 1966.

———. "The Trivialization of the Bill of Rights: One Historian's View of How the Purposes of the First Ten Amendments Have Been Defiled." *Wm. and Mary L. Rev.* 31 (1990): 287, 292.

Safire, William. *Lend Me Your Ears: Great Speeches in History.* New York: W. W. Norton, 1992.

Scalia, Antonin. *A Matter of Interpretation*. Princeton, N.J.: Princeton University Press, 1997.

———. "Originalism: The Lesser Evil." *U. Cin. L. Rev.* 57 (1989): 849–865.

Scanlan, James P. "'The Federalist' and Human Nature." *The Review of Politics* 21 (1959): 657–677.

Schachner, Nathan. *Alexander Hamilton.* New York: D. Appleton-Century Co., 1946.

———. "Alexander Hamilton Viewed by His Friends: The Narratives of Robert Troup and Hercules Mulligan." *Wm. and Mary Q.* 4 (1947): 203–225.

Schauer, Frederick. "Easy Cases." *S. Cal. L. Rev.* 58 (1985): 399–440.

Schutz, John, and Douglass Adair, eds. *The Spur of Fame: Dialogues of John Adams and Benjamin Rush, 1805–1813.* Indianapolis: Liberty Fund, 2000.

Sellers, M.N.S. *American Republicanism: Roman Ideology in the United States Constitution.* New York: New York University Press, 1994.

Shaw, Samuel, and Josiah Quincy. *The Journals of Major Samuel Shaw: The First American Consul at Canton: With a Life of the Author.* Boston: Wm. Crosby and H. P. Nichols, 1847.

Sheldon, Garrett Ward. *The Political Philosophy of James Madison.* Baltimore: Johns Hopkins University Press, 2001.

Slonim, Shlomo. "Federalist No. 78 and Brutus' Neglected Thesis on Judicial Supremacy." *Const. Comm.* 23 (2006): 7–31.

Smith, Margaret Bayard, and Gaillard Hunt. *The First Forty Years of Washington Society.* New York: Scribner's, 1906.

Smith, Peter. "Sources of Federalism: An Empirical Analysis of the Court's Quest for Original Meaning." *U.C.L.A. Rev.* 52 (2004): 217–287.

Sparks, Jared. *The Life of Gouverneur Morris.* Boston: Gray & Bowen, 1832.

———, ed. *The Writings of George Washington.* Boston: Little, Brown, 1855.

Spaulding, Ernest W. *New York in the Critical Period, 1783–1789.* New York: Columbia University Press, 1932.

Spurlin, Paul Merrill. *Montesquieu in America, 1760–1801.* New York: Octagon, 1940.

Stahr, Walter. *John Jay: Founding Father.* New York: Palgrave Macmillan, 2005.

Swan, Robert. "Prelude and Aftermath of the Doctors' Riot of 1788." *New York History* 81 (2000): 417–456.

tenBroek, Jacobus. "Use by the United States Supreme Court of Extrinsic Aids in Constitutional Construction." *Cal. L. Rev.* 27 (1939): 157.

Tiefer, Charles. "Can Appropriation Riders Speed Our Exit From Iraq?" *Stan. J. Int. L.* 42 (2006): 291–341.

Tillman, Seth B. "The Federalist Papers as Reliable Historical Source Material for Constitutional Interpretation." *W. Va. L. Rev.* 2003 (105): 601–619.

Treanor, William M. "Judicial Review Before Marbury." *Stan. L. Rev.* 58 (2005): 455–562.

Trees, Andrew S. *The Founding Fathers and the Politics of Character.* Princeton, N.J.: Princeton University Press, 2004.

U.S. Department of State. *Documentary History of the Constitution of the United States of America, 1786–1870.* Washington, D.C.: Government Printing Office, 1901.

Veit, Helen E., et al., eds. *Creating the Bill of Rights: The Documentary Record from the First Federal Congress.* Baltimore: Johns Hopkins University Press, 1991.

Venit, Abraham H. "An Unwritten Federalist History." *New England Quarterly* 21 (1948): 241–252.

Verplanck, William E., and Moses W. Collyer. *Sloops of the Hudson River.* Port Washington, N.Y. : I. J. Friedman, 1968.

Ward, George Washington. *Early Development of Chesapeake and Ohio Canal Project.* Baltimore: Johns Hopkins University Press, 1899.

Webster, Noah. *Collection of Papers on Political, Literary and Moral Subjects.* Salem, N.H: Ayer, 1968. (Originally published 1843)

Whealy, Mervin B. "'The Revolution Is Not Over': The Annapolis Convention of 1786." *Maryland Historical Magazine* 81 (1986): 228–240.

White, Morton G. *Philosophy, the Federalist, and the Constitution.* New York: Oxford University Press, 1987.

Williams, Charles R., and William H. Smith. *Life of Rutherford Birchard Hayes.* Boston: Houghton Mifflin, 1914.

Wills, Garry. *Explaining America: The Federalist.* New York: Penguin Books, 1982.

———. *James Madison.* New York: Times Books, 2002.

Wilson, James G. "The Most Sacred Text: The Supreme Court's Use of the Federalist Papers." *B.Y.U. L. Rev.* (1985): 65–135.

Wood, Gordon S. *The Creation of the American Republic, 1776–1787.* Chapel Hill: University of North Carolina Press, 1969.

———. *Revolutionary Characters: What Made the Founders Different.* New York: Penguin, 2006.

Wood, John, and John Henry Sherburne. *The Suppressed History of the Administration of John Adams.* Salem, N.H.: Ayer, 1968. (Originally published 1846)

INDEX